*The Gathering Storm
in the Churches*

The Gathering Storm in the Churches

JEFFREY K. HADDEN

Doubleday & Company, Inc.
Garden City, New York
1969

Table from "White Attitudes Toward the Negro" by Paul B. Sheatsley, from the Winter 1966 issue of *Daedalus*. Reprinted by permission of the American Academy of Arts and Sciences.

Gallup Poll tables reprinted by permission of the American Institute of Public Opinion.

Table from "A Comparison of Major Religious Groups" by Bernard Lazerwitz, from the September 1961 issue of the *Journal of the American Statistical Association*. Reprinted by permission of the author and the American Statistical Association.

Table from "The American Dilemma: An Empirical Test" by Frank R. Westie, from the August 1965 issue of *American Sociological Review*. Reprinted by permission of the author and the American Sociological Association.

Excerpt from "The Uncomfortable Pew" from the May 11, 1966 issue of *The Christian Century*. Copyright © 1966 by Christian Century Foundation. Reprinted by permission of the publisher.

Excerpt from *The Noise of Solemn Assemblies* by Peter L. Berger. Copyright © 1961 by Peter L. Berger. Reprinted by permission of Doubleday & Company, Inc.

Figures from a Louis Harris Survey reprinted by permission of Louis Harris and Associates, Inc.

Excerpt from *My People is the Enemy* by William Stringfellow. Copyright © 1964 by William Stringfellow. Reprinted by permission of Holt, Rinehart and Winston, Inc.

Material from tables from *Religion and Society in Tension* by Charles Glock and Rodney Stark. Reprinted by permission of Rand McNally & Company.

Table from *American Piety: The Nature of Religious Commitment* by Rodney Stark and Charles Y. Glock. Reprinted by permission of the University of California Press.

DEDICATED TO

KENNETH UNDERWOOD

(1918–1968)

whose encouragement and patience
helped move me beyond tabulating
data to ponder their meaning

Acknowledgments

I have often read through lengthy acknowledgments in books with a somewhat jaundiced eye. In the process of developing the material for this volume I have developed an appreciation for how much indebtedness one can accumulate in developing research and how feeble a few words of acknowledgment can be in expressing the gratitude and appreciation an author has for those who have in one way or another contributed to his work. While acknowledging one's indebtedness to others cannot even begin to constitute repayment of that debt, it is at least a modest way of saying thanks to those who have helped. It goes without saying, of course, that those who are acknowledged should in no way be held responsible for my shortcomings.

My greatest debt is to Kenneth Underwood, who initially encouraged me to study clergymen and through his role as the director of the Danforth Study of Campus Ministries provided the financial resources to make this study possible. But my indebtedness to him goes far beyond this. He has been in every sense a truly remarkable teacher, colleague and friend. I can only hope that in the course of my own career I will be able to provide the kind of encouragement and intellectual stimulation to young scholars that Ken Underwood provided for me.

I also owe a significant debt to Raymond C. Rymph of Purdue University. In the initial development of the manuscript we spent many long sessions together hammering through some of the central issues that are developed here. We had initially planned to collaborate on this volume, but my move to Case Western Reserve University while the volume was still at a formative stage made collaboration impractical. His initial contribution in sifting the grain from the chaff was an important contribution to the development of this volume. The first section of Chapter V, which reports a case study of the Urban Training Center for Christian Mission, was initially published in collaboration with Rymph.

John Calloway, Public Affairs Director of radio station WBBM in Chicago, was in part responsible for the initiation of this study. His award-winning thirteen-week documentary program, "A House Divided," served to make me more aware of the involvement of clergymen in the civil rights struggle. He gave generously of his time and insights and loaned me his notes and transcripts for careful study.

An expression of debt and gratitude is also due to almost 10,000 clergymen who have contributed the data which is reported here. The large proportion of this 10,000 contributed by completing a lengthy questionnaire, which was in itself a heroic accomplishment. Several hundred more gave of their time for personal interviews which often ran many hours. Without the openness, honesty, and generosity of these clergymen, this volume could never have emerged. Far more clergymen than I can possibly mention here went far beyond "the call of duty" in opening up their files, personal correspondence, sermons, and indeed their lives for my perusal and digesting. While I feel I have learned a great deal about them, I have also learned a great deal from them. Among the many who have helped, several deserve a special word of thanks: Robert Bonthius, Frances Geddes, Wayne C. Hartmire, Jr., Ray Miklethun, James Morton, Nick Ristad, Glenn Sampson, Paul Stoppenhagen, Gerald Trigg, and Jim L. Waits.

Many of my academic colleagues and friends have left their mark on this manuscript. To try and record the specific ways in which they have done so would almost certainly result in some glaring omissions, so I won't even try. But this does not diminish my appreciation. A special word of thanks is extended to the following: Earl R. Babbie, N. Jay Demerath III, Charles Y. Glock, Jerald Hage, Phillip E. Hammond, Marie Haug, Richard J. Hill, Benton Johnson, Paul Kramer, Kenneth Lutterman, Robert McNamara, S.J., Martin Marty, Gerald Marwell, Richard L. Means, Hoyt Oliver, Parker Palmer, Robert Perrucci, Richard Peterson, Glenn Trimble, Oliver R. Whitley, and J. Alan Winter. A special word of thanks is due to Rod Stark, who has served as a critical sounding board since the inception of this project. Also, special thanks is due to Edgar W. Mills for a very careful and thorough reading of an earlier draft of the entire manuscript. In addition, the work of a few scholars has been particularly informative and helpful in the development of this book. They include: Peter Berger, Edgar F. Borgatta, Ernest Q. Campbell, Benjamin Nelson, Thomas Pettigrew, and Liston Pope.

My students have also contributed in many ways to the development of this volume. Not only have they served as a critical sounding board, many have volunteered their time as research assistants long after the financial resources for the project were exhausted. These include: Jim Beard, Gene Calvert, Alan Chesney, Jerome Corsi, Charlene Stringer Knuckman, Sue Morgan, and Andrew J. White. A special word of thanks is extended to William Horvath, who for a period of two years volunteered a significant proportion of his summers and vacation periods as a research assistant.

Appreciation is also extended to Marlene Forster and Dawn Mc-Caghy for the many hours they spent doing data analysis and the tedious task of transcribing data analyses into table form. Dawn McCaghy also spent much time assisting in the proofreading of this manuscript, for which I also thank her.

The contributions of my wife, Joy, have also been invaluable. Since the inception of the clergy study in the fall of 1964, she has worked time and a half as a "voluntary" assistant. She removed much co-ordination and detail work from my shoulders, which has been of enormous help. At the same time, I should make it clear at this point that I absolve her of responsibility for any mistakes or omissions which result from my failure to pay attention to detail. It goes without saying that the sacrifices she and my children, Nora and Donna, have made for the sake of my work have been considerable. They have not gone unappreciated.

As noted above, the national clergy survey was initiated under the auspices of the Danforth Foundation's Study of Campus Ministries. Kenneth Underwood and the members of the Danforth Study Commission were enormously tolerant in permitting me to go off in directions that were often not easy to justify as relevant to the campus ministry study. While only a little attention is devoted to campus clergymen in this volume, I hope their centrality to the emerging crises in the church will be understood. Similarly, I hope that the institutional role of the Danforth Foundation's support of campus ministries will be understood by the Foundation.

Other institutions and foundations have contributed to the financial support of this study. An institutional grant from the National Science Foundation to Case Western Reserve University provided the funds for the national survey of the public's attitudes toward clergy involvement in civil rights. The President's Fund at Purdue University provided a liberal grant to cover computer services. The Christian Faith and Higher Education Institute, the Dyer-Ives Foundation, and the Society for the Psychological Study of Social Issues provided funds for some of the case studies. Their support was greatly appreciated.

Contents

Tables

Preface

In a broad sense, this is a book about the church's struggle to come to grips with the racial crisis. But in a still broader sense, it is a book about the church's struggle to come to grips with itself in a modern, secular world. What does it believe? What is its meaning and purpose for being? What is its basis of authority? What is the role of the traditional leadership—the clergy—and how do they function in an institution and world in which the traditional conceptions of belief, purpose, and authority are being shattered?

An outline of the thesis of this book is spelled out in Chapter I. In this preface I would like to accomplish two objectives. First of all, the theme of *crisis* runs through the entirety of the book. Because of the widespread use of the word crisis in our world today, I believe it may be subject to misunderstanding and impotency. I want to comment on the meaning of the concept and why I feel it is an appropriate term to describe what is happening in the churches as well as in our world. Secondly, I want to comment on the intellectuals' role—particularly the sociologists'—in studying religion. These comments may be unnecessary for some readers, but my experience as a teacher, lecturer, and scholar have led me to the conclusion that the concepts and methods of sociological inquiry are broadly misunderstood in our culture. Indeed, our inability to grasp the meaning of *social structure* is a critical part of our inability to understand the racial crisis in America. I hope that my comments will be helpful to some in "putting the record straight" as to both the possibilities and limitations of sociological inquiry.

On the Meaning of Crisis

The widespread use of the concept "crisis" calls for a sober appraisal of the very term and the reasons why it is used so freely. To be sure, it is not a term that is used with any degree of scientific precision. Yet, we live in an age in which it seems that one can examine almost any institution or structured interaction in society and conclude that the state of affairs of these institutions or groups is one of deep and entangling crisis. We describe the struggle of emerging nations to achieve economic and industrial development as a crisis. Similarly, the rapid rate of population increase on this planet is viewed by many as a grave crisis. On the domestic scene, we speak of urban problems, race relations, crime, education, and a whole host of other phenomena as constituting crises.

The dictionary definitions of crisis back up the assumptions implicit in these uses of the term. A crisis can be a turning point in the course of anything, as in a disease, or it can be a critical situation whose outcome determines whether possible bad consequences will follow. The sense of a critical turning point and of the threat of harmful consequences is felt in discussions of social crises.

Why, though, does this particular age see the world filled with crisis? In one sense, man has always lived in crisis, but never before have the expectations and the resources to eliminate problems been so abundant. Perhaps we cry crisis because the pace at which we are moving toward the accomplishment of our goals is slow when compared with human expectations. On the other hand, the human community may truly be living in the midst of a critical period in history, in which the outcome of the immediate years ahead is not at all certain and the stakes are no less than the continuation of life on this planet.

Human progress has always been a double-edged sword, and if the prospects for the next century are greater than they have been in any previous age, so are the problems and dangers. Man has not yet put an end to war, and the possibility of unleashing nuclear holocaust constitutes a problem and responsibility that human beings have never had to confront before. Man has not eliminated poverty, and the problems involved in doing so appear to be quite serious. If man fails to achieve this goal, the consequences are almost certain to be grave. The poor are increasingly concentrated in urban areas where their expectations for a better life are rising. Failure to eliminate poverty must inevitably result in continued social unrest or the creation of a garrison caste society which is strongly at variance with the major ideological thrusts of Western civilization.

And so it goes with many of the social problems which we label with the concept "crisis." Failure to meet the multitude of social challenges which twentieth-century man confronts will, at the very least, result in consequences which we view as detrimental to the human condition. Thus, crisis is perhaps an appropriate word, for it conveys something of the seriousness of our situation and the need to find solutions. At the same time, it should be recognized that excessive use or misuse of a concept may result in a weakening of its impact. The word crisis calls for a response, and if it becomes commonplace it may no longer convey a sense of urgency. Yet, so many of the problems that modern man faces do demand this sense of urgency. To suggest that we call a moratorium on the use of the concept would seem to convey a rather naïve assumption that if we ignore problems they will go away. Thus, in spite of its ambiguity and the threat of overuse and misuse, it is a concept which we must live with for some time, for it is a concept which reflects the urgency, seriousness, and complexity of the human condition.

The word crisis, as it is used by commentators on the contemporary scene, has at least two distinct meanings which parallel the connotations discussed above. The first usually refers to an immediate situation which, for the moment, has disrupted or seriously threatens to disrupt the ongoing activities of the society or some significant aspect of it. This immediacy is like the critical turning point in a disease. The Cuban crisis of 1962 threatened all of human society, while the educational crisis at Berkeley in 1964 immediately disrupted only one major university. Both were characterized with a sense of need for immediate action in order to prevent a total breakdown in the system. But when some action is taken so that the immediacy of the disruption has passed, the crisis is considered over.

For most people, these crises tend to be forgotten when the flurry of publicity is over. But some see the immediate crisis as a result of an underlying problem which had existed long before and still remains after the incident.

This leads to a second use of the term. Crisis can also apply to situations which, if left unaltered over a longer period of time, threaten irreparable consequences to a system or some segment thereof. It is in this context that scholars usually use the term. It is a much more ambiguous usage because the urgency of a situation is often understood by only a few and the immediate consequences are generally not felt by many, or if the consequences are immediately apparent, they are not perceived as the result of a broader crisis. The latter is illustrated by the crisis of the world's exploding population. Individuals do not perceive that their own unemployment, hunger, suffering, and hope of nothing but the same for their children are the consequence of the excess fertility of millions like themselves.

It is in this second sense that the term crisis has been used in this volume. It is not employed lightly or without some misgivings, but I believe it is a term which appropriately describes the condition of the Protestant churches today. Unless more serious attention is given to the implications of the situations that are now brewing in the churches, the future may well produce the most grave consequences. My concern here is something much more serious than the demise of the institutional church. If the churches should go under, or be radically altered so that they cease to have any relevance for modern society, what institution(s) would replace the churches as a value-creating, value-carrying, and value-legitimizing force in society?[1]

The churches have not yet reached a crisis of the magnitude of the racial struggle in America today. But I believe that "crisis" is an appropriate word to describe what is happening in the churches today. If those who have a vested interest in the survival of the churches fail to see the gathering storm as such, it is questionable whether there will be a Christian church in the next century. I hope that this volume will succeed in clarifying the magnitude of the problems that the churches face.

Some Thoughts of the Nature of a Sociological Perspective

One hears a lot of talk about "sociological studies" and "sociological perspectives" among clergy and church administrators today. But if one listens carefully it soon becomes apparent that the term "sociological" is often little more than popular jargon. It seems to have replaced the mystical quality of the "psychological perspectives" of the forties and fifties. Those who use the jargon often have only the vaguest notion of what the concept implies. In religious circles it has become a catchall phrase which embraces nearly everything that is not theological.

While the term sociology is currently in vogue, the research and writings of sociologists are more often than not either ignored or panned in religious publications as the trivial elaboration of the obvious, or shallow in their perception of complex issues. These criticisms are sometimes justified, but other times, from the sociologists' perspective, they are not.

There are a number of understandable reasons for skepticism among the critics of the sociology of religion. While there is a very rich and provocative history of theoretical thought in the sociology of religion, systematic empirical studies of religion have begun to emerge only very recently. Similarly, until very recently, there had been a long dearth of significant theoretical development. Sociologists have long acclaimed the centrality of religious institutions in the socialization process, by which society's values and norms are transmitted, and integrative process, by which each area of an individual's life is provided for. Yet, one can quickly compile a long list of social institutions that have been studied by sociologists with much greater care. It is beyond the scope of this discussion to elaborate all the reasons why sociologists have not systematically studied religion, but the relatively recent interest of sociologists in religious phenomena needs to be emphasized.[2]

At the same time, I believe that it is appropriate to point out that during the past quarter of a century there has emerged a large body of literature which has been called sociology of religion, in large part produced under the auspices of denominational research departments, which has been little more than unimaginative head-counting and marketing studies.

Such studies have, no doubt, been valuable for church planners, but they have not done a great deal to enhance the status of sociology as a useful perspective for understanding religious phenomena. What is, I believe, much more important in understanding the jaundiced view of sociological research is the fact that many people do not have a very clear understanding of sociological perspective.

For a variety of reasons, our culture is psychologically oriented. We seek to find causes in terms of personality and deep-seated, psychic motivation. Even when we understand sociological phenomena, we tend to express them in psychological terms. Even sociologists are "guilty" of psychologizing sociological phenomena. This is obviously not the place to develop an elaborate essay on the meaning of sociology, but some brief comments are in order.

Sociology is a discipline that studies *institutions* and *social structure*. The sociologist *does not* attempt to predict human behavior in terms of personality, psychic motivation, and the like, but rather attempts to account for behavior in terms of the social context in which an individual functions. He looks at the individual as a member of a group(s) which possesses certain social characteristics, and causal relationships are sought in the structural properties of groups and in the individual's structural relationships to groups. The sociologist may be interested in personality, motivation, and ideology, but he attempts to explain these phenomena in social-structural terms, or he introduces them to account for variance that cannot be explained from his own unique perspective.

To be sure, sociology is not a monolithic intellectual perspective. What is sociological to one sociologist is social psychology to another, and sheer nonsense to yet a third, though we need not go into a discussion of the major sociological orientations or theoretical perspectives here. Suffice it to say that sociology is still a young discipline and the "schools," if indeed such exist, are still in the process of emerging. Most sociologists are rather eclectic and draw from a number of theoretical orientations as they are appropriate for describing or explaining the phenomena being studied.

The development of systematic integrated theory depends on the prior task of description. As a young discipline, a good deal of the sociological enterprise is oriented to description without a tight commitment to any theoretical orientation. This often results in poohpoohing the "common-sense trivia" that the sociologist "discovers." While such criticism is sometimes justified, the "fact-finding" endeavors of sociologists can clearly be justified and must be expanded if we are to establish an integrated body of knowledge and theory. At the present moment we are accumulating a large inventory of "common-sense" findings which are diametrically opposed to other "common-sense" notions of the nature of social reality. Theories may explain "common-sense" ideas about the nature of society without necessarily corresponding to empirical reality. Such explanations may not only be wrong, they can also be deleterious if they are accepted as truth and their implications translated into public policy. Thus, the sociologists, like all scientists, must maintain a delicate balance between the development of theory and the gathering of facts. Since there are so many aspects of society that are not yet empirically known, the fact-finding endeavors of sociologists will continue for a long time. To a considerable extent, this volume is a fact-finding endeavor.

It also needs to be emphasized that the sociological perspective represents a radical break from the psychological ideology of our society. To be sure, we are gradually assimilating some popular sociological perspectives in the mass culture. For example, when middle-class college students descend on Fort Lauderdale in the spring and raise hell for a week, we say that they are nice kids who are just "blowing off a little steam." This explanation is a popular sociological interpretation. What it says, in essence, is that college students spend most of the year working in a highly competitive and tension-producing environment and thus this form of tension release is understandable and even tolerable if it is "contained." But if the behavior of the deviant is beyond the limits of cultural toleration, and we are unable personally to identify with the individual, we introduce a psychological explanation. No matter how the life chances (social structure) may be stacked against a person, we are likely to agree with the explanation presented in the "Gee, Officer Krupke" song in *West Side Story*—"deep down inside him, he's no good."

In a psychologically oriented culture, we are wed to the ideology of individual responsibility. To assert that behavior is predictable in terms of the social conditions of a society is not only foreign, it is personally disturbing because it places the burden of the ills of society on MAN, writ large, and not simply on a minority of "bad" individuals. It bears repeating that the sociologist has never claimed that *all* deviance can be explained in terms of social structure. Nor does his "cultural" explanation dismiss the role of individual responsibility. He is merely saying that if you want to understand (control, explain, predict, change) individual behavior, you must understand the social context within which behavior occurs.

I hope the implications of these comments will become clearer as the findings of the volume unfold. To give one example which will be analyzed in some detail in Chapter V, we will see that for most clergymen, involvement in an activist role in the civil rights movement cannot be accounted for solely in terms of the minister's own personal convictions about racial justice, or his unique personality characteristics, but rather must take into account the nature of his social context. Depending on the nature of his position, his denominational background, and several other social-contextual variables, he may or may not be "structurally free" to pursue an activist role. Social structure may allow, indeed encourage him to be deviant, or it may prohibit him from being so with the threat of serious reprisals.

The Role of the Sociologist in Understanding Religious Beliefs and Behavior

If non-sociological thought processes are deep-seated in American culture, non-scientific thought is widespread among scholars of religion. To many church scholars, the scientific or objective study of religion is a misnomer. They hold that religion, and its various aspects that are manifest through the church, is fundamentally a spiritual quality which transcends understanding in the same way that one may understand other belief systems and institutions. While many religionists have turned to sociology in recent years to gain additional insight as to the nature of the church and religious faith, there remains a significant number of church scholars who fundamentally believe that sociology is irrelevant, or at best peripheral, to an understanding of religion. This position is succinctly summarized by sociologist J. Milton Yinger:

> It is the conviction of many thoughtful men that the objective study of religion is at best impossible, and at worst dangerous. How is it possible, they may ask, to "see" a stained-glass window from the outside? Its whole meaning is apparent only as the light shines through, just as the true meaning of religion is visible only to one on the inside. What can be the consequences, moreover, of an objective study of religion, based as religion is on faith, but the weakening of that faith?[3]

Oliver Whitley, a theologian who is also a sociologist, points out that this battle has historical antecedents which raged long before the emergence of sociology as a discipline.

Just as the theologians disagreed about the visibility or invisibility of Jesus Christ, so in the modern views of the church we have virtually the same two extremes. The Docetists say that "the church" refers to only spiritual, invisible aspects of transcendent reality. What is real about the church is, in its essence, not empirically observable. The Arians argue that, on the contrary, we should exclude from the notion of the church everything that we cannot account for through empirical observation. . . . It is not too far wrong to suggest that in discussing the church the religionists and/or theologians are Docetists and the sociologists are Arians.[4]

Whitley does not view Docetism and Arianism as absolute positions, but rather as tendencies which can be ordered along a continuum. Theologians probably tend more toward the Docetic end of the continuum while most sociologists are nearer the Arian position, but "pure types" are probably as difficult to locate as types derived from any kind of theoretical construct. To attack one position or the other is to set out on a venture which is not unlike the infamous adventures of Don Quixote.

In light of various approaches to the nature of religious institutions and religious beliefs, it is important at the onset that my own position, as a sociologist, be made clear. I see no inherent reason why religious beliefs and institutions cannot be studied much in the same way as any belief system or institution is studied. Religious institutions have an organization, both formal and informal; they have a membership which is stratified in terms of involvement and functions performed; they have goals which are pursued; they are founded on a commitment to an ideology; etc. That goals or ideologies are not uniformly agreed upon is no different than what one finds in other institutions, and an examination of dissensus is one legitimate problem which a sociologist may choose to study.

I am by no means committed to the proposition that a sociological perspective is the only legitimate or useful approach to studying religion. I would argue that it is an indispensable approach if one wishes to understand religious institutions and religious behavior, but it is only one approach, which quite obviously has some rather serious limitations. Clearly, letting the light shine through the stained-glass window provides one perspective on the beauty of the church, but this is a rather narrow perspective from which to examine the full beauty and architectural complexity of a magnificent cathedral.

Whether it is necessary to "believe" in order fully to understand religion is a metaphysical question which I feel need not concern us since no claim to "full understanding" has been asserted. It is interesting to note, however, that most of those who would claim that it is necessary to believe the canons of a religious tradition in order to understand it would not hold that belief is a necessary prerequisite for understanding the Third Reich or the John Birch Society. To the contrary, most would argue that commitment to the ideologies of these movements would blind one's perspective to understand objectively the nature and implications of these movements. If this is true of extremist ideologies, why doesn't the same argument apply to all ideological systems? Indeed, the fact that most religious ideologies are "less deviant" than the groups mentioned above might well give rise to the argument that the subtle influences of the ideology will be more difficult to detect, and thus objectivity will be even more difficult for the "insider."

But again, the argument enters a metaphysical realm, though I would argue that becoming a participant observer of the John Birch Society, without accepting the ideology, would provide a certain understanding (*Gestalt*) of the movement which could not be grasped from simply reading what is written about and by members of the group. In short, I fully accept the validity of multiple approaches to knowledge, and I have no basic quarrel with those who argue that a sociological perspective has some rather serious limitations. I would only remind those who are critical of sociology that the same can be said of every other scholarly perspective.

But what is a legitimate sociological question in the general area of religion, and what is it that is clearly outside the sociologist's realm of concern? Let me begin with the second part of the question, for it is easier to define what is outside the sociologist's domain than to describe all that a sociological perspective includes. Most importantly, the sociologist does not attempt to compete with the theologian or the social ethicist in the normative task of defining truth and morality. This is not to say that a sociologist never makes normative pronouncements or that his scholarship is entirely "value-free." To be sure, sociologists do occasionally traverse into the normative realm from time to time, but this is seldom the critic's bone of contention. If anything, critics are generally concerned that the sociologist does not devote more attention to an explication of the normative implications of his findings.

Much criticism of sociological studies results from a basic misunderstanding of what it is that a sociologist does. When a sociologist asks a sample of people "Do you believe in the physical resurrection of Christ?" he is *not* attempting to explore the validity of that particular doctrine. The "truth" of a religious doctrine cannot be determined by a sociological survey or a public opinion poll. But an answer to that question does say something about how closely the group studied does or does not adhere to a traditional orthodox Christian doctrine. This simple question may or may not be a good indicator of an individual's adherence to a whole set of doctrinal principles. This is an empirical question subject to careful examination in the same way as the response to the single question must be analyzed.

Suppose, for example, we have six doctrinal issues about the Christian faith and discover that a particular individual indicates that he doesn't accept any of them. What does this mean? We may discover that the respondent is Jewish, and hence we are not surprised to learn that he rejects statements about the Christian faith. But suppose the respondent is a Protestant clergyman. Does this mean he is a heretic? It might, and certainly many orthodox believers would be inclined to interpret the results in this way, although this is probably a hasty conclusion considering the fact that a clergyman has taken sacred vows. But suppose we discover that a whole group of clergy reject our statements of orthodoxy and on further examination we discover that they have a whole range of characteristics in common, such as where they received their theological training, theologians they most admire, age, denomination, etc. It may be that they are having difficulty in identifying their own theological beliefs in terms of our categories. Does this mean that our questions are faulty? It might, but on the other hand, if other clergy do not have the same problems and if our questions accurately reflect on orthodox position, we would be inclined to conclude that our results reveal a very basic theological reorientation that is taking place. But as we have stated the problem, it is still not clear what the essence of the new theology is. We only know something it is not, and thus our task of understanding what clergy believe is incomplete. Nevertheless, we should not minimize what we have discovered, namely that traditional expressions of Christian theology do not adequately express the beliefs of clergy with certain characteristics, while this theology does seem adequate for clergy with other characteristics.

But discovering the nature of theological belief and certain background characteristics which may be related to particular beliefs constitutes only one aspect of the sociological inquiry. The sociologist may postulate that what one believes about theology is systematically related to what one believes about social issues. Or a person's social class, occupation, or any number of other characteristics may be systematically related to belief. Theoretically, the number and kinds of questions that a sociologist can raise are limited only by his imagination and familiarity with the subject matter he wishes to study. The perceptiveness of his understanding, on the other hand, is limited by the validity and reliability of his techniques for measurement. "Theological orientation" may be more difficult to measure than, say, prejudice against Negroes, but in either case, the sociologist must constantly scrutinize the adequacy of his measuring devices.

To return to the specific nature and task of sociological inquiry in the area of religion, we know, for example, that 95 to 97 per cent of the American public respond affirmatively to the question "Do you believe in God?" But probably no one would feel that this is an adequate description of religious belief in America. We need also to ask, "What kind of concept of God? How is this belief manifest in terms of religious practice? How strongly do you feel about your religious beliefs? How much do you know about the doctrines of the religious faith you adhere to? What are the consequences of your religious beliefs in your daily life? What else do you believe that complements or conflicts with your religious beliefs?" In other words, to know how Americans respond to the question "Do you believe in God?" does not tell us much about the character of religion in the society. By probing for answers to these other questions, however, the nature of religion in American life becomes much clearer. Again, it should be clear that answers to these questions do not exhaust all there is to know about religion, nor all that is within the legitimate domain of the sociologist to explore, but to answer them adequately will take us further down the road to understanding.

The structure of religious belief and religious institutions is enormously complex, and the material which follows is in no sense an adequate description of this complexity. It is only a beginning. I cannot even claim that all the significant or important issues are raised in this volume. However, I do hope that the nature of the questions raised is considerably more sophisticated than the question "Do you believe in God?" and that the evidence presented sheds some light on issues which have heretofore only been the subject of speculation.

I

The Threefold Crisis

The Christian churches today are in the midst of a struggle which has every evidence of being the most serious ferment in Christendom since the Protestant Reformation. Some have even spoken of the developments of the past few years as the "New Reformation." The general mood of liberal church leaders has been one of euphoria over the prospects of reuniting Christians who have for centuries been divided over disagreements regarding doctrinal issues. *But those who have been unfalteringly optimistic about the prospects of Christian unity have turned their backs on other developments which have been taking place simultaneously—developments which are threatening seriously to disrupt or alter existing church structures.*

The optimists have assumed that the ecumenical spirit is a reflection of emerging doctrinal unity, an assumption which the evidence of this volume will prove to be unfounded. But more important, they have largely ignored at least two alternative explanations of ecumenicism. First of all, is it possible that theological differences have not so much disappeared as they have become *irrelevant?* If traditional theological doctrines of the Christian churches have become irrelevant, one must ask what it is that has become relevant. And whatever the new relevancy may be, one must further ask if the rank and file of those who call themselves Christians share this new relevance. If the church is in the process of becoming a "new thing" one must ask what this new thing is, as well as the basis of its authority. It is clear that the historical church gathered its authority from many sources, but its strength cannot be divorced from the fact that central to its authority was an elaborate system of rewards and sanctions. The church held the keys to heaven and hell and could say, "No man cometh unto the Father but by me."

If the rational-scientific world has not shattered this concept of traditional authority, it has certainly shaken the foundations. Earlier generations of Christians accepted their religious heritage as the given nature of the social order. Contemporary man, on the other hand, is more acutely aware of the dimensions of *faith,* and that his acceptance represents a commitment to one of several explanations of ultimate meaning in a complex social order. Contemporary man is increasingly a pragmatic being, and his acceptance of a particular world view cannot be divorced from pragmatic motivations. If his "faith" demands too much of him, or makes demands which conflict with other goals or values which he holds, what is to keep him firmly in the fold of believers? This has become a particularly acute issue in an age in which men are having increasing doubts as to whether the church holds the keys to heaven and hell—and, in fact, doubt that such places even exist, or that such concepts are relevant to understanding the human condition.

This leads to a second interpretation of the meaning of the ecumenical thrust which is not frequently discussed by the proponents of unity. In the broadest sense, organizations unite for one of two reasons: either their unity can provide an advantage, i.e., better chances of accomplishing goals, or it is a necessity in order for one or both of the merging organizations to survive. The phenomenal post-World War II growth of church real estate and membership may make the "merge to survive" thesis seem preposterous to some. However, a more careful examination of what is happening in Protestantism today may lend greater tenability to this thesis than is apparent on the surface.[1]

The purpose of this book is to describe and interpret sociologically the central developments that are emerging in contemporary religious institutions. Sociology provides a rich theoretical and historical perspective for understanding religion. While this volume is informed by this tradition, it does not attempt to integrate or even summarize that branch of intellectual thought which is called the sociology of religion. Although such an exercise would provide a broader perspective for interpreting and understanding the central thesis of this volume, it is not essential for understanding this volume. This volume attempts to document contemporary evidence of the crisis of religious institutions. For a fuller understanding of the historical origins of this crisis, the reader will need to turn elsewhere. Hopefully, those who are stimulated by this volume will be encouraged to do so. Peter Berger's book *The Sacred Canopy: Elements of a Sociological Theory of Religion* provides an invaluable historical and theoretical understanding of the broader implications of what is attempted here.[2]

The central thesis of this volume is that the Protestant churches are involved in a deep and entangling crisis which in the years ahead may seriously disrupt or alter the very nature of the church. The civil rights crisis in this nation is seen as the central issue which has served as a catalyst to unleash the sources of latent conflict which have been gathering in Protestantism for more than a half century. In the broadest sense, these sources of conflict are as old as Protestantism itself.

From a narrow perspective, this is a study of the church's response to the civil rights confrontation in this nation, but the broader objective is to understand why the church has responded to civil rights as it has, as well as the implications of this response. While the study focuses almost exclusively on Protestant churches, the social forces which are reshaping Protestantism seem also to be at work within Roman Catholicism. No systematic attempt is made to develop this latter thesis, but anyone familiar with developments within Catholicism will be able to see the parallel developments.

Because of the decentralized nature of Protestantism, many church leaders and the vast majority of the churchgoing public have not really grasped the depth and complexity of the growing crisis. In the high councils of churches one hears innuendoes about the "silent revolution" and an "underground church," but private conversation with many church executives has led me to question whether those who speak of revolution fully understand the significance of what is happening. Only a few seem to grasp the implications of the warning of one high church official who privately told me, "The crisis confronting the churches today has arisen because we have not faced up to the consequences and implications of the fact that we have too long been deceiving the polity."

The deception, though I would argue that this is not really the appropriate word, cuts deeply along two dimensions. The first dimension is a struggle over the very *purpose* and *meaning* of the church. Clergy have developed a new meaning of the nature of the church; but for a variety of reasons, laity have not shared in the development of this new meaning. Today, laity are beginning to realize that something is different, and for many this is a source of the gravest concern, for the new image is in sharp conflict with their own concept of the meaning and purpose of the church. The second dimension of unrest in the churches is a crisis of *belief*. As the data presented in this study dramatically reveal, Christian theology has been shaken at the foundation. But again, the laity have largely been left out of this painful struggle to reinterpret the meaning of the Christian theological heritage for contemporary society.

Yet a third dimension of crisis in the church grows out of the first two, and that is a struggle over *authority*. Clergy have long been vested with authority to run the church as they have seen fit. Today, laity are discovering that they have grave reservations about the way clergy have handled their authority, and the evidences of power struggles are beginning to be apparent.

The Crisis of Meaning and Purpose

The struggle over meaning and purpose in the churches today is perhaps best summarized in the title of a recently published study of Episcopalians, *To Comfort and to Challenge*.[3] To many, the church is a source of *comfort* and help in a troubled world, but to an increasing number, labeled by theologian Harvey Cox as the "New Breed,"[4] the church has become an institution to *challenge* men to put an end to social injustice in this world. As the New Breed pushes for greater commitment to the challenge role, growing evidence suggests that there is an inherent conflict between the roles of comforter and challenger.

The emergence of the challenge orientation has a long history, but it has largely been isolated and alienated from the mainstream of church life. However, during the 1960s cries of discontent have begun to lash out as never before. Norman Vincent Peale's popular "peace of mind" brand of Christianity has been blasted as a "cult of reassurance." Billy Graham, Mr. Evangelism, has been accused of distorting the gospel and encouraging pietist content and self-righteousness, and thus diverting the church from its true mission of servanthood in the world. *Together*, a popular Methodist magazine, has been criticized for creating an image of Christ that is "indistinguishable from the rest of the lonely crowd." And so the criticism goes. Phrases like "suburban captivity," "solemn assemblies," and "the comfortable pew" have become household terms which symbolize the increasingly uneasy status of contemporary religious institutions. The critics have left few sacred stones unturned.

Of all the areas of criticism, the lack of aggressive action in race relations has emerged as the most critical indicator of the church's commitment to the status quo. The picture of eleven o'clock on Sunday morning as the most racially segregated hour in America has flashed across the nation and around the world as a symbol of American religion.

While the number of critics calling for social change in the church is large, a few names stand out among the many as spokesmen for a new church. A brief review of the writing of some of these men will illustrate the scope and nature of their criticism. It will also illumine the nature of the conflict to which this book is addressed.

William Stringfellow is a white Episcopalian layman who, upon graduation from Harvard Law School, took up residence in a Harlem tenement and for seven years devoted his professional skills to helping poor Negroes and Puerto Ricans in the Manhattan ghetto. *My People Is The Enemy* is a penetrating autobiographical account of his life in Harlem.[5] Few white men have grasped the depth and complexity of the never-ending struggle for survival in the ghetto as Stringfellow has. It is understandable, therefore, that his major quarrel with the church is its failure to face up to the race issue. The church's failure, Stringfellow says, is much deeper than simply barring its doors to Negro participation. For four centuries the church has, in a variety of ways, supported the racial status quo. Even those who have professed to care and understand the problem have by their words and actions revealed how little they understand the nature of the problem. "Mainly, they have repeated the empty dogmas of humanism and the platitudes of tolerance."[6] Even the thousands of white clergymen and church members who participated in the August 1963 March on Washington have no reason for pride. Their entry into the struggle was too late and with too little understanding to make a decisive difference. The initiative had already passed from the hands of the white man.

But even though the church has entered into the struggle, albeit late, ". . . most white churches and their members are still uninvolved and uncommitted."[7] Much of Stringfellow's criticism is directed at the church's failure to realize the *latent* consequences of its economic policies. The following passage illustrates the nature of his criticism:

> . . . The churches have, with few exceptions, refused to risk their wealth or use their enormous economic power in American society in the racial struggle, except as they continue to commit it intentionally, or by default, to segregation and discrimination. The churches of main-line, predominantly white American Protestantism have investments of staggering magnitude in business and industry, not only endowments controlled and invested by denominational mission boards, but also investments held by regional jurisdictions and by the larger parishes in the cities and the suburbs. How many of them have ever even examined their investment portfolios to find out whether the enterprises in which they have substantial holdings practice discrimination in hiring or job training? A few have, but most have not even considered such an involvement in the struggle; among those who have given this consideration, the view has usually been taken that it is inappropriate for the churches to use their economic power for social ends. They overlook the fact that their economic power *is* already committed to social ends wherever it is part of the investment in enterprises which practice segregation and discrimination. And they overlook the fact that the most effective weapon in the racial crisis has not been legislation, or even court decision, or demonstrations, or federal troops, but economic sanctions.[8]

Another critic who elaborates the latent consequences of church policy is Gibson Winter. In his book *The Suburban Captivity of the Churches* Winter describes how the church's exodus from the central city has left the metropolis without responsible moral leadership at a time in history when it has never been needed more.[9] Winter notes that the modern metropolis in America has evolved two fundamental, underlying principles of social organization. The first is increasing political and economic *interdependence.* Yet in the midst of increasing functional interdependence the life of the metropolis is being fragmented by a growing pattern of *communal insulation,* ". . . a pattern of segregated communities of personal association shapes the neighborhoods of the metropolis; skin color, style of life, manners, and even religious ties create autonomous ghettos of people from a similar occupational level and ethnic background."[10]

These realities of the emerging shape of the metropolis are well documented in dozens of sociological studies. What is unique in Winter's argument is his contention that white Protestants have been the vanguard of the suburban exodus. Furthermore, this pattern is not new. Native white Protestants first began the exodus in response to large numbers of Roman Catholic immigrants. Later, Jews and foreign-born Protestant ethnic groups were to accelerate the flow from the central city. Thus, the most recent suburban flight in response to the large urban influx of Negroes is only a repetition of a pattern that has been occurring for over half a century. The native white Protestants have been joined more recently by Jews, Catholics, and the immigrant Protestant groups. In their escape from the central city, each group is struggling desperately to maintain an insulated community of people who in terms of social, ethnic, and religious characteristics are alike. Winter sees this as a fundamentally pathological attempt to "set the clock back a hundred years."[11]

Furthermore, Winter argues that the religious congregation has become the symbol around which people have attempted to maintain some semblance of a common life. "The search for identity in the churches seems to be a grasp for traditional symbols by an uprooted and alienated social class. . . ."[12] This ghettoization of socially different groups has created a fundamental paradox for Protestantism: "How can an inclusive message be mediated through an exclusive group, when the principle of exclusiveness is social-class identity rather than a gift of faith which is open to all?"[13] Protestantism, thus, rather than serving as a transforming and integrating force in the metropolis, has simply mirrored the patterns of segregation, following the lines of least resistance.

Winter feels that this is a betrayal of the early Christian church, which was socially inclusive. *"The churches can only embody or mediate a true identity to their members when the fellowship of members represents the interdependencies of human life. Inclusiveness is intrinsic and not accidental to the nature of the church."*[14]

Winter does not argue that the church's disengagement from the central city was a cunning and deliberate strategy. Rather, it has resulted from its failure to consider the implications of the forces of social change. While many congregations have had good intentions, the effect of their exodus from the central city has been an abdication of Christian responsibility where it is most needed. ". . . congregations are disengaged from answerable relations with the metropolis;

they are autonomous bodies which claim to be answerable to God, yet seem to be answerable only to their own survival as organizations."[15]

Of the several contemporary books that have criticized the church, none is more disturbing than Peter Berger's *The Noise of Solemn Assemblies*.[16] Like other critics, Berger posits as his central thesis that the church has ignored its mission of social responsibility in the world. Christian responsibility, Berger argues, involves not only concern for the problems of individuals but also a vital commitment to attempt to change the very social structures which have created human problems.

Berger builds his argument in two directions. First, he develops a theological defense of the contention that the church ought to be more vitally involved in the transformation of the world. One of his central arguments on the nature of involvement in the world pivots on Jesus' charge to his disciples to be "wise as serpents and innocent as doves" (Matthew 10:16). Berger argues that this passage has not been properly understood as an explanation of the *nature* of involvement, but rather in being misunderstood has become a justification for ignorance and abdication of responsibility in the world. His position is well summarized in the following passage:

> . . . What is characteristic of our church life today is not "innocence" in this sense of religious passion; it is rather in the common American sense of the word "innocent" as a quality of being intellectually untouched, as a euphemism for plain ignorance and obtusiveness, as another way of saying "born yesterday." Religion then becomes a starry-eyed optimism, a naive credulity in the ideologies of the *status quo,* something that goes together with an unthinking if benign conservatism in all areas of life. When all is said and done, religion then becomes a solemn ratification of an existence of trying to get along with a minimum of awareness. This is not only humanly reprehensible. It is an offense against the integrity of the Christian commitment.[17]

But Berger's most penetrating critique is his sociological analysis of the nature of the religious establishment. His analysis not only draws from a theoretical tradition in sociology and anthropology but also represents an outstanding attempt to integrate and interpret research findings by social scientists. Berger's conclusion is that religion in American culture has become enthralled in a complex set of symbols of social integration, social control, and justification for the existing social order. Religion is a leisure-time activity which, having been consumed on Sunday, bears no relevance to the life and work of Christians on Monday. Religion is hopelessly bound to social class, and the "upper-strata individuals who 'consume,' say, Congregationalism . . . [do so] . . . in the same way and for the same reason that they 'consume' *filet mignon,* tailored suits, and winter vacations in the Caribbean."[18] ". . . it ratifies the routines, sanctifies the values by which the social roles are rationalized, comforts the individual if personal crises threaten his social adjustment."[19] In short, religion has lost its cutting edge to transform individuals and social structures into agents vitally committed to making the world into an authentic Christian experience.

In 1963 Ernest Harrison, representing the General Board of Religion of the Anglican Church of Canada, approached Pierre Berton, a Canadian journalist and television personality, about writing a Lenten study book for 1965. Harrison explained that the Anglicans had not had much success with their Lenten books and they felt that a "name" writer might produce something that was both critical and stimulating. The intriguing aspect of this request was that Berton was not a member of the Anglican Church or any other church. He was, at best, what theologian Paul Tillich called a member of the "latent church."

Berton's book, *The Comfortable Pew,* was destined to be born in controversy, and when it was published in the United States some six months after its appearance in Canada, 150,000 copies had already been printed, a figure well beyond any other book ever published in Canada.[20] *The Comfortable Pew* quickly became a controversial best seller in the United States.

Berton's major contention was that the voice of the church had simply become "weak, tardy, equivocal, and irrelevant."[21] "The Church to its opponents has become a straw man, scarcely worth a bullet."[22] To Berton, the church was rapidly growing bankrupt and might very well cease to function within the next century. His quarrel with the church was not simply that he disagreed with the church's position on a wide range of social issues, but rather that the church had failed to move even after the general public and most other social institutions had reached consensus on changing realities in the world.

Unlike some of the other critics, who concentrated their attacks on a single issue, Berton's shotgun blasted in many directions. The following partial list of chapter titles is illustrative of the range of his criticism: "Was God Really on Our Side?" "What Colour Was Christ?" "Is Good Business the Church's Business?" and "Can Christian Morality be Pre-Packaged?" Like other critics Berton indicts the church for its marriage to the status quo:

> It has all but been forgotten that Christianity began as a revolutionary religion whose followers embraced an entirely different set of values from those held by other members of society. Those original values are still in conflict with the values of contemporary society; yet religion today has become as conservative a force as the original Christians were in conflict with.[23]

But the critics of the "stand pat" church have not been satisfied to confine their criticism to written words. During the 1960s the New Breed began to express their views in direct action, in defiance of church authorities and laity who saw no role for the church in direct confrontations of power and social protest. The civil rights movement had dramatized the persistence of social injustice for Negroes in our society, and an increasing number of clergymen had come to feel that there was an enormous disparity between the teaching and practices of the Christian church.

In early 1961 the first sizable show of clerical collars appeared in the historic integrated Freedom Rides through the Deep South. The rides were effective, for they not only dramatized the overt bigotry, hostility, and violence in the South but also caused the Interstate Commerce Commission to issue a ruling calling for desegregation of bus, train, and air terminal facilities. Fresh from a political and moral victory in the South, clergy returned north to participate in the struggle to desegregate restaurant and motel facilities along U.S. Route 40 between New York and Washington, D.C.

During the summer of 1962 white clergymen participated in the racial struggle in Albany, Georgia. In 1963 the National Council of Churches created the Commission on Religion and Race, and this office was to become the heart of the church's struggle for involvement in the civil rights movement. In August of that same year, several thousand clergymen were among the crowds that descended on our nation's capital for the historic March on Washington. From that point on, the clerical collar has become as much a part of the imagery of the civil rights protest as the bearded students in sandals and Bull Connor with his dogs and fire hoses. In the years which have followed, the efforts of clergy to change existing social conditions have taken many forms, and there can be little doubt that the number of clergy who have become involved has steadily increased.

The forces of the status quo in the churches were not to remain silent. The more active the clergy became in the civil rights struggle, the more their opposition within the church began to fight back. One of the most outspoken critics of church involvement in social issues is J. Howard Pew, chairman of the board of Sun Oil Company and vice-president of the board of trustees of the general assembly of the United Presbyterian Church in the U.S.A. In a *Reader's Digest* article, Pew indicts the church for "meddling" in civil affairs.[24] Pew feels that the church's involvement in secular matters is directly traceable to a "creeping tendency to downgrade the Bible as the infallible Word of God."[25] "I go to church," says Pew, "to hear heralded the mind of Christ, not the mind of man. I want to hear expounded the timeless truth contained in the Scripture, the kind of preaching that gets its power from 'Thus saith the Lord.' "[26]

Pew feels that by teaching Christian principles, individuals will be able to relate these principles to secular matters. However, for the clergy or the church as a corporate body to engage in secular issues is to meddle and thus subvert the basic purpose of the church, which is "to preach the Gospel" and "convert men to a personal faith in Jesus Christ." Pew goes on to say, "To commit the church as a corporate body to controversial positions on which its members differ sharply is to divide the church into warring camps, stirring dissensions into one place where spiritual unity should prevail."[27]

Pew concludes by pledging resistance to the involvement of clergy in social issues: "If the church's 'social activists' are to be halted from plunging the church again into areas where it has no jurisdiction, its concerned laymen and clergymen will have to make their voices heard more clearly in the high councils of their denominations."[28]

The Christian Century, a moderately liberal ecumenical weekly, responded angrily with an editorial entitled "The Uncomfortable Pew."

We do not usually review and criticize fantasy but in this case we cannot ignore the challenge. For Mr. Pew's "springboard for discussion" will be widely quoted as unassailable proof that the church should abandon its crusades for justice in the world and return to spiritual things. Ironically, social conservatives and religious fundamentalists will conclude that Mr. Pew's astonishing success in what he calls the secular world somehow enables him to designate for the church its "God-ordained jurisdiction." We expect that the appearance of this article in a large-circulation popular magazine will produce more mischief with one blow than the God-is-Dead fury produced with several.

We said "fantasy" not in malice but seriously and by design. The world Mr. Pew envisions and the Christian Gospel to which he appeals in his defense of monastic ethereal Christianity exists solely in his and kindred minds and has no basis in reality. Mr. Pew's world is a segmented one in which the economic, civil, political and ecclesiastical parts are rigidly isolated from each other and in which the church should address itself only to things ecclesiastical—such as man's eternal well-being and his post-historical destiny. In his compartmentalized world the church becomes a sacred precinct, a religious enclave, a fortress in which men may retire from the morassness of the world but from which they can advance only one by one in attacking the world's injustices. Mr. Pew allows the *individual* Christian "to relate his conscience to the problems of the secular society of which he is a part" but if two or three Christians are gathered together to protest collectively the war in Vietnam, racial discrimination in Alabama, exploitation of fruit pickers in California, then Christ cannot be in the midst of them.

The Christian Gospel knows no such disjunction in man's affairs. The world into which Christ came, in which the church as his body remains and into which Christ sent his disciples is not an ecclesiastical province, but man and all of man's affairs, the whole human empire and not one of its minor colonies. This is the world "God so Loved," and for which He gave His Son—total man in his total setting. . . .

Mr. Pew's segmented world is inhabited by curiously stratified men, men whose lives are divided horizontally into an upper story where they keep things spiritual and a ground floor where they live among things secular. . . . To the Gospel, man is neither spiritual nor secular, nor is he a bifurcated spiritual-secular being. He is man. The restoration of his wholeness as man is one part the salvation of Jesus Christ brings him. When the church treats man as though he were spiritual in one part and secular in another, angel when he kneels in prayer and devil when he dances, morally responsible personally but morally irresponsible collectively, a saint when he worships and a sinner when he plays, clean when he disciplines his body but unclean when he celebrates its pleasures—when the church thus makes religious schizoids out of men it thwarts the saving power of the Christ who came to make men whole.[29]

Mr. Pew's pledge to make his and other voices heard more clearly in the high councils of the denominations was not an empty threat. At the time of his article in *Reader's Digest* he was already on the board of directors of an organization called Presbyterian Lay Committee, Inc., which has as one of its goals the discouragement of public pronouncements by church leaders on political, social, and economic issues. Mr. Pew and his group of Presbyterian laymen are not alone. Similar organizations have been formed by laymen in other denominations, including the Methodists and the Episcopalians.

In short, the struggle over the meaning and purpose of the church shows every evidence of intensifying. On the one hand are a growing number of clergy, supported by a minority of laymen, who are no longer content to see the church remain an institution where the socially and economically advantaged can seek comfort and reassurance that their view of the world is really right. On the other side stand laity and clergy who see no need radically to redirect the nature and purpose of the church. This, then, is part of the basis of the struggle for authority which we shall return to later in this chapter.

Crisis of Belief

The crisis over meaning and purpose is complicated by an increasing crisis of belief. The most striking evidence of doubt and uncertainty about the traditional doctrines of the Christian faith has been the emergence of a small group of theologians who call themselves "Christian atheists" and proclaim the "Death of God."

The amount of attention this group has received is far out of proportion to its size. As far as the popular press is concerned, the controversy largely centers around three young theologians: Thomas J. J. Altizer of Emory, Paul VanBuren of Temple, and William Hamilton of Colgate Rochester Divinity School. To this point, their disciples appear to be few in number but curiosity and interest run high. Religious periodicals, whether sympathetic or in staunch opposition, have found it impossible to ignore this group. Similarly, the mass media have found that the catchy and provocative phrase makes good copy.

Moving beyond the cloud of controversy to an understanding of what the "Death of God" theologians are saying is not an easy task. Two things, however, are clear. First, not all of the "Death of God" theologians are saying the same thing and there is some question as to whether some of the individuals are saying the same thing from one publication to the next.[30] Secondly, not everyone is hearing the same thing. What one interprets as old-fashioned atheism in polysyllabic terms is interpreted as symbolic rhetoric by another.

It is beyond my task to attempt to unravel the complexities of the "Death of God" debate, or to speculate about the enduring theological importance of this development. What does seem apparent, however, is that this development has served to dramatize the growing *crisis of imagery* in Christian theology.

In this sense, the "Death of God" theology can be viewed as simply another manifestation of the growing dissatisfaction with the traditional imagery of God. The "Death of God" theologians are, in another way, wrestling with the same problems as the most heralded theologians of the mid-twentieth century. The struggle is to find a meaningful theology which is both true to the Christian heritage and relevant to the realities of contemporary secular society.

This struggle, which has been taking place for many years in the theological schools, has now become a public debate. But the "Death of God" theologians are not the only ones responsible for airing this theological struggle in the public arena.

In early 1963 the Student Christian Movement Press in London published a little book by the Bishop of Woolwich, John A. T. Robinson, entitled *Honest to God*.[31] In just a matter of weeks this volume became a best seller in Britain and the United States. Bishop Robinson's message was at best fairly simple and unoriginal: "Our image of God must go." He was not denying God, but rather repudiating the traditional images of God that have been taken for granted by a large segment of the Christian world. In many respects the Bishop's book does not represent original theological thought, but rather is an attempt to synthesize and translate the works of a number of contemporary theologians for an audience that does not normally devour theology for pleasure or as a scholarly discipline. Robinson draws heavily from the thought of three outstanding theologians of this century, Paul Tillich, Dietrich Bonhoeffer, and Rudolf Bultmann.

Honest to God was praised as a courageous and imaginative expression of contemporary thought and condemned as a betrayal of virtually every basic Christian doctrine. A second edited volume, entitled *The Honest to God Debate,* reflects the range of response.[32] Eric Routley, a Congregational minister and historian, writes, "I cannot write objectively and dispassionately about this. I can only record that the reading of it gave me more comfort, more encouragement, and more sense that life is worth living, and the ministry worth exercising, than any book I have read for years and years."[33]

Journalist T. E. Utely, on the other hand, views Robinson's book with alarm and sees in it the deepest roots of heresy:

> What should happen to an Anglican Bishop who does not believe in God? This, I hold, is the condition of the Bishop of Woolwich, as revealed in his paperback, *Honest to God,* and it raises, I maintain, a question of Church discipline which cannot be shirked without the greatest repercussions on the whole Anglican Communion. . . .
>
> It is one thing to restate the eternal truths of religion in contemporary language and quite another expressly to repudiate fundamental doctrines which were believed by those who learnt Christianity from the lips of Christ. It is not always clear, indeed, whether the Bishop's aim is to convince agnostics that they can conscientiously go to church or to persuade Christians that there is no need to do so. At the lowest, he seems to be violating the principles of honest commerce by trying to see as Christian a commodity that bears no relation to the historical and accepted meaning of that word.[34]

Others, however, have failed to see anything startling or new in *Honest to God.* The late C. S. Lewis, for example, wrote, "The Bishop of Woolwich will disturb most of us Christian laymen less than he anticipates. We have long abandoned belief in a God who sits on a throne in a localized heaven. We call that belief anthropomorphism, and it was officially condemned before our time."[35]

But most readers have not responded to Bishop Robinson with such casual indifference. Wherever the theologians have gone during this century in search of God, most laity and a large proportion of the clergy have continued to live with the conception of a deity who is either "up there" or "out there." The Tillichian conception of God as the "Ground of our being" had not penetrated far beyond the circles of intellectual elites, and thus Robinson's book resulted in a storm of controversy. Many clergy have felt that the struggle to re-interpret the Christian theology should be carefully guarded and kept from laity for fear that they would abandon the church. This view is reflected in the response of the Rector of Birmingham to *Honest to God:*

> . . . The Bishop has written a dangerous tract published in a paperback edition. Anyone, whether equipped or not to understand it, can easily buy it and read it and they probably will in great num-bers because of all the publicity and outcry resulting from its pub-lication. This is a pity, because really the book is not intended for everyone. All parsons should read it and all well-educated laymen who are interested in Christianity. Other people may well be more hindered than helped by the tentative, exploratory, question-raising nature of the book. Before a new restatement of the Christian faith can be offered to ordinary men and women who are seeking faith for daily living, a long theological task lies before the scholars of the Christian churches. Until then ordinary Christians must use the old categories in their prayers and and in their preaching, allowing their lives to bear witness to the truth.[36]

To some laymen the appearance of *Honest to God* was a re-freshing revelation. But to others it was a shocking confirmation of what they had long suspected—that theologians had abandoned the most fundamental doctrines which have been held to be the very basis of the Christian heritage.

Before the storm over *Honest to God* had settled, a new storm hit the Christian world with nearly the same force as the Robinson book. In early 1965 a young Baptist theologian, Harvey Cox, pub-lished *The Secular City.*[37] A few weeks after the publication of this book, a noted theologian, Paul Lehmann, addressed an assembly of college and university chaplains on the campus of Cornell University. In his opening comments he stated, "It is not often one reads a book that both changes one's mind and alters one's habits of thought. Harvey Cox's *The Secular City* has done this both *for* me and *to* me."[38]

Again, as with *Honest to God,* it was only a short time before

The Secular City was on the paperback best seller list and one of the most talked-about books of the year. Cox's thesis pivots on four themes which may be interpreted as the consequences of urbanization and secularization: *anonymity, mobility, pragmatism,* and *profanity.* Most intellectuals, including theologians, have viewed these developments with a good deal of consternation and despondency. For Cox, they are the forces of human liberation. With urbanization and secularization, man has become free from the bondage of traditional moral sanctions and ideologies which have focused his attention on supernatural concerns. Secular man is free and charged with the responsibility to make of the world what he will.

> The Kingdom of God, concentrated in the Life of Jesus of Nazareth, remains the fullest possible disclosure of the partnership of God and man in history. Our struggle for the shaping of the secular city represents the way we respond faithfully to this reality in our times.[39]

But Cox does more than challenge a whole history of anti-urban intellectual thought. He views the forces of secularization as largely rendering traditional religion irrelevant. Furthermore, we ought to celebrate rather than disparage this development.

> The forces of secularization have no serious interest in persecuting religion. Secularization simply bypasses and undercuts religion and goes on to other things. . . . The age of the secular city, the epoch whose ethos is quickly spreading into every corner of the globe, is an age of "no religion at all." It no longer looks to religious rules and rituals for its morality or its meaning. . . . It will do no good to cling to our religious and metaphysical versions of Christianity in the hope that one day religion or metaphysics will once again be back. They are disappearing forever and that means we can now let it go and immerse ourselves in the new world of the secular city.[40]

Again, the response to *The Secular City* has been vigorous and mixed. On the one hand are those who stand with Paul Lehmann, proclaiming that this book has changed their lives. Others find nothing but confusion and heresy in *The Secular City* and lump Cox in the same camp with the "Death of God" writers.

One of the interesting aspects of these two books is that neither authors nor publishers anticipated the public response. Both were written for student audiences. Both had very small initial printings.

Both have exceeded a half-million sales to date. While perhaps expressing modesty, Bishop Robinson reflects considerable insight as to the "publicity explosion" in a comment in *The Honest to God Debate*. He states, "It is a safe assumption that a best-seller tells one more about the state of the market than [about] the quality of the product."[41]

Without diminishing the significance of these books, it would seem that the public response has to be understood as a reflection of the growing doubt and uncertainty about the traditional expressions of Christian belief and of the desire to discover new and acceptable images.

This growing doubt about orthodox theology is also reflected in sociological studies of the beliefs of Christians. In a recent study conducted in the San Francisco Bay Area, Charles Y. Glock and Rodney Stark found striking differences in the beliefs of Christian laity.[42] They found that in matters even as basic as belief in the existence of God, more diversity of belief was found among the denominations than was found to exist between Protestants and Catholics. On many doctrinal issues, the range of beliefs professed was as much as seventy percentage points. Furthermore, there was no single doctrinal issue raised by Glock and Stark on which Protestants even approached unanimity. When the mean was computed to determine the belief of the "average Protestant" there was often no single denomination that even came close to this hypothetical average.

Glock and Stark, thus, challenge the assumption of emerging doctrinal unity, and propose rather the emergence of a "New Denominationalism" which they suggest may be fragmenting the very core of the Protestant heritage. They conclude that:

> The new cleavages are not over such matters as how to worship God properly, but whether or not there is a God of the sort it makes any sense to worship; not over whether the bread and wine of communion become the actual blood and body of Christ through transubstantiation, or are only symbolic, but over whether or not Jesus was merely a man.[43]

In Chapter III we will examine the beliefs of clergy in six major Protestant denominations. The results, as we shall see, reveal an amazing similarity to the beliefs of laity. Differences in theological beliefs are great both between and within denominations. Of the six Protestant denominations studied, only one even approached a consensus of belief.

Thus, the crisis of doubt and ambiguity of belief is not confined to the theologians but rather penetrates into the rank and file of both clergy and laity. Among the Protestant laity in the Glock and Stark study, 29 per cent had at least some doubts about the existence of God, 43 per cent were not completely convinced that Jesus was born of a virgin, and 35 per cent had some doubt as to the possibility of a life beyond death. Among Congregationalists, the most liberal denomination in the study, the proportion who expressed doubt regarding fundamental orthodox beliefs ran much higher. Fifty-nine per cent had some doubts about the existence of God, 79 per cent expressed some doubt about the virgin conception of Jesus, and 64 per cent were not altogether certain that there is a life after death.

Clergy have the same difficulty accepting orthodox Christian doctrine. Twenty-six per cent of the clergy are not completely convinced that the birth of Jesus was a biological miracle, and 18 per cent cannot affirm the doctrine of divine judgment after death where some will be rewarded and others punished. Perhaps even more important is the fact that 62 per cent of the clergy indicate that they would expect a *thinking* Christian to have doubts about the existence of God; with doubt comes rejection of certain specific doctrines.

Of course, it can be argued that rejection of orthodox doctrine does not necessarily represent a crisis of belief. In modern theology, myth and symbol have replaced literalism as the basis for interpreting and understanding the Christian heritage. Thus, one may reject literalism and not reject the faith, but rather accept a new basis for understanding it.

While this may be true, it ignores some important consequential implications. In the first place, among literalists there is a consensus, or near consensus. But when symbol and myth are introduced as the basis for understanding the foundation of a faith, consensus is shattered. What is myth to one is literal to another, and while there may be consensus that a particular passage of scripture may be symbolic, the interpretation may vary. And who is to say which interpretation is correct, or what is acceptable and unacceptable? In short, when a group can no longer proclaim "Thus saith the Lord," the basis of authority has been challenged. We will return to the implications of this later, but at present it is sufficient to note that the absence of authority constitutes an important dimension of the growing crisis of belief. Among theologians, clergy, and laity we see the evidence of this doubt. What is central doctrine to some is unimportant to others. The boundaries that divide Christians on matters of belief are only partially denominational. Within denominations and single congregations are many varieties of belief.

There are still other ways in which this growing doubt can be seen. Church attendance is one of the most important indicators of religious convictions and involvement. A person may participate in religious activities for reasons other than belief, but failure to participate at all suggests that a person either has doubts about the importance of his religious faith or that in his priorities of values, other things are more important. Independent of the content of belief, religion is an overarching, all-embracing system of values which defines the nature of ultimate reality.[44] If one fully accepts the values of a religious system, participation in the activities of that system is a critical way in which acceptance and support is manifest and through which the doctrines of the system are learned and rein-

TABLE 1

CHURCH ATTENDANCE SHOWS
GRADUAL DECLINE SINCE 1955

% Attending Church During an Average Week, 1955–66

1955	49%
1956	46%
1957	47%
1958	49%
1959	47%
1960	47%
1961	47%
1962	46%
1963	46%
1964	45%
1965	44%
1966	44%

Source: George Gallup Poll as quoted in *Information Service,*
Vol. XLVI, No. 2, January 28, 1967.

forced. In short, participation in religious activities is a barometer of the strength of the faith.

In 1958 church attendance reached a peak in American society. According to the Gallup Poll, 49 per cent of all Americans attended church in an "average" week. Since 1958, the proportion of Americans who attend church regularly has slowly but consistently declined. During 1966, only 44 per cent of the American public attended church during an average week.[45]

Certainly caution must be exercised in interpreting these figures. However, examination of additional data from the Gallup survey suggests some fairly regular patterns which are logically consistent with the trend toward declining church attendance. To begin with, the figure of 44 per cent attendance during an average week masks diversity within major religious groups.

Catholics are by far the most regular attenders in American society. During an average week 68 per cent of the Catholics attend religious services, compared with only 38 per cent of the Protestants. Members of the Jewish faith are by far the least frequent attenders, with only about one in five indicating that they attend religious services weekly.

TABLE 2

ATTENDANCE VARIES AMONG RELIGIOUS GROUPS

% Attending Church During an Average Week in 1966

National	44%
Religion:	
Catholic	68%
Protestant	38%
Jewish	22%

Source: George Gallup Poll as quoted in *Information Service,* Vol. XLVI, No. 2, January 28, 1967.

Moreover, the proportion attending religious services also varies considerably within Protestantism, with the more theologically conservative churches showing the highest levels of attendance. Forty-three per cent of the Lutherans report attending church during an average week, compared with 34 and 31 per cent respectively for Methodists and Episcopalians. In other words, church attendance is lowest among those denominations where doubt or rejection of orthodoxy is highest.

TABLE 3

ATTENDANCE VARIES WITHIN PROTESTANTISM

% Attending Church During an Average Week in 1966

National	44%
All Protestants	38%
Denominations:	
Lutheran	43%
Baptist	37%
Presbyterian	36%
Methodist	34%
Episcopal	31%

Source: George Gallup Poll as quoted in *Information Service,*
Vol. XLVI, No. 2, January 28, 1967.

Finally, church attendance varies with age. Older persons attend with greater frequency than younger age groups. In the most recent Gallup Poll 47 per cent of those fifty years of age and over reported attending church weekly, as compared with 37 per cent in the 20–29 age group.

These various figures on church attendance lend at least inferential support to the thesis that the long-range trend is toward declining church participation and that this decline reflects growing doubt as to the centrality of religious faith in an individual's life. We will return to a discussion of this issue later in the book.

Perhaps even more important than the figures which show a gradual decline in church participation is the fact that Americans *perceive* that religion is losing its influence. Over a period of eleven years George Gallup asked the American public, "At the present time, do you think religion as a whole is increasing its influence on American life, or losing its influence?" In 1957, 69 per cent of the public felt that the influence of religion was increasing. Five years later the proportion who felt the influence of religion was increasing dropped sharply to 45 per cent. The percentage dropped again in 1965 and by 1967 only 23 per cent of the public felt the influence of religion was increasing. During the same eleven-year period, the proportion who felt that religion was losing its influence rose dramatically from only 14 per cent in 1957 to 57 per cent in 1967.

TABLE 4

AMERICANS FEEL RELIGION IS LOSING ITS INFLUENCE

*At the present time, do you think religion as a
whole is increasing its influence on American life,
or losing its influence?*

	1957 %	1962 %	1965 %	1967 %
Increasing	69	45	33	23
Losing	14	31	45	57
No difference	10	17	13	14
No opinion	7	7	9	6

Source: George Gallup Poll as quoted in *The Cleveland Press*,
April 18, 1967.

Younger people are more likely to feel that religion is losing its
influence than older people (63 per cent under thirty years of age,
compared with 53 per cent of those fifty and over). Also, education
is associated with feeling that religion is losing its influence. Sixty
per cent of the public with some college training, as compared with
52 per cent of the public with a grade school or less education, felt
religion is losing ground.

TABLE 5

YOUNGER PEOPLE AND THE EDUCATED ARE MORE LIKELY
TO FEEL THAT RELIGION IS LOSING ITS INFLUENCE

% Saying Religion Is Losing Its Influence, 1967

AGE:
21–29 years	63%
30–49 years	57%
50 and over	53%

EDUCATION:
College	60%
High School	59%
Grade School	52%

Source: George Gallup Poll as quoted in *The Cleveland Press*,
April 18, 1967.

Sociologists have written a good deal about concepts such as the
"definition of the situation," and the "self-fulfilling prophecy." The

gist of these concepts is perhaps most succinctly communicated by one of the founding fathers of sociology. In 1918, W. I. Thomas wrote, *"if men define situations as real they are real in their consequences."*[46] In other words, the very fact that Americans feel that religion is less influential may have consequences which affect the role of religious institutions in our society.

Finally, public opinion polls indicate that the prestige of clergy in America is perhaps at an all-time low. Lou Harris recently found that only 45 per cent of the American public expressed confidence in the clergy.[47] This can be compared with 74 per cent for physicians and 62 per cent for educators. Politicians, who have always been subject to suspicion and distrust by the American public, rank only one percentage point worse than the clergy.

To summarize, we have seen a number of indicators which suggest that religion in America is facing a crisis of belief. Theologies which a few years ago would have been thought of as heresy are now being received with interest and even enthusiasm in some circles. Among clergy and laity there is a great deal of doubt and division of opinion as to what constitutes appropriate belief. This doubt is also reflected in America's changing habits of church attendance. Furthermore, attendance is lowest among those who reject traditional religious orthodoxy. Finally, the majority of Americans feel that religion is losing its influence, and this is accompanied by declining confidence in clergymen.

Crisis of Authority

The growing crisis over the purpose and meaning of the church and the emergence of doubt and theological reorientation have led to a third crisis in the church, namely a struggle over *authority*. In Protestantism, the struggle over authority appears less dramatic than in the Roman Catholic Church, where authority has been centralized for centuries. But the challenging of authority in Catholicism should not overshadow equally significant power struggles that are occurring in Protestantism. The battleground of this struggle does not conform to traditional boundaries of conflict between the major faiths or denominations, but rather is splintering denominations, congregations, and church councils. While the schism cuts in many directions, perhaps the greatest conflict is between clergy and laity.

We have already noted that laity who disapprove of the pronouncements and involvement of clergy in social issues have begun to exert their influence to prevent such activity. To understand the nature of this conflict requires an examination of the church as an organization and clergymen as its professional leaders.

To begin with, religious organizations are *voluntary associations*.[48] By this is meant that individuals choose to participate out of their own volition and not because of some external force which compels them to membership. The distinction between a voluntary and a non-voluntary association can sometimes be ambiguous. In some nations and at some points in history, the church has been much less a voluntary association than is the case in contemporary American society. To those who view their personal salvation as inextricably bound to participation in the church, it may not seem like a voluntary association. And in some social environments very strong informal pressures are exerted to force conformity to a set of socially prescribed behaviors which include participation in a particular religious group. Nevertheless, there is a strong and growing element of voluntarism in the individual's participation patterns in a religious group. Frequency of attendance, amount of financial support, and the intensity of adherence to the doctrines and goals of a particular religious group are, to a large extent, voluntary and private decisions. If an individual strongly objects to some aspect of the particular religious group to which he belongs, he is, in most cases, free to join another religious group or withdraw from participation in a religious group altogether. Thus, our description of religious institutions as voluntary associations must be understood in a broad, general descriptive sense and not as an absolute principle. As we shall see, a number of factors determine the degree of a religious organization's voluntariness.

From what we have said thus far, it follows that the ongoing functioning of a voluntary association depends on a basic consensus among the membership as to the goals or purposes of the organization. That is to say, if an organization is completely voluntary, its membership must, in a broad sense, accept the organization's goals. Without some rewards or sense of satisfaction, there are no forces to sustain an individual's participation. It is important to recognize, however, that the rewards or satisfactions that a person derives from participation in a voluntary association may be secondary or latent to the formally stated goals. Thus, for example, a member of a bridge club may not be a particularly good bridge player and as such may not derive a great deal of satisfaction from playing bridge. However, the ongoing satisfaction of sociability with a group of friends may be more than adequate reward to sustain membership in the group. But when a person who doesn't play bridge well ceases to enjoy the company of the other players, there is little reason to continue membership in the group and the chances are pretty great that this person will drop out. The point is simply this: A person who derives nothing from participating in a voluntary association is not likely to continue to participate. Similarly, if the negative factors involved in participation are perceived to outweigh the positive benefits, membership, or at least commitment, is likely to be curtailed.

Turning from the individual participants to the leaders of a voluntary association, it follows that one of the tasks of the leadership is to see that the organization continues to provide its membership with rewards that are satisfactory to assure their continued participation. If the leadership chooses to redefine the goals and rewards, they must either convince the membership of the efficacy of the new goals and rewards or they must seek to recruit new members who share their definition of the organization. Failure to achieve one or the other of these tasks will result either in the demise of the organization or in their loss of the leadership role.

Leadership in a voluntary association, thus, involves a greater element of precariousness than in non-voluntary organizations. Voluntary associations are less likely to give their leaders a mandate to develop their own goals for the organization. The leader must operate within the boundaries of his prescribed role as leader. To deviate beyond the role prescriptions of his office is to invite conflict with the membership.

At this point we need to introduce some additional concepts to understand the precarious nature of the leader's role in a voluntary association. The first concept is *power,* by which we mean the ability of an individual or a coalition of individuals to exercise their will in a group with respect to some goal or activity. *Authority,* on the other hand, is the legitimate right to exercise power. The Congress, for example, has the legal right to declare war. When a President wages an undeclared war he does so by virtue of the fact that he has the informal power to persuade Congress to appropriate funds to the military. If enough congressmen disapprove of the war so that they refuse to appropriate expenditures to the military, then the President cannot pursue war because he lacks the *authority*.

Sociologist Max Weber has described three ways by which a leader may gain authority.[49] The first of these is *tradition*. Over a period of time certain rights and powers come to be associated with an office, i.e., leadership position. Therefore, the incumbent of an office assumes authority because traditionally the holder of that office has assumed authority with respect to specific tasks. A second type of authority described by Weber is *rational-legal* and accrues to a specific office because the group has established laws or rules which specify that the office legally embraces certain specific authority. A third type of authority is called *charismatic* and accrues to an individual leader because he possesses traits which inspire confidence and a willingness on the part of the members of the group to follow his directives, independent of what tradition and law may define as the means of authority.

Paul Harrison, in his study of the American Baptist Convention, described a fourth type of authority, which he calls *rational-pragmatic*.[50] This is power that is not legitimately authorized, but rather is "power grasped" because the holder of an office finds it expedient to exercise power in a vacuum where power has not legally been authorized. These types of authority, to be sure, are only ideal-type constructs, and a careful scrutiny of the types reveals that they are not necessarily independent types. Nevertheless, they are useful for the present discussion.

While the study of complex organizations is a young intellectual enterprise and as such lacks a well-developed and empirically verifiable theoretical framework, it is our contention that different types of authority tend to develop in different types of organizations. Specifically, voluntary associations are less likely to develop elaborate specifications of *rational-legal* authority for their leadership. Thus, the leader in a voluntary association must rely more on his own charismatic qualities and his ability to grasp *rational-pragmatic* authority.

In the Protestant churches the leadership is predominantly made up of clergymen. While Protestantism presumably differs from Catholicism in its adherence to the theological doctrine of the priesthood of every believer, in reality the major bulk of the planning, pro-

graming, and decision-making in Protestantism has been entrusted
to a professional leadership group—the clergy. Harrison describes
well the difference between theory and reality in the American Baptist Convention, a denomination which is particularly sensitive to
the role of laity and the autonomy of the local church. The theory
provides an integral role for laity and the local church in decision-
making processes of the denomination. In reality, however, laity
and the local congregation participate in policy formation in only a
most perfunctory way. The major power in the denomination rests in
the hands of church executives, usually clergy, who have little legal
authority but have enormous pragmatic influence. While the organizational structure of the American Baptist Convention may be
unique in the degree of its failure to grant legitimate authority to
positions of leadership, the same phenomena can be clearly observed in other denominations.

In the past, laity have not objected seriously to the authority
structure in their churches. To the extent that they have even been
aware of the fact that the clergy were calling most of the shots, they
have not been particularly disturbed. But when the rank and file of a
voluntary association object to the direction in which the leadership
is moving the organization, they begin to exercise their own authority. In Protestantism today, laity, who have entrusted authority to professional leaders, have come to have grave doubts about
how the authority has been used, and are beginning to assert their
own influence.

An examination of the ways in which this is happening points
up the importance of our comments about the church as a voluntary
association. Because the church is a voluntary association, laity have
very significant authority vis-à-vis their ability to withhold or control the nature of their support. The collective annual budgets of
the Protestant churches in America total several hundred million
dollars. While some of these operating expenses come from foundations, endowments, and investments, by far the greatest source of
operating revenue comes from the ongoing voluntary contributions
of the membership. Without these voluntary contributions, most
churches would close their doors in a matter of weeks. But this is
not the only source of power that the laity hold. In many denominations they have the immediate authority to hire and fire a minister,
and in those denominations where this task is removed from the

local congregation, they can still exercise influence by threatening to withhold their financial contributions. And finally, the layman can exercise influence by threatening to withdraw membership from the organization. One layman whose financial contribution to the church is relatively small may have relatively little power if he chooses to oppose his local pastor. But several members or a single member whose contribution constitutes a significant proportion of the congregation's budget must be contended with.

Thus, by virtue of the fact that a church is a voluntary association, it must operate within boundaries that are acceptable to its membership. When it begins to move outside these boundaries, conflict becomes inevitable. The evidence of this conflict has become increasingly apparent during the past few years in Protestantism.

Mr. Pew, whom we mentioned earlier, is only symbolic of the growing discontent among laity. In the New York Episcopal Diocese, one layman withdrew a $600,000 pledge because of his opposition to clergymen's involvement in civil rights. In the same diocese a similar financial sum was lost in pledges to the building fund of the Cathedral of St. John the Divine. Bishop Horace W. B. Donegan admitted that the Cathedral's position on racial justice, including the hiring of a Negro priest, was the major cause for the withdrawal of pledges. Another Episcopal diocese reportedly suffered a loss of 25 per cent of its pledges, largely in opposition to the liberal stance that the Bishop had taken on a number of social issues. At least two Episcopal lay groups, "Episcopalians for the Faith" and "Episcopalians for Christ," have been organized to resist the rising tide of church pronouncements and involvement in social issues. Father Lester Kinsolving, co-chairman of the legislative division of the Episcopal Diocese of California, writes that "the possibility of a right-wing take-over is a critical issue today in hundreds of local Episcopal churches."[51]

These are only examples, and not an exhaustive catalogue, but the Episcopal Church is not alone in this conflict. In the American Baptist Convention, one of its largest and wealthiest congregations withdrew in protest to the denominational affiliation with the National Council of Churches. In a Washington suburb, the assignment of a Negro minister to an all-white Methodist congregation brought a 50 per cent decline in attendance and a similar reduction in financial contributions, in spite of the fact that the pulpit committee had voted unanimously to accept a minister "regardless of race." In Shaker Heights, Ohio, a wealthy Cleveland suburb, a multiple-staff Presbyterian church was forced to let one of its ministers go because of a decline in contributions. The decline in funds resulted from the fact that two of the associate pastors had signed a statement calling for the resignation of school board members in Cleveland during the school crisis of early 1964 which saw the death of another young Presbyterian minister. At least two other Shaker Heights ministers resigned as a result of their congregations' opposition to their involvement in the same crisis.

Because much of the conflict over authority is decentralized, it is difficult to determine just how widespread the episodes have been. My own clipping of newspapers and interviews with hundreds of clergy over the past three years, however, would suggest that the actual extent of confrontations is much broader than is generally believed. Furthermore, I see little evidence that the basis for continued conflict will be eliminated soon. If anything, the full impact of the latent conflict has not yet been felt.

This, then, is what this book is all about. In recent years, three crises have been emerging in the Protestant churches; a crisis over its very meaning and purpose for being, a crisis of belief, and a crisis of authority. The three crises are obviously interrelated. Clergy have challenged the traditional role of the church in society because they have reinterpreted the theological basis of their faith and in so doing have come to feel that their faith involves a much more vital commitment to the problems of this world. Laity have challenged the authority of clergy because they do not share their understanding of the meaning and purpose of the church. The shattering of traditional doctrines has weakened the authority of the clergy, for it is no longer certain that they hold the keys to the kingdom.

Examination of this conflict leads us in a number of directions, which hopefully will provide a deeper understanding of the crisis. Chapter II examines the nature of religious beliefs and attempts to document more thoroughly the sources and nature of ambiguity and doubt that have been raised in this chapter. The focus of this examination is the beliefs of Protestant clergymen, but other sources of data are introduced to demonstrate that this crisis is not confined to clergy.

Chapter III explores the relationship between theology and social issues. It attempts to answer the question: "Do one's beliefs about theological doctrines affect the way one feels about social issues?" For clergy, the answer is an emphatic yes. While the data for laity are less adequate, religious beliefs seem to operate independent of beliefs about social issues. This provides an initial basis for understanding the conflict between clergy and laity.

Chapter IV zeroes in on civil rights, the issue which has generated so much conflict between clergy and laity. Data are examined which reveal the beliefs of both groups toward civil rights. In addition, the attitudes of laity toward the involvement of clergy in civil rights are examined.

Chapter V looks at the processes by which clergy have become involved in the civil rights struggle. In addition to ideology, we examine group dynamics and the ways in which organizational structures have facilitated involvement. This provides a broader basis for understanding how the conflict has emerged and why it cannot be easily resolved.

The final chapter attempts to integrate and interpret the results of the study. Strictly speaking, it represents a departure from the role of an objective scholar unfolding the results of his inquiry and attempts to speculate about the meaning and implications of the findings.

II

The Nature of Religious Belief

In the introductory chapter we reviewed a broad range of evidence which is indicative of belief patterns in Protestantism. The purpose of this chapter is to explore this issue in more depth by examining the religious beliefs of clergy and laity, and to speculate about the implications of this theological disunity. Major emphasis is devoted to the beliefs of clergy. This examination represents a preliminary report of a comprehensive survey of the beliefs of campus and parish clergy conducted by the author under the auspices of the Danforth Study of Campus Ministries directed by Dr. Kenneth Underwood. The data reported here deal only with parish clergy. Briefly, the purpose of the broader study is to describe the relationships between ministers' theological orientation, perception of their calling, their professional responsibilities, their attitudes toward public issues, their social backgrounds, and their personalities.[1] More detailed description of the results of this study will be presented in subsequent volumes. The examination of laity beliefs presented here is based primarily, though not exclusively, on the recently published findings of Charles Y. Glock and Rodney Stark, mentioned in the introductory chapter.

The Religious Beliefs of Protestant Clergy

DESCRIPTION OF THE SAMPLE. The data on the beliefs of clergy were gathered early in 1965 by a mail questionnaire which was sent to a "random" sample of parish clergy and the entire population of campus clergy in six major Protestant denominations: American Baptist, American Lutheran, Episcopalian, Methodist, Missouri Synod Lutheran, and Presbyterian, U.S.A. The sampling procedure involved the random selection of a number (N) and then drawing the name of every Nth full-time parish clergyman from the official roster of each denomination. The data reported here are based on the responses of 7441 parish clergy. The over-all response rate for the study was 67 per cent. Individual denominational response rates ranged from 60 per cent for Episcopalians to 73 per cent for Presbyterians. Considering the length of the questionnaire (524 questions) the response rate is unusually high. This was achieved with a persistent follow-up of five letters encouraging co-operation with the study. Comparison of the first five hundred questionnaires returned with the last five hundred returned revealed no systematic differences on responses of these two groups of clergy. However, an examination of the background characteristics of the non-respondents indicated that these clergy tended to be somewhat older, theologically more conservative, and likely to serve smaller churches in rural areas. However, in terms of the over-all picture of the beliefs of clergy, this does not constitute a significant bias in the findings reported here.[2]

The attitude or belief items in this study were responded to on a six-point continuum, i.e., clergy were asked to choose one of six categories which most nearly represented their response to the attitude statement: definitely agree, agree, probably agree, probably disagree, disagree, and definitely disagree. This range of response categories is very useful for certain types of statistical analysis. In addition, this approach captures a greater sense of the saliency of an item than simply asking a person to "agree" or "disagree" with a statement. However, the presentation of all six response categories in percentage tables is very cumbersome and confusing for the lay reader. Therefore, unless otherwise noted, the percentages reported in this volume combine the definitely agree and agree categories. At some points, the splitting of these two categories or the addition of the probably agree response adds some depth to the analysis. Such cases are noted in the text.

INTERPRETATION OF THE BIBLE. The Bible is considered to be the central document that informs Christians of their heritage and faith. While the literal authenticity of the Bible has long been challenged, its central place in Christian history has not. Therefore, it is appropriate that our analysis of religious beliefs begin with an examination of ministers' views of the role of the Bible in understanding the Christian faith.

Of the many questions in the study which deal with religious beliefs, four items are addressed to the question of how the scriptures are to be interpreted. The response of clergy to these four statements dramatically reveals that contemporary Protestant ministers substantially disagree in matters as basic as how the Bible should be used and interpreted.

The first statement reads, "I believe in a literal or nearly literal interpretation of the Bible" (Table 6). Denominational differences are immediately apparent. Only 11 per cent of the Episcopal clergy said that they believe in a literal or nearly literal interpretation of scripture. The proportion of literalists increases to approximately one in five among Methodist and Presbyterian ministers. Moving on down the table, 43 per cent of the American Baptist and American Lutheran clergy report that they accept the scriptures literally. Finally, more than three quarters of the Missouri Synod Lutheran clergy believe that the Bible is to be accepted as literal truth. The difference separating the Episcopalians, the most liberal group on this item, and the Missouri Synod Lutherans, the most conservative, is 65 percentage points.

TABLE 6

SCRIPTURES SHOULD BE INTERPRETED LITERALLY

"I believe in a literal or nearly literal interpretation of the Bible."	% Agreeing
Methodist (N = 2515)*	18
Episcopalian (N = 1270)	11
Presbyterian (N = 1198)	19
American Baptist (N = 654)	43
American Lutheran (N = 908)	43
Missouri Synod Lutheran (N = 895)	76

* N = Number of respondents on which the percentage is based.

A second statement attempts to apply the general principle of literalism to a specific biblical passage, namely the miraculous account of creation (Table 7). The item reads, "Adam and Eve were individual historical persons." In four of the six denominations the percentage who reported that they believe scriptures should be interpreted literally corresponds very closely to the percentage that believe that Adam and Eve were real persons. While 11 per cent of the Episcopalians say they believe in a literal or nearly literal interpretation of scripture, only 3 per cent are prepared to accept the Genesis account of creation. In contrast, while 76 per cent of the Missouri Synod Lutherans believe scripture should be interpreted literally, 90 per cent believe in the authenticity of the creation of man. In other words, approximately a half of the Missouri Synod clergy who reject the idea that scriptures are to be understood literally *do not* reject the biblical account of the creation of Adam and Eve. Thus, the differences which separated the six denominations on the first statement become even greater when a specific scriptural text is examined.

TABLE 7

CREATION STORY IS LITERALLY TRUE

"Adam and Eve were individual historical persons."	% *Agreeing*
Methodist	18
Episcopalian	3
Presbyterian	16
American Baptist	45
American Lutheran	49
Missouri Synod Lutheran	90

A third statement attempts to explore the authenticity and authority of scriptures for understanding historical, natural, and secular events (Table 8). It reads, "Scriptures are the inspired and inerrant Word of God not only in matters of faith but also in historical, geographical, and other secular matters." The same broad range of response is apparent across denominations, but some notable differences appear. Perhaps most interesting is the fact that in all but one denomination the per cent agreeing with this proposition is less than the per cent who believe the story of Adam and Eve. Similarly, the per cent agreeing with this item is less than the per cent who agree that scriptures should be interpreted literally (Table 6). Thus, two important observations are apparent. First, to say that scriptures should be interpreted literally does not mean that their authority is without limitation when applied to matters that do not strictly deal with faith. Second, the principle of literalism can be rejected without implying rejection of a specific liberal doctrine—even though the doctrine may be subject to serious challenge by scientific evidence.

This raises the very interesting question of the processes by which some doctrines are accepted and others rejected. What is essential to belief and what is optional to the individual? Other than to raise this question, it is beyond our task and available data to explore the issue in detail here. However, as specific doctrines are examined in this chapter it is difficult to escape the conclusion that this is a highly ambiguous matter and that there is really no consensus.

TABLE 8

AUTHORITY OF BIBLE IS NOT LIMITED TO MATTERS OF FAITH

"Scriptures are the inspired and inerrant Word of God not only in matters of faith but also in historical, geographical, and other secular matters."	% Agreeing
Methodist	13
Episcopalian	5
Presbyterian	12
American Baptist	33
American Lutheran	23
Missouri Synod Lutheran	76

A final item introduces the role of myth and symbolism in interpreting the Bible (Table 9). The statement reads, "An understanding of the language of myth and symbol is as important for interpreting Biblical literature as are history and archaeology." The literature of conservative Protestant traditions has, to a considerable degree, acknowledged the proposition that archaeology and historical documents other than the Bible could be useful for increasing the world's understanding of the origins and nature of the Christian faith. They have been reluctant, as is suggested in Table 6, to introduce mythology and symbolism as legitimate sources of understanding. Table 9 is largely a confirmation of Table 6. If the percentage believing in a literal interpretation of scripture (Table 6) is added to the percentage who find myth and symbol informative (Table 9), the resulting sum approaches 100 per cent, suggesting that clergy tend to see the Bible in either literal or symbolic terms. The only major exception to this pattern is the Missouri Synod Lutherans. Adding the two responses together results in a total of 110 per cent. This may indicate the strain and tension in attempting to have it both ways. Their theological tradition has taught literalism, but on the other hand there is now considerable evidence which calls for symbolic understanding.

TABLE 9

MYTH AND SYMBOL ARE IMPORTANT FOR
UNDERSTANDING SCRIPTURE

"An understanding of the language of myth and symbol is as important for interpreting Biblical literature as are history and archaeology."	% Agreeing
Methodist	77
Episcopalian	88
Presbyterian	76
American Baptist	62
American Lutheran	62
Missouri Synod Lutheran	34

In summary, these four statements dramatically reveal that in matters as fundamental as understanding and using the Bible as a source of authority, the various denominations substantially disagree. While the Missouri Synod Lutherans are clearly in most radical disagreement with the other denominations, the distance between the other groups is considerable and cannot be easily dismissed. This wide range of response may not be particularly surprising to those who are familiar with the doctrinal positions of these denominations. However, several important factors should be kept in mind. First of all, while these differences have been suspected by some, others have argued that denominational differences in belief have ceased to be an important consideration in Protestantism. The data reported here are the first attempt of its kind to document the beliefs of clergy. While some may consider it to be a documentation of the obvious, there exists a substantial body of speculative literature which is made invalid by these findings. Secondly, while the differences across denominations are great, it should be emphasized that differences *within* denominations are also very substantial. As we explore other areas of belief, we will see that the implications of these differences are extremely important.

DOCTRINE OF LITERALISM. With the exception of the Adam and Eve statement, the items we have examined thus far have dealt with the issue of how scriptures should be used and the scope of their authority. We turn now to a consideration of several Christian beliefs. Specifically, six traditional theological doctrines are examined: the virgin birth of Jesus, the physical resurrection of Christ, life after death, hell, the devil, and original sin. The items selected do not exhaust the religious beliefs examined in the study. Indeed, the religious belief section of the questionnaire contained 115 statements. These particular items were selected because of their centrality in traditional orthodoxy. That these doctrines are no longer central in the thinking of some Christians does not detract from their historical importance. Indeed, they remain central to many Christians and the fact that they are not central to others is a source of deep concern and, at the least, latent conflict in the churches. On the basis of what we have seen above, the readers should not be surprised to find widespread disagreement on these doctrines. Our task here is to demonstrate the extent and nature of this disagreement.

The first doctrinal statement deals with the miraculous conception of Jesus and reads as follows: "I believe that the virgin birth of Jesus was a biological miracle" (Table 10). Only 40 per cent of the Methodist clergy assent to this statement. In other words, the majority of Methodist clergy either do not believe in the virgin birth of Jesus or they attach some significance to this scriptural story other than as a miracle. Among Episcopalians and Presbyterians the percentage accepting this position is slightly more than half. Still, nearly half are unwilling to acknowledge belief in this doctrine. Only in the two Lutheran groups does the percentage accepting the virgin birth doctrine approach a substantial majority. Eighty-one per cent of the American Lutherans agree with the statement, and virtual consensus is attained among Missouri Synod clergy, with 95 per cent saying that the virgin birth was a biological miracle.

TABLE 10

JESUS WAS BORN OF A VIRGIN

"I believe that the virgin birth of Jesus was a biological miracle."	% *Agreeing*
Methodist	40
Episcopalian	56
Presbyterian	51
American Baptist	66
American Lutheran	81
Missouri Synod Lutheran	95

The Bible tells that not only the birth but the death of the founder of the Christian faith was steeped in the miraculous. Having been crucified and buried, on the third day Jesus Christ arose from the dead and dwelt among his disciples. Because this incident has been subjected to symbolic interpretation, the wording of the statement attempted to exclude symbolic interpretation. It was worded as follows: "I accept Jesus' physical resurrection as an objective historical fact in the same sense that Lincoln's physical death was a historical fact" (Table 11). In other words, the resurrection really happened and was not simply a symbolic happening in which his followers were grasped by the spirit and meaning of his life.

Again, the Methodists are the most likely to reject the literal interpretation of this doctrine. Only half (49 per cent) of the Methodist clergy believe in a literal physical resurrection. At the other end of the continuum, 93 per cent of the Missouri Synod Lutherans believe that this is the way it happened. While the over-all picture is one of greater belief in this doctrine than in the virgin birth, considerable doubt or disbelief is present. Moreover, the conservative denominations are more likely to respond "strongly agree" than the more liberal denominations. Thus, while denominational differences are clearly apparent in Table 11, the combining of the two "agree" categories tend somewhat to camouflage the range of response to this statement. It is also interesting to note that while Episcopalians are the least likely to report belief in a literal interpretation of scripture, this particular doctrine is important to them in its literal form. Seventy per cent of the Episcopal clergy report that they believe in the physical resurrection as an objective historical fact.

TABLE 11

JESUS ROSE PHYSICALLY FROM THE GRAVE

"I accept Jesus' physical resurrection as an objective historical fact in the same sense that Lincoln's physical death was a historical fact."	% Agreeing
Methodist	49
Episcopalian	70
Presbyterian	65
American Baptist	67
American Lutheran	87
Missouri Synod Lutheran	93

The doctrine of divine judgment has also been central to the Christian tradition. The third doctrinal statement asserts the reality of salvation and damnation: "I believe in a divine judgment after death where some shall be rewarded and others punished" (Table 12). Again, denominational differences are broad, ranging from 52 per cent of the Methodists who believe in divine judgment to 94 per cent of the Missouri Synod Lutherans. Also note that for three of the denominations the percentage of clergy who accept the doctrine of divine judgment is only slightly larger than the per cent who do not accept this belief.

TABLE 12

AFTER DEATH COMES DIVINE JUDGMENT

"I believe in a divine judgment after death where some shall be rewarded and others punished."	% Agreeing
Methodist	52
Episcopalian	55
Presbyterian	57
American Baptist	71
American Lutheran	91
Missouri Synod Lutheran	94

The next item introduces a symbolic interpretation of hell. Rather than asking clergy if they believe in hell as a special place where people burn eternally or otherwise suffer, the statement asserts that hell refers to a mental state in this life. The item reads, "Hell does not refer to a special location after death, but to the experience of self-estrangement, guilt, and meaninglessness in this life." Sixty per cent of the Episcopalians accept this highly non-literal interpretation of the meaning of hell. They are followed closely by the Methodists, with just 2 per cent less agreeing with this position, and 54 per cent of the Presbyterians feel that hell is to be defined in terms of mental anguish and meaninglessness in this life. Approximately one third of the Baptists and one in five of the American Lutherans interpret hell in these terms. By far the most literal group on this item is the Missouri Synod Lutherans, with only 6 per cent agreeing with the interpretation of hell suggested in the statement.

TABLE 13

HELL REFERS TO A CONDITION IN THIS LIFE,
NOT AN AFTERLIFE

"Hell does not refer to a special location after death, but to the experience of self-estrangement, guilt, and meaninglessness in this life."	% *Agreeing*
Methodist	58
Episcopalian	60
Presbyterian	54
American Baptist	35
American Lutheran	22
Missouri Synod Lutheran	6

The doctrine of a demonic force in the world, like the doctrine of hell, has been subjected to a good deal of demythologizing. The statement in the clergy survey reads as follows: "I believe in the demonic as a personal power in the world" (Table 14). While the wording of this statement leaves room for a broad range of interpretations of the meaning of a demonic force in the world, and thus increases the possibility that persons holding both symbolic and literal views would agree with this statement, the denominational spread remains wide. Agreement with this statement ranges from

38 per cent among Methodists to 91 per cent among Missouri Synod Lutherans, with the other denominations being rather widely spread between these two positions.

TABLE 14

THE DEMONIC IS A REAL FORCE IN THE WORLD

"I believe in the demonic as a personal power in the world."	% Agreeing
Methodist	38
Episcopalian	63
Presbyterian	53
American Baptist	67
American Lutheran	86
Missouri Synod Lutheran	91

A final doctrinal statement deals with original sin: "Man by himself is incapable of anything but sin" (Table 15). Once again, Missouri Synod Lutheran clergy are almost unanimous in agreeing with this statement (85 per cent). Agreement falls off sharply in other denominations. Among American Lutherans, slightly less than three quarters agree with the stated position. All other groups fall below 50 per cent, with only 36 per cent of the Methodists agreeing that man by himself is destined to be a sinner. The spread of belief on the doctrine of original sin is the greatest of any of the six doctrinal statements: 49 percentage points separate the extremes.

TABLE 15

MAN IS GUILTY OF ORIGINAL SIN

"Man by himself is incapable of anything but sin."	% Agreeing
Methodist	36
Episcopalian	45
Presbyterian	47
American Baptist	40
American Lutheran	73
Missouri Synod Lutheran	85

Several general observations on religious beliefs follow from our examination of these six statements. First of all, note that the Methodists have replaced the Episcopalians as the most liberal denomination on these issues. Where the Episcopalians are the most liberal in rejecting a literal *interpretation* of scripture, fewer Episcopalians than Methodists are actually willing to reject specific literalist doctrine. On four of the six statements the Episcopal clergy are more conservative than the Presbyterians, and 70 per cent of the Episcopalians accept the physical resurrection of Jesus, a greater proportion than the Baptists show. Thus, while more liberal in asserting . that scriptures should not be interpreted literally, Episcopalians are more likely than some of the other groups to accept literal interpretations of the specific doctrines examined here, particularly those doctrines dealing with the miraculous.

The Methodists, more than any of the groups, have jettisoned orthodox beliefs. Only 36 per cent believe in original sin; 38 per cent accept the notion of the demonic; 40 per cent believe in the virgin birth; and 49 per cent say that they believe in Christ's physical resurrection. Only on the doctrine of divine judgment after death do more than half of the Methodists agree with an orthodox position. On that item 52 per cent agree.

The Missouri Synod Lutherans, on the other hand, remain consistently the most conservative or literalist denomination. On all six items 85 per cent or more of the Missouri Synod Lutherans interpreted the scriptures literally. Their sister church, the American Lutheran, was the next most conservative church, with approximately 75 per cent or more accepting the literal view of the scripture. The spread between Methodists and Missouri Synod Lutherans is no less than 42 percentage points (divine judgment) and ranges as wide as 55 per cent (virgin birth).

On the initial items dealing with how scriptures should be interpreted, Baptists and American Lutherans were close together; on actual interpretation of doctrine, however, the American Lutherans stand nearer the fundamentalist Missouri Synod Lutherans, and the Baptists nearer the moderate Presbyterians.

While Glock and Stark's laity study and this study of ministers cover many of the same theological issues, the wording of the questions does not permit a direct comparison of responses. In addition, the survey of laymen used a four-point response scale, ranging from "completely true" to "definitely not true," and the study of clergymen used a differently worded six-point scale. Nevertheless, three statements are nearly parallel, permitting some comparison. These deal with the virgin birth, the devil, and the innately evil nature of man (Table 16).

The results show a remarkable similarity on these items between laity and clergy within each denomination. Although the figures seem

TABLE 16

COMPARISON OF BELIEF STATEMENTS OF
LAITY AND CLERGY

	Methodist	Episcopalian	Presbyterian	American Baptist	American Lutheran	Missouri Synod Lutheran
VIRGIN BIRTH						
Laity:						
"Jesus was born of a virgin."						
(% answering "completely true")	34	39	57	69	66	92
Ministers:						
"I believe that the virgin birth of Jesus was a biological miracle."						
(% answering "definitely agree")	28	40	36	58	68	90
DEVIL						
Laity:						
"The devil actually exists."						
(% answering "completely true")	13	17	31	49	49	77
Ministers:						
"I believe in the demonic as a personal power in the world."						
(% answering "definitely agree")	21	38	30	49	66	78
EVIL NATURE OF MAN						
Laity:						
"Man cannot help doing evil."						
(% answering "completely true")	22	30	35	36	52	63
Ministers:						
"Man by himself is incapable of anything but sin."						
(% answering "definitely agree")	19	25	25	22	53	72

Source for Laity data: Charles Y. Glock and Rodney Stark, *Religion and Society in Tension* (Chicago: Rand McNally & Co., 1965), Chapter 5, Tables 3, 5, and 6.

to indicate that the clergy are more liberal than laity, one should hazard only cautious comparisons because of the dissimilarities between the studies mentioned above, and because of the small number of questions.

More important is the evidence that the liberal-to-fundamentalist order of denominations among ministers corresponds to that found among laymen by Glock and Stark. The Episcopal and Methodist clergymen, like laymen, are the most liberal. The Missouri Synod Lutheran clergy, like laymen, are the most fundamentalist. The few deviations that occur in the middle denominations involve only a few percentage points.

These data strongly suggest that where theological reorientation is taking place, it is happening for both clergy and laity and in about the same proportion. However, it will be argued later that clergy and laity are not shifting their theological outlooks for the same reasons, nor are the consequences of their change the same.

AGE AND CONSENSUS. Thus far, the data from this study of clergy strongly support Glock and Stark's conclusion that Protestants do not have a common-core creed. Theological issues that divide laity also divide clergy, and with approximately the same magnitude. Furthermore, differences are wide within as well as between denominations. Thus, whatever the reasons for increasing interdenominational co-operation, ecumenicism does not appear to emerge from any growing doctrinal unity, as some have postulated.

However, the data from both studies are for a single point in time, so there is no way of knowing how far apart the denominations under consideration were, say, twenty-five years ago. While never an adequate substitute for a study over time, an examination of different age groups may provide some clues as to possible changes in theological views. If there is any basis for the thesis of emerging doctrinal unity, we would expect to find younger ministers, irrespective of denomination, moving toward a consensus on doctrinal issues.

To examine this thesis we shall return to the belief statements which were examined earlier and look at the responses by age groups. Turning first to the statement "I believe in a literal or nearly literal interpretation of the Bible," we see in Table 17 an unambiguous movement by the younger ministers toward a non-literal interpretation of the scriptures. In every denomination, younger clergy have a more liberal view regarding the interpretation of scripture than do older age groups. For example, only 14 per cent of the Presbyterians under age thirty-five believe in a literal interpretation of scripture, compared with 31 per cent of those over age fifty-five. The other two age groups fall in a rank order position between the youngest and oldest age groups. Minor deviations from this pattern, involving only a few percentage points, do occur for the two groups over forty-five years of age. But the consistency of the pattern is of much greater significance than the minor deviations.

TABLE 17

YOUNGER CLERGY ARE LESS LIKELY TO BELIEVE IN A LITERAL INTERPRETATION OF SCRIPTURE

"I believe in a literal or nearly literal interpretation of the Bible."	Methodist	Episcopalian	Presbyterian	American Baptist	American Lutheran	Missouri Synod Lutheran
			% Agreeing			
Under 35	11	5	14	27	24	72
35–44	16	11	16	41	43	73
45–54	23	14	23	55	60	79
Over 55	23	14	31	47	74	84

In four of the six denominations the percentage of the youngest clergy who believe in a literal interpretation of scriptures is less than half the percentage of the oldest age group holding this view. In a fifth denomination (American Baptist) the ratio of young to old who believe in scriptural literalism is nearly half. Only among the Missouri Synod Lutherans do we fail to observe significant age shifts. In this denomination 84 per cent of the oldest age group, compared with 72 per cent of the youngest age group, report that they believe in the literal interpretation of scripture.

Examining the youngest and oldest clergymen across the six denominations discloses that the youngest are generally closer together than the oldest. While the Missouri Synod Lutherans do not constitute an exception to this generalization, the differences in age groups for this denomination are much less dramatic than in other denominations. The greatest differences across denominations when age is controlled appears in a comparison of Episcopalians and American Lutherans. While 60 percentage points separate the oldest age cohorts, the youngest age groups in these denominations are separated by only 19 per cent.

Earlier in this chapter we examined three statements on the nature and authority of scripture. In order to avoid detailed and repetitive interpretation, these same items are not presented here with age controls. However, these tables do appear in a statistical appendix so that the interested reader may examine them to observe the consistency of response as well as possible interpretations that are not developed here. With only minor exceptions, the age breakdowns for the other three items conform to the same pattern observed in Table 17. This same procedure of presenting detailed statistical tables in an appendix will be followed in subsequent sections of the book.

While Table 17 shows substantial differences in response by age groups, a word of caution should be introduced regarding the interpretation of these results as real change over time. It is possible, for example, that as clergy become older they become more conservative in their views about scripture. Although this interpretation is possible, it does not seem probable in this case. On the basis of preliminary analyses of the impact of theological seminaries on the beliefs of clergymen, we found that older ministers who were educated in seminaries that were liberal forty years ago are considerably more liberal than those who were educated in more conservative seminaries.[3] Thus, it would appear that the differences observed for the various age groups does indeed represent change.

Turning from the question of how scripture should be interpreted to the specific doctrinal issues explored in Tables 10 through 15, the hypothesis of emerging theological unity among the younger generation takes on a much more complex motif. Table 18 presents clergy response to the statement "I believe that the virgin birth of Jesus was a biological miracle," divided by the four age groups. (Additional items on doctrinal issues controlling for age appear in the appendix.) While the youngest clergymen still tend to be more liberal than the older ones, the dramatic differences we observed between age groups in Table 17 are no longer apparent. Age groups are separated on the virgin birth doctrine by approximately 15 to 20 percentage points, with younger ministers being more likely to reject the literal doctrine. The *proportional* differences separating the extreme age groups is considerably less than was the case on the items dealing with how scripture should be interpreted.

TABLE 18

YOUNGER CLERGY ARE LESS LIKELY TO ACCEPT
THE DOCTRINE OF MIRACULOUS CONCEPTION OF JESUS

"I believe that the virgin birth of Jesus was a biological miracle."	Methodist	Episcopalian	Presbyterian	American Baptist	American Lutheran	Missouri Synod Lutheran
			% Agreeing			
Under 35	31	49	38	58	70	94
35–44	43	53	52	64	84	95
45–54	42	57	57	75	92	96
Over 55	48	65	61	68	92	98

On other doctrinal issues the age differences tend to be even less than the age differences on the virgin birth statement (see appendix). Only very minor age differences occur on the doctrines of physical resurrection and original sin. In several instances younger clergy accept a literal position of scripture to a greater degree than do the older clergy. For example, 97 per cent of the Missouri Synod Lutheran clergy under age thirty-five believe in the physical resurrection of Jesus, compared with 87 per cent in the over fifty-five age group. Similarly, 67 per cent of the youngest group of Episcopalians report belief in the demonic as a personal power in the world, as compared with 58 per cent of the oldest age group of Episcopalians. But these reversals in pattern are not consistent for all denominations. This would seem once again to underscore the impact of denominationalism in the educational process.

These data introduce a perspective which contrasts sharply with the interpretation we obtained in Table 17. Younger clergy are considerably more willing than older clergy to accept the general principle that the scriptures are not to be interpreted literally and to accept the idea that myth and symbol are important tools for understanding scripture. However, on the six specific doctrinal issues introduced in this study, younger clergy were not significantly more willing actually to abandon specific doctrine. In fact, on some doctrinal issues younger clergy in some denominations were more likely to hold steadfast to a literalist position than the older clergy.

The convergence of belief among younger ministers in interpreting scripture, then, largely disappears on specific doctrinal issues. In fact, among the liberal and moderate denominations the difference separating the youngest ministers of each is greater on four of the six statements than it is for the oldest age groups. *Younger ministers tend to be about as close or closer to older ministers in their own denominations than they are to ministers of their own age in other denominations.* Thus, denominationalism appears to be significant in determining what a minister actually believes about traditional theology.

While these results strongly suggest that denominationalism greatly influences a minister's theological outlook, the differences within denominations cannot be ignored. On almost every issue, the Methodists are about equally divided in acceptance or rejection of the traditional position. A third or more of the Presbyterians and Baptists each reject a strict literalism. Only in the two Lutheran denominations do ministers approach a consensus of creed.

ECUMENICAL IMPLICATIONS. These findings would seem to have several implications for the current ecumenical movement. Some observers have ascribed the ecumenical thrust to an emerging belief in a common core of American Protestantism. But as noted in Chapter I, this assumption has been challenged by Glock and Stark's study.[4]

They argue that should ecumenicism be central to contemporary Protestantism, little concern for the old disputes like infant baptism and the virgin birth would be found; new awareness of Christian unity would appear instead. But no such unity was found. They suggest two possible interpretations of their findings, which stand in sharp contradiction to the accelerated pace of ecumenical discussion and make difficult any explanation of its progress and prospects. Glock and Stark concluded:

> The denominations simply may not realize the extent of their disagreement on basic doctrine. If so, negotiations aimed at unification may break down sooner or later.
> Concern with theological issues as such may be lessening. Doctrinal barriers may not be seen as especially significant.[5]

However, there remains the question of what other factors may illuminate the sources of ecumenicism. Our findings so far point to three tentative observations:

> First, the denominations are widely divided concerning doctrinal issues, in the pulpit as well as in the pews. Consequently, the ecumenical movement proceeds not from any doctrinal unity, but in spite of it. Protestants are divided; the age of their spiritual leaders makes little difference.
> Second, all the denominations except the Lutherans have a substantial body of clergymen who reject dogmatic literalist theology. It seems appropriate to speculate that this more liberal group is leading efforts toward ecumenical co-operation. Having rejected a dogmatic literalist theology, these liberal ministers may stand ready to co-operate with others of different theological traditions in pursuit of common goals.
> Third, the essence of the ecumenical spirit may have little to do with doctrinal matters.

Our data shed no light directly on ecumenical leadership, but they do indicate that the theological liberals are more open than are conservatives to communication with traditions differing from their own. These statements in the questionnaire were designed to measure tolerance or acceptance of those who doubt or reject Christian teachings. These items read as follows:

(1) "Ambiguity and uncertainty as to what one is to believe and do are signs of faithlessness and indifference to God";
(2) "I would expect a thinking Christian to have doubts about the existence of God"; and
(3) "I have greater admiration for an honest agnostic seeking truth than for a man who is certain that he has the complete truth."

When responses to these statements were cross-tabulated with the six doctrinal belief items, we found that those who reject literal interpretations of scripture are considerably more likely to accept the doubter or disbeliever than are the scriptural literalists. In Table 19 we have constructed a Biblical Literalism Index, which is a summary or composition score of the six doctrinal statements (virgin birth, physical resurrection, life after death, hell, the demonic, and original sin). For each of the six items, rejection of the literalist position was scored 0, uncertainty was given a value of 1, and acceptance of the literal interpretation was scored 2. Thus, a score of 12 would represent the highest possible score on the index, meaning that the individual accepted the literal interpretation of every item, and 0 would represent total rejection of the literalist position. For convenience and clarity of presentation, this thirteen-point scale is collapsed to three positions: high (12–9), medium (8–4), and low (3–0).

The results in Table 19 are quite clear. Those who reject biblical literalism manifest considerably more tolerance and appreciation for those who live with doubts and uncertainty regarding their religious convictions. Similarly, they are much more likely to admire the nonbeliever who is honestly seeking truth than they are to admire a person who is certain that he has completely grasped truth.

The biblical literalist, on the other hand, is much more skeptical of the place of doubt in the Christian faith. For example, 66 per cent of those scoring low in the biblical literalism index indicated that they would expect a thinking Christian to have doubts about the existence of God, as compared with only 38 per cent of those scoring high on the index. Similarly, 82 per cent of those scoring low on the index of biblical literalism, as compared with 44 per cent scoring high, report that they have greater admiration for an honest agnostic seeking truth than for a man who is certain that he has the complete truth.

In sum, these results clearly indicate that tolerance of doubt and even unbelief is strongly related to rejecting literal interpretations of scripture. It would also seem probable that this same group would be more willing to tolerate interpretations of Christian theology different from their own. Although this study has no data on the clergy's involvement in ecumenical activities, the results suggest that such activity is highest among those who have rejected biblical literalism.

This leads to the third observation: The essence of the ecumenical spirit may have little to do with doctrinal matters. Unity may pivot

TABLE 19

BIBLICAL LITERALISTS ARE LESS TOLERANT OF DOUBTERS AND DISBELIEVERS

	BIBLICAL LITERALISM INDEX		
	LOW (3–0)	MEDIUM (8–4)	HIGH (12–9)
	% Agreeing		
"Ambiguity and uncertainty as to what one is to believe and do are signs of faithlessness and indifference to God."	6	12	25
"I would expect a thinking Christian to have doubts about the existence of God."	66	53	38
"I have greater admiration for an honest agnostic seeking truth than for a man who is certain that he has the complete truth."	82	66	44

on a common understanding of the church's place in society. To explore this thesis, we examined the clergy's response to two questions, one which expresses the sentiment that the church should exist *for* the world, and the other which says that the church should withdraw *from* the world.

The first item states, "The Christian church can only be its true self as it exists for humanity" (Table 20). Admittedly, the statement is vaguely worded, and implementation may take a variety of forms,

TABLE 20

THE CHURCH SHOULD EXIST FOR MAN

"The Christian church can only be its true self as it exists for humanity."	% Agreeing
Methodist	75
Episcopalian	61
Presbyterian	72
American Baptist	75
American Lutheran	74
Missouri Synod Lutheran	71

but denominational differences among the respondents have virtually disappeared. With the exception of the Episcopalians, approximately three quarters of the clergy responded affirmatively to this statement.

A second item takes quite a different view from the first, namely that the church ought to withdraw from the world. The statement reads, "The primary task of the church is to live the Christian life among its own membership and activities rather than try and reform the world" (Table 21). This position is strongly rejected by clergy in every denomination. Even the Missouri Synod Lutherans, who have consistently been at odds with other Protestant groups, are essentially in agreement with the proposition that the church should not withdraw from the world.

TABLE 21

THE CHURCH SHOULD WITHDRAW FROM THE WORLD

"The primary task of the church is to live the Christian life among its own membership and activities rather than try and reform the world."	% Agreeing
Methodist	6
Episcopalian	7
Presbyterian	5
American Baptist	8
American Lutheran	10
Missouri Synod Lutheran	12

The relationship of age to understanding the church mission (not presented here) indicates a somewhat greater commitment among the young ministers to church involvement. Young Lutherans—especially the American Lutherans—are more committed to an activist role for the church than are their elders.

These figures suggest that a major source of ecumenical unity stems from a consensus that the church has a responsibility in the world and that this mission may better be accomplished together rather than through the diversified energies of many groups. In other words, the sources of ecumenicism are social rather than doctrinal.

To pursue this thesis further, we examined responses to several other statements which dealt with the social mission of the church. Only two representative examples are presented here, one dealing with the churches' responsibility for the racial issue and the other dealing with the role of the church in solving urban problems. The first statement reads, "For the most part, the churches have been woefully inadequate in facing up to the civil rights issues" (Table 22). Note that denominational differences have virtually disappeared. Agreement with this strongly worded statement ranges between 69 and 77 per cent across denominations. In other words, nearly three quarters of the clergy in every denomination acknowledge the failure of the churches in facing up to the racial issue. A similar item (not shown here) was equally strong in indicting

TABLE 22

CHURCHES HAVE BEEN INADEQUATE IN FACING UP TO CIVIL RIGHTS

"For the most part, the churches have been woefully inadequate in facing up to the civil rights issues."	% Agreeing
Methodist	76
Episcopalian	70
Presbyterian	76
American Baptist	77
American Lutheran	70
Missouri Synod Lutheran	69

Christians for their attitudes on racial justice. The item stated, "Many whites pretend to be very Christian while in reality their attitudes demonstrate their lack of or misunderstanding of Christianity." Agreement with this item ranged from 78 per cent among Missouri Synod Lutheran clergy to 84 per cent among American Baptists.

This concern for the relevance of the church in facing social issues goes beyond the racial question. Another item states "Christian education needs to bring laymen face to face with urban problems and propose solutions" (Table 23). A substantial majority believe that this is a responsibility of Christian education. The range of agreement is from 64 per cent among Missouri Synod Lutherans and Episcopalians to 74 per cent among Methodists. While the percentage of agreement is somewhat lower than on the civil rights statement, the denominational range is quite narrow. The lower level of agreement probably arises out of the fact that this statement is more specific in suggesting constructive action rather than simply pointing out a problem. We will return to the implications of this observation in Chapter V. But for the moment, our most important conclusion is that at the level of expressing concern about social issues, denominational differences, which have thus far characterized the data in this chapter, have virtually disappeared. A large majority in all denominations agree that the church should be involved in the world. Moreover, a significant majority in all denominations feel that the churches have not been altogether adequate in facing up to such issues as race and urban problems.

TABLE 23

CHRISTIAN EDUCATION SHOULD CONFRONT
URBAN PROBLEMS

"Christian education needs to bring laymen face to face with urban problems and propose solutions."	% Agreeing
Methodist	74
Episcopalian	64
Presbyterian	68
American Baptist	67
American Lutheran	68
Missouri Synod Lutheran	64

This general level of consensus should not, however, be interpreted as support for any specific program. It should be fairly obvious, for example, that denominations are deeply split on exactly what the Christian position should be on many social issues. This split exists both within individual denominations as well as across denominational lines. There is a wide range of disagreement regarding what kinds of solutions the churches should be offering to urban problems, on how the churches should be working for world peace or racial justice, etc. What is important, however, is the fact that the various denominations agree that these are matters which the church should be concerned with. And it may very well be that it is this broad consensus which provides at least one important basis for ecumenical dialogue.

ROOTS IN HERITAGE. But beyond joint concern for current social issues, a heritage of Christian faith is also shared. The supernatural interpretation of Christ's life may be accepted by some men of the cloth and rejected by others, but there is a common heritage professing the relevancy of Jesus for modern man. Regardless of how one views the sacred works of Christianity, all churchmen hold that the life and teachings of Christ fundamentally inform man in the appropriate relationships between God and man and among fellow men. This is not to say specific doctrine is irrelevant; the data presented here demonstrate quite the opposite. But apparently the roots of interdenominational co-operation go deeper than a common creed. The broad consensus is that God is both hidden and revealed in the life and the works of Christ. Since no one possesses the whole truth of Christian faith, tolerance of diversity becomes tenable. The earnest agnostic is more admired by our sample than the convinced dogmatist.

In a profound sense, the Christian religion, for an increasing number of clergy, is a faith professing a heritage which instructs men in the meaning of life rather than a dogmatic tradition proclaiming to possess ultimate reality.

The sources of this greater tolerance obviously are many. Modern science has not only created doubt regarding the plausibility of specific religious doctrines, but has in a real sense introduced the dimension of doubt and uncertainty. The Christian is more profoundly aware of the fact that his convictions are a matter of faith than he has ever been before. Empirical certainty and faith are independent dimensions that have never been so clearly perceived as such.

Christianity exists in an increasingly pluralistic world. Mass movements of people during the past two hundred years have created mixed human communities. Television, magazines, and films have exposed the diversity of world views. More than ever before, Christianity exists in a world where it cannot impose its view on people aware of other persuasions. Freedom of religion increasingly means not only choice among a variety of faiths, but also freedom from religion. The church has been forced to alter its doctrine to remain viable in a changing world. Ecumenicism, therefore, represents, on the one hand, the thrust of an institution for survival, and on the other, dramatic realization that the doctrines that splintered the church are secondary to the common heritage—man's pursuit of the meaning of life, that which is beyond his empirical grasp. But how much strength does this common heritage have to unite Christians in confronting the critical social issues of our day, such as the civil rights crisis? This question, at least implicitly, is carried throughout the duration of this volume.

The Religious Beliefs of Protestant Laity

The study by Glock and Stark of Christian laity was mentioned in the introductory chapter and again in this chapter in making some comparisons between clergy and laity.[6] This is an important study and merits a closer look.

The Glock and Stark study involved a random sample of some three thousand church members residing in the four metropolitan counties of the San Francisco Bay Area.[7] While the initial published reports on this study were primarily concerned with differences in beliefs *among* denominations, an examination of the data reveals that sharp differences exist *within* denominations as well. Table 24 reproduces just a few of the responses to Glock and Stark's multi-faceted exploration of religious belief. The questions included here cover a wide range of doctrines, including belief in God, the divinity of Christ, miracles, and life after death.

A word of explanation is necessary regarding the interpretation of the responses in Table 24. On the first three statements, respondents were asked "Which of the following statements comes closest to expressing what you believe about (God, Jesus, miracles)?" The responses presented represent the orthodox or literalist position. The other response alternatives involve varying degrees of doubt to rejection of belief in the Christian doctrine. For example, on the question regarding belief in God, the responses range from unfaltering acknowledgment of the existence of God ("I know God really exists and I have no doubt about it") to rejection of the existence of God ("I don't believe in God"). The final statement in the table is taken from a check list of specific doctrines in which respondents were asked to respond on a four-point continuum as follows: "completely true," "probably true," "probably not true," and "definitely not true."

Table 24 dramatically demonstrates the diversity of belief patterns across denominations. The pattern is highly similar to the one we have already observed for clergy. The additional denominations included in the Glock and Stark study provide a perspective for placing the six denominations included in the clergy study. Congregationalists are consistently the most liberal group, and the Southern Baptists and sects are consistently the most conservative groups on religious beliefs.

In the laity study only among Southern Baptists and sectarian groups is there a consensus of belief on these doctrinal issues. Missouri Synod Lutherans are also highly orthodox, but a minority at least have doubts about orthodox doctrine. No other denomination even approaches consensus on doctrine, either in terms of accepting or rejecting the orthodox position. Congregationalists are the least willing to accept orthodox doctrine. But even among Congregationalists there is a significant minority who do adhere to a literalist position.

Denominationalism is clearly a powerful force in influencing what

TABLE 24

LAITY ALSO SHOW WIDE RANGE OF BELIEFS ON RELIGIOUS DOCTRINES

	Congregational	Methodist	Episcopalian	Presbyterian	Disciples of Christ	American Lutheran	American Baptist	Missouri Synod Lutheran	Southern Baptist	Sects	Total Protestant	Catholics
BELIEF IN GOD *"I know God really exists and I have no doubts about it."*	41	60	63	76	75	73	78	81	99	96	71	81
BELIEF IN DIVINITY OF JESUS *"Jesus is the Divine Son of God and I have no doubts about it."*	50	54	59	74	72	74	76	93	99	97	69	86
MIRACLES *"Miracles actually happened just as the Bible says they did."*	28	37	41	62	58	69	62	89	92	92	57	74
LIFE BEYOND DEATH *"There is a life beyond death."* (% who answered "completely true.")	36	49	53	64	69	70	72	84	97	94	69	75

Source: Charles Y. Glock and Rodney Stark, *Religion and Society in Tension* (Chicago: Rand McNally & Company, 1965), Chapter 5, "The New Denominationialism," Tables 1, 2, 4, and 5.

people believe about Christian doctrine. But perhaps even more important is the fact that within denominations and even within individual congregations there is a significant degree of dissensus. This diversity of belief can perhaps best be seen by examining the responses of Christian laity in a single congregation. The data come from a large Lutheran church (Lutheran Church in America) located in a Minneapolis suburb. A total of 1628 laymen of Faith Lutheran Church, representing approximately 80 per cent of the adult congregation, completed questionnaires in the fall of 1966 which explored the nature of their religious beliefs.[8] The Faith Lutheran study included one hundred statements which were designed to explore the nature of religious belief. Members were asked to respond to the belief statements in the same manner as the clergy study—a six-point continuum ranging from "strongly agree" to "strongly disagree." We need not present a detailed analysis of their religious beliefs here, but a few selected issues will serve to demonstrate the varieties of belief that exist even within a single congregation of a conservative denomination.[9]

Eighty-seven per cent of the Faith Lutheran respondents agreed with the statement "I believe in a Supreme Being who sees and knows everything." An additional 8 per cent indicated that they probably agree with the statement. The response to this question, thus, is similar to national polls which ask, "Do you believe in God?" But while the Faith Lutheran members affirm the existence of God, they are widely divided on their views of what God is like and the extent to which God is revealed in the Christian religion. Only half (49 per cent) of the respondents positively affirmed the statement "Only in Christianity is the one true God revealed." In a similar vein, 44 per cent said, "It is not important what religion one believes in, because all religions worship the same God even though they speak of the divine differently." In short, roughly half of the members of this congregation take a very broad view of their religious faith and do not exclude the possibility that other religious faiths constitute an equally legitimate source of knowledge of the deity. For the other half, Christianity constitutes a unique faith through which God's truth has been revealed. The significance of this divergence cannot be easily dismissed, for it suggests that the saliency with which any specific doctrine is held will vary considerably. Keep in mind also that the Lutherans are among the most conservative groups. If these issues are not salient for Lutherans, we can hardly expect them to be so for more liberal traditions.

This becomes clear when we examine their responses to questions about the doctrine of salvation. What does salvation mean? What meaning does the traditional doctrine of eternal life have for contemporary Christians? What happens to man when his physical body dies? Examination of five different statements dealing with the doctrine of salvation reveals that the issue is a perplexing one for the Faith Lutheran congregation. Only slightly more than half (52 per cent) of the members are able to affirm with certainty that "There is a divine judgment after death where some will be rewarded and others punished." But even this affirmation must reflect a certain amount of tenuousness since slightly less than half (46 per cent) feel that "Every man has an immortal soul that lives on after death." Approximately half of the members, thus, believe in some kind of immortal soul which is subject to judgment and half the members express varying degrees of doubt or disbelief in this doctrine.

Just what this immortal soul is like, however, is unclear. Some possible clarification may be added by the statement "I expect to have a bodily existence after death in which I will be recognizable to myself and others." Eighteen per cent agreed with this proposition and another 18 per cent indicated that they probably agreed. When asked if they thought heaven and hell were geographical places, 84 per cent said they were not. At the same time, only about a third (36 per cent) were able to affirm the modernist view that "Salvation in the Christian sense refers to the possibility of living a fully human life." Yet, 53 per cent agree and 22 per cent probably agree that "Salvation means winning heaven and escaping hell."

The doctrine of salvation, thus, is at best a perplexing one for Faith Lutheran laity. They approach consensus only in rejecting heaven and hell as geographical places. In spite of rejecting heaven and hell as geographical places, a third express some anticipation of a corporate existence somewhere "out there." Another third see salvation in terms of deeper meaning in this life. Still another group (again approximately one third) seem to suggest by their responses that salvation is not a very salient issue, having rejected both tradition and symbolic conceptions of salvation.

Although this same dissensus is apparent in almost every theological issue raised in the study of the Faith Lutheran congregation, we need not belabor this point with a detailed description. The central theme of the Glock and Stark data, our clergy data, and the Faith Lutheran data is the same: *Christians join together in a common expression of faith when in reality there is no shared consensus regarding the nature of that faith.*

Observing this wide range of adherence to Christian doctrine is one matter. Interpreting the significance of the findings is another. Clearly these findings cannot be divorced from a theological perspective. We know that theology has been undergoing a very radical reinterpretation for many years. The central doctrinal issues of yesterday are, for many Christians, no longer the most critical issues today. But to dismiss the responses to the doctrinal issues raised here as irrelevant or meaningless because they do not tap the frontiers of theological thought is to miss the significance of what the data tell us. While the doctrinal issues raised may not be critical to some, it is quite apparent that they are terribly important to others. And herein lies the dilemma of contemporary Protestantism: *There is no consensus as to what is believed, as to what is central and what is peripheral, nor is there any clear authority to resolve the uncertainty.*

The question of authority looms very large. As a doctrine of infallible truth, Christianity possesses enormous authority. It is a belief system which professes to hold the essence of truth about the nature and meaning of life, a system which offers rewards for those who believe and practice this doctrine of truth and punishes those who reject it. But when the foundations of this belief system are no longer certain, what happens to its authority? Without certainty of belief, is it possible for the institution to exercise the kind of authority which will keep its membership firmly committed to the institution and its programs?

The Gallup Poll data presented in Chapter I suggest an answer to this question. The Gallup data show that church attendance is highest in the theologically conservative denominations and lowest in those denominations where rejection of orthodox theology is the greatest. As doubt about the validity of Christian beliefs emerges, commitment to ritual participation in religious institutions declines. In other words, with doubt comes a rejection of the church's authority to demand regular participation in the life of the church.

This is, perhaps, reading too much into the Gallup Poll figures, but a second volume recently published by Stark and Glock[10] lends overwhelming evidence to support this thesis. Stark and Glock examine the relationship between denominationalism and involvement in a wide range of ritual activities, including church attendance, membership in church organizations, time spent in religious activities, listening and watching religious programs in the mass media, financial contributions to the church, perceived importance of church membership, and private ritual including prayer, reading the Bible and devotional literature, and table grace. On every single indicator of ritual involvement, the theologically liberal denominations scored lower than the conservative denominations. Stark and Glock conclude that "a general corrosion of commitment presently accompanies the acceptance of a modernized, liberal theology."[11]

> The authors elaborate their conclusion as follows: . . . the majority of members of liberal bodies are dormant Christians. They have adopted the theology of the new reformation, but at the same time they have stopped attending church, stopped participating in church acitvities, stopped contributing funds, stopped praying, and are uninformed about religion. Furthermore, only a minority of members of the liberal bodies feel that their religious perspective provides them with the answers to the meaning and purpose of life, while the overwhelming majority of conservatives feel theirs does supply the answers. Finally, the liberal congregations resemble theater audiences, their members are mainly strangers to each other, while conservative congregations resemble primary groups, united by bonds of personal friendships.[12]

Perhaps most revealing in terms of the implications for the sustained institutional life of the church are figures on financial contributions. Fifty-nine per cent of the Southern Baptists reported that they gave $7.50 a week or more to the church, compared with only 15 per cent of the Congregationalists who reported giving that much. These figures become even more dramatic if one considers the fact that Congregationalists have a higher income level than Southern Baptists. None of the Southern Baptists, compared with 23 per cent of the Congregationalists, in the Stark and Glock study had an income of $16,000 a year or greater. Yet 32 per cent of the Southern Baptists, compared with only 1 per cent of the Congregationalists, reported contributions of $15 a week or more. In brief, those who believe in the literal teachings of scripture are much more deeply involved in every phase of church life, including financial support.

Moreover, Stark and Glock find a general shift in membership away from conservative toward liberal church bodies.

The implications of these data will be explored more fully in a later chapter, but it should be clear that commitment to and recognition of the authority of the church is very much dependent on the degree to which one accepts the orthodox teachings of the Christian faith. Furthermore, there is considerable evidence of movement away from these orthodox teachings, among both clergy and laity.

Summary

The results of two major surveys, my study of clergy and the Glock and Stark study of laity, reveal that Protestantism is divided within and among denominations on the most basic issues of theological doctrine. The clergy data suggest that there may be a more basic core of humanistic concerns which unite Christians. The Stark and Glock data introduce a more complex dimension which indicates that laity commitment to the institutional life of the church is in large part a function of their adherence to orthodox Christian doctrine. The full implications of these findings, however, are not clear. Of critical importance is the relationship between religious beliefs and beliefs about social issues. Do the religiously orthodox express greater or less concern about social issues, or do the two realms of belief operate independently of each other? Chapter III addresses itself to this question.

III

Religious Beliefs and Social Issues

The text at the top of the page is partially visible and illegible.

Introduction

Given the wide diversity of religious beliefs that we have seen, among both clergy and laity, the next task in our quest to understand the storm that is gathering in the churches over the civil rights issue is to examine the relationship between religious beliefs and beliefs about social issues. In essence, the question we are concerned with is whether theological beliefs are systematically associated with beliefs about the nature of the social order, or whether the two realms of ideology operate independently of each other. In this chapter, our concern with social issues will focus on economic and political ideology in the broadest sense as they are reflected in party affiliation and preference for political candidates. In the next chapter we will turn to the relationship between religious beliefs and beliefs about the civil rights issue. The broader picture of social ideology presented in this chapter provides a necessary context for viewing beliefs about civil rights in the next chapter.

Three developments in this decade have served to heighten interest in the relationship between religion and political behavior in particular. The first was the election of a Catholic president in 1960. The second development has been the alliance between radical right-wing political groups and a number of religious figures. The third development has been the unprecedented involvement of clergy in a variety of expressions of protest for social justice.

For a large proportion of the public, this involvement of clergy in picketing and other forms of social protest represents an alignment with the radical left. As long as the marching ministers are unknown, it is easy to dismiss them as an element of the lunatic fringe who are not significantly different from the clergy on the far right who lend their support to groups like the John Birch Society. However, when one's own minister joins the picket line or expresses sympathy for the protesters from the pulpit, the problem of understanding the reasons for this involvement becomes more complex. Thus, the heightened interest in understanding the relationship between religious and social beliefs is seen both from the viewpoint of a public that is confused by developments during this decade and the social scientist who is interested in the more general question of the relationships between ideologies.

Social scientists have been slow to explore the relationships between religious beliefs and social ideologies. While Professor Paul Lazarsfeld of Columbia University and his colleagues reported in studies conducted as early as 1940 that religious identification was related to a person's choice of a political party, social scientists remained skeptical of these findings.[1] Others argued that the observed relationship could be accounted for by social class differences and ethnic-minority statuses.[2] As late as 1959 one of the leading pollsters in this nation sought to dispel the "myth of the Catholic vote."[3]

Numerous studies and polls have demonstrated the strong tendency for Protestants to identify with and vote for Republican candidates, while Catholics and Jews are more frequently aligned with the Democratic party.[4] However, there have been few attempts to explore voting variance *within* any of the major religious faiths. If theological belief is related to political ideology, then this represents a serious limitation on the value of these earlier studies, since we have seen that religious belief varies significantly both within and among denominations.

In a sense, examining the relationship between political preference or voting behavior and broad religious categories (i.e., Protestant, Catholic, and Jew) may be analogous to asking the question "Do you believe in God?" It may give us some very general clues as to the relationship between religion and political ideology, but there is much that remains unanswered. The task of this chapter is to move as far beyond these broad categories as available data will permit.

Thus far, Benton Johnson is the only scholar who has attempted to move beyond the broad categories of religious identification, and his work is particularly important in clarifying the relationship between religion and political preference.[5] Focusing within Protestantism, Johnson has argued that individuals who adhere strongly to the theological tradition which Weber described as "ascetic" Protestantism will be inclined to support political traditions which emphasize free enterprise, limited government, and individualism.[6] Moving from the theoretical to the practical level, this means that persons who adhere to a fundamentalist or conservative theology (orthodoxy or literalism as we have used the terms to this point) are likely to identify with the conservative political tradition of the Republican party.

In two parallel studies of church laity in Oregon and Florida, and a study of clergy in two denominations in Oregon, Johnson found considerable support for this thesis. While the fact that he found the same results in three settings suggests that the same relationship may exist in the general population, the limited samples in Johnson's studies necessitate cautious interpretation. The data from our national study, however, do provide the opportunity for a more thorough examination of the findings reported by Johnson.

For the purposes of this inquiry, theological belief is measured by the clergy's own self-designation. Several theological categories were presented on the questionnaire and clergy were asked to check the category which best described their own theological position.[7] It should be pointed out that this is only one of several ways in which theological belief might be measured. In Chapter II, for example, we used a Biblical Literalism Index which combined responses to six doctrinal statements. Actually, the Biblical Literalism Index and the minister's self-designated theological position are highly correlated. Ministers who say they subscribe to a particular theology tend to believe on specific issues as do others in the same theological category. That is, fundamentalists score high on literalism and liberals score low, with conservatives being closer to the fundamentalists and neo-orthodox being closer to liberals. Thus, our results are not essentially altered by using one measure of religious belief rather than the other.

The Religious and Social Beliefs of Clergy

Our analysis begins by examining the relationship between the minister's theological position and his preference for political party.

Table 25 confirms the findings of Johnson in the smaller regional sample. Fundamentalists and conservatives are much more likely to identify with the Republican party than are neo-orthodox or liberals.

TABLE 25

PARTY PREFERENCE IS RELATED TO
THEOLOGICAL POSITION

		REPUBLICAN	INDEPENDENT	DEMOCRAT
Fundamentalist	N = (342)	68%	18%	13%
Conservative	N = (3182)	62%	22%	15%
Neo-orthodox	N = (2032)	39%	26%	35%
Liberal	N = (1560)	36%	28%	36%

N = Number of cases. The number of cases does not total 7441 as reported in Chapter II because persons responding "Universalist-Unitarian" and "other" were not included in this analysis.

Sixty-eight and 62 per cent respectively indicated that the Republican party was their usual party preference, compared with 39 and 36 per cent of those calling themselves neo-orthodox and liberal.

Similarly, persons identifying themselves as liberals and neo-orthodox were more likely to claim usual preference for the Democratic party. Thirty-six and 35 per cent respectively of the latter two groups indicated a Democratic preference. Only 13 and 15 per cent of the fundamentalists and conservatives indicated a Democratic party preference, and this is partially accounted for by persons in the sample from the South.

However, neo-orthodox ministers choose the Republican party with a slightly greater frequency than they select the Democratic party.

Approximately one fifth in all theological groups indicate that they are political independents, but the proportion is slightly higher for the liberals. The most dramatic differences are clearly between the fundamentalist-conservative groups on the one hand and the neo-orthodox-liberal groups on the other.

Table 26 shows the relationship between theological position and party preference for each denomination. While there is noticeable denominational variance, the pattern remains essentially the same for all groups. In every denomination, the fundamentalists and conservatives identify with the Republican party to a much greater extent than do the neo-orthodox and liberal groups. This difference is least in the Methodist and Episcopalian denominations, which, again, can be partially accounted for by the fact that these two groups have large representations in the South, while the other denominations do not.

With the exception of the Baptists, fundamentalists are more likely to select the Republican party than are the conservatives. Neo-orthodox and liberals are more likely to identify with the

TABLE 26

PARTY PREFERENCE IS RELATED TO
THEOLOGICAL POSITION WITHIN EACH DENOMINATION

		REPUBLICAN %	INDEPENDENT %	DEMOCRAT %
Methodist				
Fundamentalist	N = 84	44	27	29
Conservative	N = 734	43	28	29
Neo-orthodox	N = 799	31	28	41
Liberal	N = 850	34	29	37
Episcopalian				
Fundamentalist	N = 3	*	*	*
Conservative	N = 340	40	22	27
Neo-orthodox	N = 382	35	26	39
Liberal	N = 326	31	31	38
Presbyterian				
Fundamentalist	N = 17	82	6	12
Conservative	N = 449	75	15	10
Neo-orthodox	N = 493	49	21	29
Liberal	N = 221	49	22	30
American Baptist				
Fundamentalist	N = 49	62	20	18
Conservative	N = 369	70	20	10
Neo-orthodox	N = 101	40	31	30
Liberal	N = 117	38	29	33
American Lutheran				
Fundamentalist	N = 59	80	12	9
Conservative	N = 593	69	22	9
Neo-orthodox	N = 213	49	28	23
Liberal	N = 117	31	34	34
Missouri Synod Lutheran				
Fundamentalist	N = 130	79	17	4
Conservative	N = 697	69	23	9
Neo-orthodox	N = 44	43	36	20
Liberal	N = 12	*	*	*

* The number of cases is too small to compute statistically reliable percentages.

Democratic party, with liberals tending to select the Democratic party with a somewhat greater frequency than those calling themselves neo-orthodox. While there tends to be a linear order from fundamentalist to liberal, the sharpest break is clearly between the conservatives and neo-orthodox. Conservatives respond more like fundamentalists and neo-orthodox respond more like liberals.

The proportion identifying with the Democratic party does not approach 50 per cent for any group. However, the more theologically liberal are more likely to consider themselves independent. These observations suggest the possible influence of their middle-class congregations, who are probably predominantly Republican. We will return to this question later.

In summary, the findings from the national survey strongly corroborate the regional conclusions of Benton Johnson. Fundamentalist and conservative clergymen are much more likely to identify with the Republican party, while neo-orthodox and liberals are more likely to claim loyalty to the Democratic party.

While the relationship between conservatism in theology and conservatism in politics may appear obvious and self-evident to some readers, two words of caution are in order. First, with the exception of the limited studies of Johnson, this relationship has not previously been established in empirical studies. Second, obvious though the relationship may seem, we will see a little later that it does *not* hold for laity.

It is important to emphasize that the hypothesized relationship between conservative theology and preference for the Republican party is derived from the historic value orientations of "ascetic" Protestantism, which proclaimed the virtuousness of free enterprise and individualism. In other words, the logic of the hypothesis is that preference for the Republican party is only an *indicator* of an underlying political ideology. If this is correct, we would expect conservative theology to be even more strongly aligned with *value statements* that represent this ideology.

Three items in the questionnaire explore the extent to which theological belief is related to belief in free enterprise and individualism. The first statement reads, "The free enterprise system is the single economic system compatible with the requirements of personal freedom and constitutional government" (Table 27).

It is clear from an inspection of Table 27 that there is a strong

TABLE 27

CONSERVATIVE THEOLOGICAL BELIEFS ARE ASSOCIATED WITH UNFALTERING COMMITMENT TO FREE ENTERPRISE

"The free enterprise system is the single economic system compatible with the requirements of personal freedom and constitutional government."	Methodist	Episcopalian	Presbyterian	American Baptist	American Lutheran	Missouri Synod Lutheran
				% Agreeing		
Fundamentalist	71%	*	88%	82%	76%	76%
Conservative	61%	45%	52%	65%	51%	56%
Neo-orthodox	38%	29%	24%	31%	28%	20%
Liberal	33%	28%	26%	18%	29%	*

* The number of cases is too small to compute statistically reliable percentages.

relationship between belief in free enterprise and adherence to conservative theological beliefs. For every denomination there is a sharp break in the percentage who agree with the statement as theological position shifts. For example, among American Baptists, 82 per cent of those calling themselves fundamentalists agree that free enterprise is the only economic system which is compatible with the idea of freedom and constitutional government. The proportion agreeing with this position drops to 65 per cent among the conservatives, 31 per cent among the neo-orthodox, and only 18 per cent among the theologically liberal. This same general pattern of step-progression can be observed in every denomination. The proportion of fundamentalists who agree with this statement ranges from 71 per cent in the Methodist group to 88 per cent among Presbyterians. At the other end of the theological continuum, the proportion of liberals who agree with this position ranges from a low of 18 per cent among Baptists to a high of 33 per cent among the Methodists.

When these responses are compared with party affiliation in Table 25, it is seen that the proportion of fundamentalists and conservatives who agree with the free enterprise statement is *greater* than the proportion indicating preference for the Republican party. Also, the proportion of neo-orthodox and liberals who agree with the statement is *less* than the proportion in these groups who identify with the Republican party.

While the figures are not shown here, it should be mentioned that if the "probably agree" response is added to the "agree" response on this item, the proportion of fundamentalists agreeing and tending to agree ranges from 88 per cent to 100 per cent across the denominations. Furthermore, the proportion who "probably agree" with the statement is greater for the two conservative groups than for the two more liberal groups, thus increasing even further the distance between conservatives and liberals. These findings are clearly consistent with the hypothesized relationship between theological orientation and political ideology.

The reader should not lose sight of the fact that this is a strongly worded statement. How the clergyman interprets the concept of a "free enterprise system" may vary. What is important is that to agree with this statement is to believe that free enterprise is in juxtaposition to other economic systems and that all other systems are incompatible with the ideals of personal freedom and constitutional government. Clergymen who hold conservative theological views are very much inclined to believe this is true. Clergymen whose theological beliefs are more liberal tend very much to doubt or reject the validity of this point of view.

The next statement dealing with government and the economic order is much less radical in its ideological content. It reads, "The government is providing too many services that should be left to private enterprise" (Table 28). It does not imply a rejection of the validity of the role of government in providing public service, but rather sees the current government as too heavily involved in activities that might better or more appropriately be handled by the private sector.

Again the proportion agreeing with the statement varies dramatically with theological position. Approximately three fourths of the fundamentalists agree, as compared with only about one fourth of the liberals. Though slightly less dramatic than the response to the first statement, the pattern of response is identical. As was reported for the statement above, if the percentage who reported that they

TABLE 28

THEOLOGICAL CONSERVATIVES BELIEVE GOVERNMENT IS
INVADING THE DOMAIN OF THE PRIVATE SECTOR

"The government is providing too many services that should be left to private enterprise."	Methodist	Episcopalian	Presbyterian	American Baptist	American Lutheran	Missouri Synod Lutheran
			% Agreeing			
Fundamentalist	68%	*	76%	70%	75%	88%
Conservative	55%	47%	56%	62%	62%	63%
Neo-orthodox	32%	34%	24%	33%	40%	25%
Liberal	27%	26%	22%	14%	26%	*

* The number of cases is too small to compute statistically reliable percentages.

"probably agree" had been included, the distance separating the more conservative theological groups from the more liberal groups would be even greater.

A third statement deals with the fundamental question of the source of poverty. The item in the questionnaire posits that the individual is responsible: "Most people who live in poverty could do something about their situation if they really wanted to" (Table 29).

The distribution of responses to this item is much less dramatic than it is in the first two statements, but the pattern is the same. The more conservative a minister's theology, the more likely he is to agree with the statement. There are a number of explanations which may account for the failure of this item to elicit as wide a range of responses as the other two items. Probably most important is the fact that the mass media have made Americans increasingly aware of the plight of the poor, not only in this nation, but throughout the world. What the response to this statement suggests is that sensitivity to the dilemma of poverty, and the complex forces which produce poverty, is significantly influenced by a person's ideology. In other words, conservative theology tends to limit one's awareness to an underlying cause of poverty.

This position was convincingly argued by Stark and Glock in a

TABLE 29

THEOLOGICAL CONSERVATIVES TEND TO BELIEVE
POVERTY-STRICKEN ARE RESPONSIBLE
FOR THEIR OWN PLIGHT

"Most people who live in poverty could do something about their situation if they really wanted to."	Methodist	Episcopalian	Presbyterian	American Baptist	American Lutheran	Missouri Synod Lutheran
				% Agreeing		
Fundamentalist	61%	*	53%	52%	51%	60%
Conservative	40%	54%	26%	39%	37%	36%
Neo-orthodox	22%	16%	12%	17%	19%	14%
Liberal	19%	16%	11%	14%	23%	*

* The number of cases is too small to compute statistically reliable percentages.

paper presented at the University of California Centennial Symposium on Patterns of American Prejudice.[8] Searching for underlying theological factors which might account for prejudice, Stark and Glock argue:

> Underlying all *traditional* [emphasis added] Christian thought is an image of man as a free actor, as essentially unfettered by social circumstances, free to choose and thus free to effect his own salvation. This free-will conception of man has been central to the doctrines of sin and salvation. For only if man is totally free does it seem just to hold him utterly responsible for his acts; to punish him for his sins and to demand repentance. . . . At least since the work of Max Weber, it has been widely recognized this conception of human nature has been a mainspring in the development of Western civilization and has greatly influenced our attitudes on personal accountability and the ingredients of personal success. An image of man as free and yet responsible lies behind all such notions as rugged individualism, the self-made man, and the justification of wealth on the basis of merit. In short, Christian thought and thus Western civilization is permeated with the idea that men are individually in con-

trol of, and responsible for, their own destinies. If I am really the "captain of my soul, and the master of my fate," then I have no one but myself to thank or to blame for what happens to me.[9]

Stark and Glock acknowledge that this radical form of unfettered free will has undergone considerable modification in contemporary society. Nevertheless, the persistence of this ideology, however subtle its form, is an important factor contributing to the persistence of prejudice. Specifically, Stark and Glock argue that:

> . . . radical and traditional Christian images of man prompt those who hold them to put the blame for disadvantage upon the individuals who are disadvantaged. A radical free-will image of man makes for an inability to perceive the effect of those forces outside the individual which may utterly dominate his circumstances. . . . It is not that these Christians condone the social forces that deprive Negroes, but that they simply do not recognize the existence of such forces in the world.[10]

It should be pointed out that when Stark and Glock refer to "traditional" Christian thought, they refer to those traditional theological images which we have characterized as "biblical literalism" in the previous chapter and which are embraced by the categories of "fundamentalist" and "conservative" in this chapter. While we are jumping ahead of ourselves to conclude that this conservative theology is at the root of prejudice, our data do support Stark and Glock's conclusion that theological belief is strongly associated with the way a person views the economic order and the relationship of man to that order. We will return to the implications of this observation later, but first we want to pursue the relationship between theological views and social ideology further.

The 1964 presidential election was unique inasmuch as the Republican candidate, Senator Barry Goldwater, unambiguously articulated the ideology which Weber described as "ascetic Protestantism." Goldwater's campaign attempted to appeal to an ideology as much as, if not more than, to a party. Thus, support for Goldwater can be viewed as another way of measuring the relationship between theological outlook and political ideology. We would expect support for Goldwater to be stronger among fundamentalists and conservatives than among neo-orthodox and liberals independent of party preference.

TABLE 30

SUPPORT FOR GOLDWATER WAS MUCH STRONGER AMONG
THEOLOGICAL CONSERVATIVES

% Favoring Goldwater in 1964 Presidential Election	Methodist	Episcopalian	Presbyterian	American Baptist	American Lutheran	Missouri Synod Lutheran
Fundamentalist	61%	*	76%	68%	64%	78%
Conservative	39%	39%	42%	53%	52%	66%
Neo-orthodox	15%	20%	11%	13%	23%	27%
Liberal	10%	13%	10%	6%	17%	*

* The number of cases is too small to compute statistically reliable percentages.

Table 30 shows the proportion who favored Goldwater for President controlled by theological position for each denomination. Support for Goldwater is strongest among the fundamentalists and is roughly proportional to their preference for the Republican party (comparing with Table 25). Conservatives favor Goldwater to a lesser degree than they identify with the Republican party. The proportion of theological conservatives favoring Goldwater, however, is greater than the proportion of the general population of the nation who voted for the Republican candidate. The proportion favoring Goldwater among neo-orthodox and liberals drops off very dramatically. Among Presbyterians, for example, only 11 per cent of the neo-orthodox and 10 per cent of the liberals indicate that Goldwater is their choice for President. Only 6 per cent of the liberal Baptists state a preference for Goldwater. In short, those who consider themselves theologically liberal (neo-orthodox or liberal) eschew the ideology which Goldwater represents. This is true even among theological liberals who normally consider themselves Republican.

Moving one step further, Table 31 shows the proportion favoring

Goldwater controlling for theological position and party preference. Eighty-two per cent who are fundamentalist and Republican favor Goldwater. Among those who are fundamentalist and politically independent, 56 per cent favor Goldwater. Defections from the Republican ranks are enormous among those who are neo-orthodox and liberal. Only 30 and 22 per cent of neo-orthodox and liberals respectively who are Republicans favor the Republican candidate.

TABLE 31

THEOLOGICALLY LIBERAL REJECT GOLDWATER IN SPITE
OF PARTY PREFERENCE

% FAVORING GOLDWATER

	REPUBLICAN	INDEPENDENT	DEMOCRAT
Fundamentalist	82%	56%	29%
Conservative	62%	39%	14%
Neo-orthodox	30%	12%	3%
Liberal	22%	7%	2%

Among Democrats, 29 per cent who consider themselves fundamentalist favor Goldwater, compared with only 3 per cent and 2 per cent who are theologically neo-orthodox and liberal.

In summary, the data support the thesis that both theological position and party affiliation are manifestations of a more basic ideology or world view which Weber described as "ascetic" Protestantism. While both theological position and party preference are significant indicators of this ideology, theology is a better predictor. This is especially obvious in Table 31, where theological position is a much stronger predictor of endorsement of Goldwater among Republicans.

Reciprocal Influences of Clergy and Laity

Professor Johnson's studies have also been provocative in suggesting that clergy have an influence on the political views of their congregations. Specifically, he finds that theologically liberal ministers have a liberalizing influence on the political behavior of their laity who by social status should tend toward conservative political behavior, while theologically conservative ministers have a moderating influence on laity who by social status should tend toward liberal political behavior. While Republicanism was directly related to higher social class among a sample of laity, frequent church attendance tended to reduce the class-based political differences in the direction of the minister's views. In congregations where the minister was theologically liberal, persons who attended church frequently were *less* likely to be Republican than those who attended seldom. On the other hand, in congregations where the minister was theologically conservative, persons who attended church frequently were *more* likely to be Republican than those who seldom attended church.

In other words, where active church laity are caught in a *cross pressure* between class-based political tendencies and the theological position of their ministers, there is a tendency for the minister to affect their political outlook. The result, thus, is a "muting ef-

TABLE 32

CLERGY TEND TO HOLD POLITICAL VIEWS THAT ARE OPPOSED TO THE VIEWS OF THEIR CONGREGATION

Congregation's Social Status	Party Preference		
	REPUBLICAN	INDEPENDENT	DEMOCRAT
Predominately professional and managerial N = (787)	42%	23%	35%
Majority salaried white-collar with considerable professional and managerial N = (1608)	48%	25%	27%
Majority salaried white-collar with considerable blue-collar N = (1130)	51%	25%	24%
Draws membership about equally from all occupational groups N = (1177)	50%	26%	24%
Majority blue-collar with some white-collar N = (1893)	53%	24%	23%
Predominately blue-collar N = (846)	53%	25%	23%

fect," with theologically liberal ministers tending to influence middle-class congregations away from the Republican party and theologically conservative ministers drawing working-class congregations toward the Republican party.

The data from this study lend inferential support to the Johnson thesis. While Republicanism is *positively* related to social status in the general population, Table 32 shows that among clergy, Republican party preference is *inversely* related to the social class of their parish.[11]

Forty-two per cent of the clergy serving congregations that are predominately professional and managerial indicated a preference for the Republican party, compared with 53 per cent of those serving blue-collar congregations. Preference for the Democratic party, on the other hand, is positively aligned with social status. Thirty-five per cent serving professional and managerial congregations, compared with only 23 per cent serving blue-collar congregations, stated a preference for the Democratic party.

The relationship between the social status of ministers' congregations and the choice of presidential candidates is presented in Table 33. As in the relationship between social status and party affiliation, social status is inversely related to preference for the Republican candidate. Only 21 per cent of the clergy serving professional and managerial congregations favored Goldwater, compared with 39 per cent who serve blue-collar congregations.

This consistent inverse relationship between the political views of clergy and those of the laity they serve presents a perplexing dilemma. How does it happen that organizations manage so persistently to hire professional leadership who differ dramatically from their own views regarding matters so basic as political ideology?

The dilemma, in large part, grows out of the nature of the market place of available clergy. Higher-status churches desire to recruit ministers who have acquired maximum quality education from high-status institutions. Many of the high-status and high-quality seminaries in America have long traditions as centers of liberal theology and progressive political thought. Thus, higher-status churches in seeking out clergy who have the credentials of the higher-status educational institutions are systematically hiring men who are politically more liberal than the constituency of the congregation. It will become even clearer as this manuscript develops that this is one of

TABLE 33

CLERGY IN HIGHER-STATUS CHURCHES ARE MORE LIKELY
THAN CLERGY IN LOWER-STATUS CHURCHES
TO REJECT GOLDWATER

Congregation's Social Status	Candidate Favored		
	GOLDWATER	JOHNSON	NEITHER
Predominately professional and managerial	21%	77%	2%
Majority salaried white-collar with considerable professional and managerial	28%	68%	4%
Majority salaried white-collar with considerable blue-collar	31%	66%	4%
Draws membership about equally from all occupational groups	33%	63%	4%
Majority blue-collar with some white-collar	38%	57%	5%
Predominately blue-collar	39%	57%	4%

the important built-in structural sources of conflict between clergy and laity in Protestantism. This is particularly the case in the free church tradition, where the processes of selecting ministers tend to maximize rather than reduce the possibility for conflict.

That liberal ministers should have at least a modest liberalizing influence on their congregations, as reported by Johnson, seems altogether plausible. By the same token, one would expect congregations to have a moderating influence on their ministers. This is not, however, strongly supported by the data in Tables 32 and 33, which show the relationship between congregational social status and the political views of ministers. Table 34 shows the relationship between congregational social status and clergymen's party preference and presidential candidate choice, controlling for theological position.

Again there is no strong evidence to suggest that higher-status congregations influence their ministers' political views. Thirty-four per cent of the liberal ministers serving middle-class congregations,

TABLE 34

POLITICAL VIEWS OF LAITY DO NOT NOTICEABLY
AFFECT CLERGY'S POLITICAL VIEWS

| | Neo-orthodox and Liberal | | | | Fundamentalist and Conservative | | | |
	Managerial & Professional	Middle Class	Mixed Class	Working Class	Managerial & Professional	Middle Class	Mixed Class	Working Class
PARTY PREFERENCE								
Republican	34%	38%	37%	39%	60%	63%	63%	63%
Independent	24%	28%	30%	26%	19%	21%	22%	23%
Democrat	42%	34%	33%	35%	21%	16%	15%	14%
CANDIDATE FAVORED								
Goldwater	10%	13%	14%	16%	43%	49%	51%	54%
Johnson	88%	84%	82%	81%	53%	46%	45%	40%
Neither	1%	3%	4%	3%	4%	5%	4%	5%

compared with 42 per cent who serve professional and managerial congregations, indicate a preference for the Democratic party. Liberal ministers in the two higher-status groups overwhelmingly pick Johnson as their presidential candidate. Of the liberal ministers in professional and managerial and middle-class congregations, 88 per cent and 84 per cent respectively favor Johnson. This is a stronger endorsement of Johnson than among liberal ministers in congregations of mixed and working-class status.

An examination of the relationship between ministers' political views and congregational social status among theologically conservative ministers also fails to suggest any noticeable influence of the congregation on the ministers' views. The smallest proportion of theologically conservative ministers who indicate that they are Republican is found in the group serving professional and managerial congregations. In that group the proportion who identify with the Republican party is 60 per cent. The proportion reporting that they are Republican is 63 per cent for all three other social status groups. Similarly, preference for Goldwater is inversely related to the social status of the minister's congregation. That is, the higher the social status of the congregation the less likely the clergyman will favor Goldwater.

In brief these data fail to confirm the proposition that congregations affect the political *beliefs* of their clergy. Clergy appear to remain fiercely independent in their political beliefs in the presence of laity who hold contrary views. While clergy may hold political views that are incongruent with their congregations, this does not mean that congregations do not affect their *behavior*.

We asked clergy whether they had endorsed one of the candidates for President during the 1964 campaign, either from the pulpit or in some other religious gathering. Only 14 per cent said that they did. This small percentage who endorsed a political candidate takes on significance when we consider the fact that 60 per cent of the ministers in the study believe that ministers should have a right publicly to indicate their views on political issues.

Responses to two additional statements further illumine the constraining influence of laity on their public behavior. Sixty-seven per cent of the clergy agreed with the statement "The John Birch Society and other extremist groups constitute a grave threat to our society." Furthermore, 51 per cent rejected the statement that "The identification of Goldwater with extremist groups during the recent election was nothing more than a great political smear by his opposition."[12] In other words, a large proportion of the clergy viewed extremist groups as a serious threat to our society, and furthermore refused to disidentify Goldwater from these extremist elements. Nevertheless, they did not speak out on the election, in spite of the fact that they felt that the issue was of grave importance and that they should have the right to do so. Thus, the data strongly suggest that clergy maintain a private posture which is dissonant from their public behavior. Their public behavior would seem to be significantly affected by what they perceive to be the expectations of their congregations.

SUMMARY. The results of this investigation, thus, clearly confirm the findings of Professor Johnson that conservative religious views are associated with preference for the Republican party, and similarly, that liberal theological views are associated with preference for the Democratic party. The data from this study further support the proposition that theological views and party preference are both reflections of an underlying ideology or world view.

The consistency of the findings across six denominations which represent a wide range of theological views leaves us with little reason to doubt that the findings would be replicated in clergy samples from other denominations. A possible exception might occur among a few small sectarian fundamentalist groups. Ellinson, for example, recently analyzed the content of the writings of A. A. Allen, a Pentecostal evangelist, and found that his teachings encourage withdrawal from political activities rather than espousal of right-wing political views.[13] Other sectarian groups, however, have been in the public light as strong supporters of radical right-wing political views.

The data presented in this study provide only an inferential basis for assessing the influence of clergy's views on their laity. We found that ministers who are theologically and politically liberal disproportionately serve higher-status churches, while conservative ministers are disproportionately serving lower-status churches. Thus, if clergy do influence their congregation's views, it would tend to be in the direction suggested in Professor Johnson's writing discussed above. However, other interpretations of these findings seem plausible and cannot be easily dismissed. For example, it may be that laity who find themselves in sharp disagreement with the political and social ideologies expressed by their minister become less involved in church activities. In other words, a minister draws the greatest support in terms of church attendance from those who agree with his social pronouncements. The available data are insufficient to resolve this dilemma of interpretation, but if the latter interpretation should be correct, the long-range implications are important. For example, if younger clergy continue to become more liberal in their social ideologies, we can anticipate increasing alienation and decline in support from higher-status congregations since they tend to hold more conservative political views.

While congregations seem to have little influence on a minister's political *beliefs,* the evidence is substantial that they affect his *behavior.* In spite of the fact that a large proportion of ministers feel that they should have the right to speak out on significant political issues, only a very small proportion actually do so. This discrepancy between belief and action apparently results from their desire to avoid head-on conflict with their congregations. It is as if an unwritten rule says that a minister is entitled to believe as he likes on political issues so long as he doesn't try to proselytize his own views.

The Religious and Social Beliefs of Laity

We have seen that for clergy theological beliefs are strongly associated with social ideologies. Clergymen who are theologically liberal also tend to have liberal views about social issues. Similarly, clergy who adhere to more orthodox (fundamentalist and conservative) theological views are more conservative in their views about social issues. But is this also true for laity? The answer is less clear because we do not have the same kind of detailed data for laity. However, the existing evidence would seem to suggest that for laity, religious beliefs are held relatively independent of beliefs about social issues. But this conclusion involves some inferences and is arrived at only after piecing together several divergent sources of data.

To begin with, persons of higher socioeconomic status tend to belong to Protestant denominations that are theologically more liberal. In 1957 the Bureau of the Census conducted a sample survey of religious preference in the United States. Because of political pressures, these data were never extensively analyzed, but the data that were published clearly indicate socioeconomic status varies significantly across denominations. Table 35 summarizes the relationship between religious preference and occupational status of families in the 1957 survey.

While the published data indicate only five Protestant denominations, the rank order of these denominations in terms of social status strongly parallels the Glock and Stark rank order on religious beliefs. Episcopalians and Presbyterians rank highest in terms of social status and are also among the most liberal in terms of religious beliefs. At the other end of the continuum, Lutherans and Baptists have the lowest socioeconomic level and are theologically the most conservative.[14] Table 35 shows the relationship between denomination and occupation for the census survey. Two other indicators of social status, income and education, are not shown here, but the pattern holds for these data. An earlier study reported by Schneider showed essentially the same relationship between denominationalism and social class.[15]

Voting studies have been very inadequate in terms of providing

TABLE 35

OCCUPATIONAL STATUS VARIES BY DENOMINATION

OCCUPATION	Episcopalian	Presbyterian	Methodist	Lutheran	Baptist*
Professions	23%	13%	10%	7%	6%
Owners, Managers, and Officials	23%	20%	11%	11%	11%
Clerical and Sales	17%	14%	11%	13%	9%
Skilled	12%	17%	16%	18%	19%
Semi-skilled	6%	7%	14%	14%	19%
Unskilled	4%	8%	8%	8%	8%
Farmers	2%	4%	9%	15%	12%
Without an Occupation	13%	17%	21%	14%	16%
Total	100%	100%	100%	100%	100%

(Source: Adapted from Bernard Lazerwitz, "A Comparison of Major Religious Groups," *Journal of the American Statistical Association,* Vol. 56, September 1961.)

* Negro Baptists are omitted from this group.

data for Protestants by denomination, but they are consistent in reporting that Protestants of higher socioeconomic status are significantly more likely to vote Republican than are Protestants of lower social status.[16]

Gallup Poll data in 1960 indicated that among Protestants, union members and unskilled workers were twice as likely to vote for Kennedy as professional and business persons. In that election, 52 per cent of the Protestants who were union members or unskilled laborers voted for Kennedy, compared with only 27 per cent of the Protestants in professional and business occupations.

If these various sources of data are pieced together, the apparent conclusion would seem to be that high-status Protestants are theologically liberal but politically conservative. Intriguing as this conclusion might be, the logic of causal inference does not permit us to draw this conclusion. In the first place, not all members of theologically liberal denominations are themselves liberal in their own re-

TABLE 36

HIGHER OCCUPATIONAL STATUS GROUPS TENDED
TO FAVOR NIXON IN 1960 ELECTION

Occupation	NIXON	KENNEDY
Professional and Business	73%	27%
White-collar	68%	32%
Skilled workers	56%	44%
Unskilled workers	48%	52%
Farmers	55%	45%
Union members	48%	52%

Source: Gallup Poll in *Religions in America,* Leo Roston
        (ed.) (New York: Simon and Schuster, 1963),
        p. 289.

ligious views. Secondly, not all members of theologically liberal denominations are also members of the higher socioeconomic levels. Thirdly, not all of the higher-status Protestants vote Republican. Finally, not all persons who vote Republican are conservative in their political ideology. Thus, the interaction of these four variables (denomination, religious beliefs, party preference, and political ideology) might in reality produce results that are quite contrary to the inference that seems apparent from the data presented above. By the same token, it does not follow that the inference suggested above is incorrect. We can only conclude that while the data are suggestive they are insufficient to draw the conclusion postulated above and we must search further for evidence that illumines the relationship between religious beliefs and social ideology.

A recently published study of Episcopalians, *To Comfort and to Challenge*[17] by Glock, Ringer, and Babbie, deals specifically with the relationship between religion and social ideology. However, again, one must be cautious in generalizing from the findings of the study. In the first place, the study deals only with Episcopalians. Secondly, although the book was published in 1967 the data presented in the study were then nearly fifteen years old. This latter problem, however, may not be too serious, for while the saliency of some of the specific social issues they are dealing with may have shifted somewhat since 1952, there is no compelling reason to believe that the relationship between religion and social ideology has been fundamentally altered.

The section of the Glock, Ringer, and Babbie study relevant here is an analysis of the relationship between involvement in the church and attitudes toward political activity of ministers. From a number of questionnaire items dealing with ritual, organizational, and intellectual involvement in the church, the authors constructed a "Composite Index of Involvement." A person with a high "involvement score" has indicated a high degree of participation in the ritual, organizational, and intellectual areas of church life.

A second index, called "Political Permissiveness," is again a composite of responses to several items, dealing with political activities that clergymen might engage in. The items include general non-partisan activities, such as urging citizens to vote, and range to specific partisan behavior, such as endorsing a candidate for office. Those scoring highest on "permissiveness" feel that clergy have a right to engage in a wide range of political activity, and those scoring lowest reject the idea that clergy should engage in any political activity at all.

In general, the more specific the political activity, the less likely laity are to approve of clergy involvement. But this seems to be independent of the extent of involvement. There was no relationship between scores on the involvement index and the permissiveness index. In other words, those who are deeply involved in the life of the church are no more or no less likely to approve of clergy involvement in political activity.

The authors then proceeded to examine the relationship between church involvement and laymen's attitudes toward a number of social issues, including the United Nations, immigration policy, conscientious objectors, civil liberties, labor, and government controls. All of these were issues on which the Episcopal church as a matter of public record had taken an official stand. Again, they failed to find any systematic relationship between involvement in the church and attitudes toward social issues. They conclude:

> The foregoing analysis has primarily shown that involvement . . . [in the life of the church] . . . is not related in any significant way to parishioners' social ideologies. This means, in effect, that parishioners are not prone, as a consequence of their involvement, to subscribe to social values of the church, nor does it indicate that those who subscribe to such values are more likely to become deeply involved. In a word, the two tendencies are irrelevant to one another.[18]

These findings bear a striking similarity to the results of a study by Greeley and Rossi on the impact of Catholic education on the social ideologies of American Catholics.[19] In a comprehensive national survey, Greeley and Rossi find that those who have received all or some of their education in Catholic institutions are not essentially different in their attitudes toward other groups and social issues than those Catholics who received none of their education in Catholic institutions.[20]

Judging from the way they state their conclusions, the authors apparently felt that parochially educated Catholics would be *more* intolerant. They conclude:

> Are Catholic school Catholics more rigid and intolerant than those who did not go to Catholic schools? The answer once again is negative. Catholic school Catholics are actually more tolerant with regard to civil liberties and are no more anti-Negro, anti-Semitic, or anti-Protestant.[21]

This writer has some difficulty in sharing Greeley and Rossi's conclusion that "Catholic school Catholics are actually more tolerant with regard to civil liberties . . ." On two of the four civil liberties items they present, Catholics with no parochial education manifest a higher proportion of "enlightened" (Greeley and Rossi's term) responses than do Catholics with all or some Catholic education. Thus, a more appropriate conclusion is that there are no essential differences in the social ideologies of Catholics educated in Catholic institutions and those educated in public schools.

The Faith Lutheran study, mentioned in Chapter II, provides yet another source of data to examine the relationship between religious beliefs and social ideology. Again, it should be made clear that these data are for a specific group and caution should be exercised in generalizing to other populations. However, if they are consistent with other research findings, they constitute an additional piece of evidence which lends support to the basic thesis.

The theological orientation of the Faith Lutheran laity was measured by a Biblical Literalism Index. This index is the same as the index constructed for clergy in Chapter II, and includes six traditional doctrinal statements dealing with the virgin birth, the physical resurrection of Christ, life after death, hell, the demonic, and original sin. Table 37 shows the relationship between the Biblical Literalism

Index and the same three political-economic ideology statements that appear in Tables 27, 28, and 29 for clergy. While theological beliefs are strongly related to beliefs about the political-economic order among clergy, there is no relationship between these two dimensions among the Faith Lutheran laity.

TABLE 37

BIBLICAL LITERALISM AMONG LAITY IS UNRELATED
TO BELIEFS ABOUT FREE ENTERPRISE, GOVERNMENT,
AND INDIVIDUAL RESPONSIBILITY FOR POVERTY

	BIBLICAL LITERALISM		
	HIGH	MEDIUM	LOW
	% Agreeing		
"The free enterprise system is the single economic system compatible with the requirements of personal freedom and constitutional government."	52%	53%	51%
"The government is providing too many services that should be left to private enterprise."	35%	37%	36%
"Most people who live in poverty could do something about their situation if they really wanted to."	49%	52%	48%

A little more than one third of the Faith Lutheran members feel that "The government is providing too many services that should be left to private enterprise." About one half believe that "The free enterprise system is the single economic system compatible with the requirements of personal freedom and constitutional government." And approximately the same proportion feel that "Most people who live in poverty could do something about their situation if they really wanted to." However, their views on these issues are not affected by their religious beliefs. Those who are biblical literalists are no more or no less likely to express liberal views on these issues.

Thus, from a variety of studies we find the same general finding: Laity involvement in church life bears little if any relationship to what they believe about social issues. We have cautioned throughout this section, however, that the studies cited are inadequate to draw definitive conclusions which parallel our clergy data on the relationship between theological beliefs and social ideology. While we have pointed out several methodological problems, perhaps the most troublesome is the fact that the several studies which we have cited all have different measures of church involvement. The problem posed at the beginning of the chapter had to do with the relationship between religious *belief* and social ideology. Yet the various studies cited have employed measures of church involvement *other* than belief.

The perplexing problem which remains, thus, is whether these various measures of church involvement can be used to infer something about the nature of religious belief. Glock has convincingly argued against assuming the unidimensionality of religious commitment.[22] People may express "religiousness" in different ways and these various ways (dimensions of religiosity) may operate independently of each other. Therefore, our implicit assumption that any measure of religious involvement can be used to infer something about the nature of religious belief may not be justified. Clearly sociologists have not yet adequately explored the problem of the multidimensionality which Glock has raised. Glock's own work, however, in collaboration with Stark, shows that while the dimensions he has postulated do have some independent content, the dimensions are interrelated. Table 38, which is taken from Stark and Glock's most recent volume, *American Piety,* shows the relationship between orthodox belief and six other measures of religious involvement. Stark and Glock's index of orthodox belief closely parallels the index of biblical literalism used in this volume.

Orthodoxy is strongly related to five of the six measures of religious involvement. Those who are highest on the Orthodoxy Index are also significantly higher on ritual involvement in the church, expressions of devotion, religious experience, religious knowledge, and particularistic conceptions of their faith. Similarly, low scores on orthodoxy are associated with low scores on these other measures of involvement. The only dimension which is not strongly associated with orthodox belief is an index of ethicalism, which involves believing that doing good for others and loving one's neighbor are essential criteria for salvation.

TABLE 38

ORTHODOX BELIEF IS RELATED TO
OTHER ASPECTS OF RELIGIOUS COMMITMENT

ORTHODOXY INDEX

	LOW	MEDIUM	HIGH
Per Cent High on *Ritual Involvement*			
Protestants	19%	39%	71%
N = *	(595)	(729)	(705)
Catholics	19%	36%	55%
N = *	(64)	(115)	(304)
Per Cent High on *Devotionalism*			
Protestants	20%	49%	79%
Catholics	18%	58%	80%
Per Cent High on *Religious Experience*			
Protestants	35%	57%	86%
Catholics	29%	49%	70%
Per Cent High on *Religious Knowledge*			
Protestants	15%	19%	46%
Catholics	0	5%	7%
Per Cent High on *Particularism*			
Protestants	9%	25%	60%
Catholics	15%	28%	40%
Per Cent High on *Ethicalism*			
Protestants**	47%	46%	42%
Catholics	48%	48%	56%

* With trivial variations all computations in these tables are based on this same number of cases.
** Members of Protestant sects are excluded from these computations.
Source: Rodney Stark and Charles Y. Glock, *American Piety: The Nature of Religious Commitment* (Berkeley: University of California Press, 1968), Chapter 11, Table 69, p. 214.

Thus, the Stark and Glock data are supportive of our inference that various measures of religious involvement do tap religious belief. Also, the fact that *ethicalism* is not strongly related to orthodox belief adds support to our conclusion that for laity religious beliefs and social beliefs operate relatively independently.

SUMMARY AND INTERPRETATION. Before proceeding to an examination of the relationship between religion and civil rights, a few summary and interpretive comments are in order. In Chapter II we saw that a very large proportion of both clergy and laity have rejected traditional orthodox conceptions of Christian belief. In this chapter we have seen that for clergy, rejection of orthodoxy is strongly associated with more liberal social and political ideologies. While the data for laity are not as adequate as for clergy, the evidence would seem to indicate that this relationship does not hold for laity. Orthodox laity seem to be no more or no less liberal in their social and political views than laity who have rejected orthodox doctrines.

Clergy who have rejected orthodox beliefs about the Christian heritage do not seem to have abandoned theology as a critical dimension of their faith. Their new theology has brought them to a deeper concern about the meaning and implications of Christian love and involvement in this world. For this new breed of clergy, salvation is not to be found in adherence to pietistic doctrine and unfaltering faith in the certainty of another life, but rather in the giving and involvement of oneself in this life.

That rejection of orthodox beliefs does not seem to have had the same effect for laity leaves much room for speculation as to why they have remained involved in church life at all. Perhaps the answer lies in the fact that for laymen, religion is a source of *comfort* and *help*. They are *consumers* of the church's love rather than producers of love. No matter how well they may fare socially and economically, life continually confronts them with problems and they need the church to comfort them and reassure them that they are doing the best they can. To the extent that they are producers of love, it is radiated to their family and friends who sit in the comfortable pew next to them. When they reach beyond the four walls of the church, their concern is manifest in paternalism which takes the form of bazaars, rummage sales, and modest contributions to charitable organizations. But this too is a vital part of the church's comforting role, for these paternalistic expressions reinforce the parishioner's self-image of goodness.

Perhaps laity have not so much rejected orthodox belief as they have found it irrelevant for their privatized civil religion that espouses the good, the true, and the beautiful.[23] They neither profess unalterable faith in orthodox theology nor do they reject it as untenable in a rational-scientific world. For those who fear that God may be a wrathful judge, belief is a convenient form of fire insurance. But this belief doesn't go too deep, for the New Testament emphasis on God as love has led them to feel that the Creator will not ultimately commit anyone to damnation. Acknowledgment of an Almighty is important, but specific doctrine is not. Theology is too deep and confusing for them to ponder very seriously.[24] Serious study of theological doctrine might produce anxiety and conflict over their comfortable concept of Christianity, so they avoid it.

Herein lies perhaps the most important basis of conflict between clergy and laity: The clergyman's new theology has moved him beyond the four walls of the church and prompted him to express God's love in concern for the world, particularly the underprivileged, and in the desire to change the structures of society which have ascribed to many a lower and disadvantaged status in life. The layman, on the other hand, seeks comfort and escape from the world in the sanctuary of God. He does not understand why ministers are not satisfied to restrict their concern to their own fellowship of believers, and to the extent that clergymen move outside their own flock, they pursue a collision course with laity. This thesis will be developed further in the following chapters. We turn next to a comparison of clergy and laity views on the civil rights issue.

IV

Clergy and Laity
View the Civil Rights Issue

Introduction

In this chapter we turn to the issue which has generated the greatest amount of conflict between clergy and laity—civil rights—and examine the beliefs of both toward this issue. In recent years, newspapers have abounded with stories of conflict between clergy and laity over the involvement of the latter in the civil rights struggle. While there has been a great deal of mass media coverage on this conflict, there is a dearth of systematic data on the extent and nature of the conflict. Many questions, from the perspectives of both an interested public and the social scientist, remain unanswered. Just how widespread is the conflict? How large is the group of clergy who are speaking out on controversial issues? Is this only a small minority, or are we truly experiencing the emergence of a new breed of clergymen who feel committed to translating creed into action even at the risk of seriously disrupting the institutional structure of the churches? How do church laymen generally feel about the involvement of clergy in social protest? Does the resistance to clergy involvement come from a hard-core minority of conservatives, or is dissatisfaction with clergy activism the predominant mood of Christian laity?

The purpose of this chapter is to shed as much light on these questions as existing data permit. To be more specific, this chapter examines four questions: (1) What are the attitudes of clergy about the civil rights issue? (2) What is the extent of clergy involvement in various forms of civil rights activity? (3) What are the attitudes of Christian laity about the civil rights issue? and finally, (4) How do laity feel about the involvement of clergy in civil rights activity?

The data for this chapter come principally from two sources. The first is the national survey of 7441 Protestant clergy which we utilized in Chapters II and III. The second is a national survey of the American public's reaction to clergy involvement in civil rights activity which we conducted in early 1967.[1] But other studies are drawn upon to fill in gaps in these data and to provide a broader perspective for interpretation.

Attitudes of Clergy About Civil Rights

We saw in Chapter III that theologically liberal clergy as a group hold liberal views about social and political issues. Therefore, we would expect this group to be also more liberal in their views about civil rights. We will see a little later that this is true, but perhaps the most profound finding in our study is that whatever their theology, *clergy as a group are overwhelmingly sympathetic to the general principle of achieving social justice for Negroes in America.*

Three items in the national survey of clergy attempted to solicit their attitudes in general about civil rights and how good a job they felt that the churches and Christians were doing in facing up to this problem. The first statement reads, "I basically disapprove of the civil rights movement in America" (Table 39).

TABLE 39

CLERGY STRONGLY SUPPORT THE
GENERAL PRINCIPLE OF CIVIL RIGHTS

"I basically disapprove of the civil rights movement in America."	Methodist	Episcopalian	Presbyterian	American Baptist	American Lutheran	Missouri Synod Lutheran
				% Agreeing		
	8	5	4	6	5	8

This statement is overwhelmingly rejected by clergy in every denomination. Only 4 per cent of the Presbyterian clergy agree with this statement, 5 per cent of the American Lutherans and Episcopalians, 6 per cent of the American Baptists, and 8 per cent of the

Methodists and Missouri Synod Lutherans. Even adding the "probably agree" response to this statement does not alter the basic pattern. The percentage indicating probable agreement with this position ranges from 2 per cent for Episcopalians to 6 per cent for Missouri Synod Lutherans. Thus, the proportion who even hint at a lack of sympathy with the civil rights movement is only a small minority of clergy.

Furthermore, the large majority of clergy express deep concern over the church's failure to be more influential in the whole racial crisis. Almost three quarters of the clergy agree with the strongly worded statement: "For the most part, the churches have been woefully inadequate in facing up to the civil rights issue" (Table 40).

TABLE 40

MOST CLERGY FEEL THAT CHURCHES HAVE BEEN
INADEQUATE IN FACING CIVIL RIGHTS

	Methodist	Episcopalian	Presbyterian	American Baptist	American Lutheran	Missouri Synod Lutheran
"For the most part, the churches have been woefully inadequate in facing up to the civil rights issue."						
% Agreeing	76	70	76	77	70	69

Agreement with this statement runs as high as 77 per cent among American Baptists and drops only to 69 per cent among the conservative Missouri Synod Lutherans. As pointed out in Chapter II, this seems to be one area where some measure of consensus is achieved among clergy, irrespective of the theological orientation of their denomination.

When the "probably agree" responses are added to the "agree," the over-all proportion expressing sentiment for this position increases to approximately 85 per cent. On the other hand, the highest proportion in any denomination who "definitely disagree" with this statement is only 6 per cent.

Finally, clergy are concerned that Christians have not fully understood the implications of their faith for the racial issue. The statement in Table 41 reads, "Many whites pretend to be very Christian while in reality their racial attitudes demonstrate their lack of or misunderstanding of Christianity."

TABLE 41

CLERGY FEEL CHRISTIANS MISUNDERSTAND THE IMPLICATIONS
OF CHRISTIANITY FOR RACE RELATIONS

	Methodist	Episcopalian	Presbyterian	American Baptist	American Lutheran	Missouri Synod Lutheran
"Many whites pretend to be very Christian while in reality their racial attitudes demonstrate their lack of or misunderstanding of Christianity."						
% Agreeing	79	82	83	83	80	78

Again, agreement with this statement runs quite high, ranging from 78 per cent among Missouri Synod Lutherans to 83 per cent for American Baptists and Presbyterians. Inclusion of the "probably agree" responses raises the total expressing sympathy with this statement to 90 per cent or more in every denomination.

In summary, the responses to these three attitude statements dramatically reveal that clergy are at least in principle committed to the achievement of the goals of the civil rights movement. However, much research has demonstrated that people who adhere to *general* principles are not necessarily committed to the specific implications of these principles, and that they are not willing to act, or approve of action which is directed at the achievement of goals that are implicit in general principles. There is no reason to believe that this is not also true of clergy as well as the general public. However, our data suggest that clergy do have considerable insight into the specific implications of their beliefs about civil rights.

The data from the national survey do not permit us fully to document the extent to which clergy understand and are committed to the implications of the general principles they adhere to. Nevertheless, some sense of their understanding and commitment can be seen by examining several items in the survey which attempted to tap "simplistic" solutions to the racial crisis. These items do not overtly measure racial prejudice; in fact, they may contain a partial element of truth. However, a growing body of social science knowledge as well as the conclusions of the Report of the National Advisory Commission on Civil Disorders would suggest that agreement with these statements reflects a lack of understanding of the complexity of the racial dilemma in America. The statements are as follows:

1. "The real obstacle to integration in this country is political leadership and not the people themselves."
2. "The racial crisis in America would probably be less serious if the Federal government had not intervened."
3. "Negroes would be better off if they would take advantage of the opportunities that have been made available to them rather than spending so much time protesting."
4. "Negroes could solve many of their own problems if they were not so irresponsible and carefree about life."

All of these items reflect an element of stereotyping or scapegoating. By pointing to the government or the Negro in rather condescending terms, they tend to remove the responsibility of the racial crisis from the society at large. At the very least, they reflect subtle overtones of racial prejudice which grow out of ignorance.[2]

As can be seen in Table 42, the large majority of clergy reject the solutions to the racial crisis that are implied in these statements. Less than one in five of the clergy in all denominations agree with the thesis that racial integration is being blocked by political leadership rather than the people themselves. Even fewer, approximately one in ten overall, believe that the racial crisis would have been less serious if the Federal government had not intervened.

Turning from the role of politicians and the government to Negroes themselves, the proportion who agree with these statements

TABLE 42

CLERGY REJECT SIMPLE EXPLANATIONS OF
THE RACIAL CRISIS

	Methodist	Episcopalian	Presbyterian	American Baptist	American Lutheran	Missouri Synod Lutheran
						% Agreeing
"The real obstacle to integration in this country is political leadership and not the people themselves."	17	14	12	19	11	12
"The racial crisis in this country would probably be less serious if the Federal government had not intervened."	12	9	7	12	8	17
"Negroes would be better off if they would take advantage of the opportunities that have been made available to them rather than spending so much time protesting."	22	16	13	22	21	31
"Negroes could solve many of their own problems if they were not so irresponsible and carefree about life."	26	19	15	26	21	20

is somewhat higher. Agreement with these statements may reflect a non-prejudicial sentiment that Negroes must share in the task of solving the racial problem. However, it should be noted that response to these questions begins to reflect denominational differences. The more theologically liberal denominations are somewhat less likely to agree with these statements that essentially say Negroes are responsible for their own problems. We will return to this shortly and examine the importance of theological views for determining racial attitudes.

Thus far our analysis of clergy attitudes toward civil rights has moved from a very general statement—approval or rejection of the civil rights movement—to more specific questions of responsibility for the civil rights crisis. We have seen that a large majority of clergy feel that the churches have not done everything that they might do, that they reject the idea that politicians and the government are primarily responsible for the crisis, and that most of them do not hold Negroes centrally responsible for the problems. While a substantial majority have taken a liberal position on all the statements examined thus far, as the statements have become more specific, the percentage of agreement has declined somewhat. This suggests, at least, as we move from general principles to specific acts designed to accomplish the goals implicit in the principles, that commitment will decline.

Another item in the questionnaire would seem to confirm this thesis. Clergy in the national survey were asked to respond to the following statement: "I am in basic sympathy with Northern ministers and students who have gone to the South to work for civil rights" (Table 43).

Agreement with this statement drops off sharply when compared with previous statements. In looking at this question it must be remembered that it was a salient and controversial issue at the time

TABLE 43

CLERGY TEND TO BE SYMPATHETIC WITH THOSE WHO
HAVE GONE SOUTH TO WORK FOR CIVIL RIGHTS

	Methodist	Episcopalian	Presbyterian	American Baptist	American Lutheran	Missouri Synod Lutheran
"I am in basic sympathy with Northern ministers and students who have gone to the South to work for civil rights."						
% Definitely agree + agree	46	56	65	52	47	33
% Probably agree	14	13	13	18	21	16
Total agreeing	60	69	78	70	68	49

the data were gathered. Many people who approved of civil rights in principle felt that outside interference in the South by students and clergy was an inappropriate means of achieving the goals of civil rights. Therefore, we would not expect clergy to approach consensus on this issue, nor would we want to jump to the conclusion that rejection of this specific act reflects lack of commitment to the accomplishment of racial justice. Many persons who rejected this position did so because they felt that this type of activity might result in greater hardships for Negroes.

What is perhaps surprising is that so many clergy indicated that they were sympathetic with this particular type of activism. Slightly more than half of the clergy in the study indicated that they were sympathetic with students and ministers going south to work for civil rights. When the "probably agrees" are included, almost two thirds of the total clergy sample express favorable sentiments for this type of involvement. But while a majority of clergy express sympathetic views toward this type of involvement in the civil rights struggle, they do fall short of consensus. Denominational differences begin to take on some significance. For example, 65 per cent of the Presbyterians agreed with this statement, as compared with only 33 per cent of the Missouri Synod Lutherans.

THEOLOGICAL POSITION AND CIVIL RIGHTS ATTITUDES. The reappearance of the denominational pattern serves to recall the conclusions of Stark and Glock reported in the previous chapter, namely that *traditional* theology which stresses radical free will is subtly reflected in racial attitudes. While most clergy express general sympathy with the civil rights cause, it may be that those who are theologically conservative are less committed to the fulfillment of these ideals—precisely because their deepest feelings about the nature of man tell them that the Negro is really to blame for his plight and that it is he who must solve the problem.

A look at the same attitude statements we have examined thus far in this chapter, controlling for theological position, lends considerable support to this thesis. This is illustrated in Table 44, which is the statement about Negroes' carefree and irresponsible attitudes about life.

The table shows that the more conservative a clergyman's theological views, the more likely he is to agree that "Negroes could

TABLE 44

THEOLOGICALLY CONSERVATIVE CLERGY TEND TO SEE
THE NEGROES' PROBLEMS GROWING OUT OF
AN IRRESPONSIBLE ATTITUDE TOWARD LIFE

	Methodist	Episcopalian	Presbyterian	American Baptist	American Lutheran	Missouri Synod Lutheran
"Negroes could solve many of their own problems if they would not be so irresponsible and carefree about life."			*% Agreeing*			
Fundamentalist	64	*	29	53	44	55
Conservative	39	27	25	33	22	26
Neo-orthodox	20	14	8	11	13	16
Liberal	18	18	8	9	9	*

* The number of cases is too small to compute statistically reliable percentages.

solve many of their own problems if they would not be so irresponsible and carefree about life." For example, 53 per cent of the fundamentalists among American Baptists agree with this statement, compared with 33 per cent who are conservative, 11 per cent who are neo-orthodox, and 9 per cent who are theologically liberal.

This same general pattern is observed when we examine the relationship between theological position and the other civil rights items which have been presented in this chapter (Tables 39 through 43). The repetitiveness of the pattern does not merit detailed item-by-item description. However, some interpretable differences do occur and the interested reader may examine these in the appendix.

Several general observations are apparent from Table 44 as well as from the tables in the appendix. First of all, theological liberals are almost without exception the most sympathetic in their views toward civil rights, followed closely by neo-orthodox clergy. Fundamentalists are the least sympathetic toward civil rights. However, one notable difference does occur. In Chapter III, the theologically conservative tended to be closer to fundamentalists in their views on social and political issues. On the civil rights items, the conservatives seem to have shifted away from the fundamentalists and on several items are actually closer to the neo-orthodox than the fundamentalists. However, on most items, the difference separating conservatives and neo-orthodox is still considerable.

Denominational differences persist even among those who identify themselves with the same theological label. Probably most notable is the fact that fundamentalists and conservatives among Presbyterians, one of the more theologically liberal denominations, tend to be more liberal in their views toward civil rights than are fundamentalists and conservatives in other denominations. However, the differences in beliefs which separate the theological groups are quite significant. There are only a couple of items in which conservative Presbyterians are as liberal on civil rights views as neo-orthodox clergy in other denominations, and in no case are Presbyterian conservatives more liberal on civil rights views than are neo-orthodox clergy in all of the other five denominations.

Differences between fundamentalists and liberals are smallest on the two items which deal with the responsibility of the churches and the racial attitudes of Christians. On these items the large majority of fundamentalists agree with the liberal civil rights view. Approximately two thirds of the fundamentalists feel that the churches have been woefully inadequate in facing up to the civil rights issue. The proportion of liberals agreeing with this position is about four fifths.

About three quarters of the fundamentalists feel that "Many whites pretend to be very Christian while in reality their racial attitudes demonstrate their lack of or misunderstanding of Christianity." But again, even a greater proportion of the theologically liberal (approximately 85 per cent) feel this way.

It seems apparent that fundamentalists and liberals would differ quite dramatically were we to ask them to elaborate their position on these two items. They would no doubt differ most sharply on what they feel ought to be done by the churches to face the civil rights issues squarely and to get Christians to realize what their responsibilities are. Only a little more than a fifth of the fundamentalists approve of clergy and students going south to work for civil rights, compared with about two thirds of the liberals. In several case studies I have conducted, this pattern has emerged very clearly. Liberal and neo-orthodox clergy are much more sympathetic with and more frequently involved in various forms of direct action. Fundamentalist and conservative clergy, on the other hand, are virtually absent in any form of direct action and they are much more likely to mention "preaching the gospel" and "teaching people to love one another" as solutions to the racial crisis.

But the differences between clergy of different theological persuasions are deeper than the perceived means of accomplishing change. Fundamentalist and conservative clergy are much more likely to point their finger at the government and Negroes as principal sources of the racial crisis. My personal interviews with liberal clergy clearly indicate that they are not willing to absolve government officials and the Negroes of responsibility. In fact, they are very critical of the government for not taking a more vigorous leadership role. However, they see government officials as reflecting the same lack of understanding and inertia as the general public. They do not feel that Negroes as a group are irresponsible and carefree, but they do acknowledge that this is probably true for some Negroes. However, they are usually quick to qualify their responses with historical and sociological explanations as to why this is so, and they see dramatic social change as necessary to eradicate the conditions which have made some Negroes irresponsible.

AGE AND CIVIL RIGHTS ATTITUDES. In Chapter II we saw that younger clergy tend to be more liberal in their interpretations of scripture and in Chapter III we saw that they tend to be more liberal in their views about social issues. We turn now to the question of whether age is also associated with attitudes toward civil rights. Again, because of the repetitiveness of the pattern, only one of the eight civil rights statements is presented here in the body of the text. Those who wish to examine age differences more carefully will find these tables in the appendix.

Table 45 presents the item dealing with carefree and irresponsible attitudes of Negroes toward life, controlled by age groups.

Older clergy are considerably more likely to see the Negroes' problems as arising out of a carefree and irresponsible attitude toward life than are younger clergy. The pattern is remarkably consistent. Each subsequently older age group is likely to feel this way in every

TABLE 45

OLDER CLERGY ARE MORE LIKELY TO SEE NEGRO
PROBLEMS GROWING OUT OF
AN IRRESPONSIBLE ATTITUDE TOWARD LIFE

	Methodist	Episcopalian	Presbyterian	American Baptist	American Lutheran	Missouri Synod Lutheran
"Negroes could solve many of their own problems if they would not be so irresponsible and carefree about life."				*% Agreeing*		
Under 35	18	11	8	9	14	22
35–44	22	13	9	18	17	19
45–54	31	16	20	34	23	33
Over 55	39	39	30	46	45	54

denomination. Again, the pattern may be illustrated with the American Baptist clergy: Only 9 per cent of those under age thirty-five agree with this statement, compared with 18 per cent who are between ages thirty-five and forty-four, 34 per cent in the age group fory-five to fifty-four, and 46 per cent of those fifty-five years or over.

While the other attitude statements show some variation in the pattern, the general pattern obtains for all items. Several general conclusions may be made about Table 45 and the other age tables in the appendix.

First of all, denominational differences continue to persist for every age group, including the youngest clergy. However, the distance separating younger clergy across denominations is less than for older clergy. On seven of the eight items, younger clergy of every denomination are more in agreement than are older clergy. With the exception of the statements dealing with government and Negro responsibility for the civil rights crisis, however, these differences are not large.

The differences among age groups within denominations vary by the degree of theological liberalness of denominations. The average difference between the youngest and the oldest age groups for the eight items is approximately 13 percentage points for Episcopalians, Methodists, and Presbyterians. Among American Baptists, American Lutherans, and Missouri Synod Lutherans, the youngest and oldest age groups are separated by an average of about 20 percentage points. In other words, age tends to separate less in the more theologically liberal denominations than in the conservative denominations. The largest differences are on the two items dealing with the responsibility of Negroes for solving the civil rights problems. Older clergy are more inclined to feel that Negroes are not taking advantage of opportunities and that they are irresponsible and carefree about life.

Thus far in this chapter we have seen that both theological position and age make very significant differences in clergy's views about the civil rights issue. The more liberal a clergyman's theological position, the greater his sympathy for the civil rights cause. Similarly, the younger a clergyman is, the more liberal his feelings are likely to be about civil rights. But what is the relationship between theological position and age? Are younger clergy more liberal in their theological views, and if so, which is most important in accounting for their views on civil rights?

Table 46 shows the relationship between age and theological position. The results reveal that theological position cannot be accounted for simply in terms of age, although theological position is clearly associated with age. Of those under age thirty-five, only 1 per cent identify themselves as fundamentalists. This proportion increases to

TABLE 46

THEOLOGICAL POSITION IS ASSOCIATED WITH AGE

	FUNDA-MENTALIST %	CONSERV-ATIVE %	NEO-ORTHODOX %	LIBERAL %
AGE				
Under 35	1	36	39	18
35–44	2	44	29	21
45–54	6	47	21	23
Over 55	12	43	15	24

12 per cent for those fifty-five years and over. When fundamentalists and conservatives are combined, the proportion identifying with these positions increases from 37 per cent of those under age thirty-five to 55 per cent among those fifty-five years and over. Interestingly, the proportion identifying themselves as liberals also increases slightly with age. This can be explained by the fact that the proportion identifying themselves as neo-orthodox decreases with age. Only 15 per cent of those fifty-five years of age and over identify with the neo-orthodox label, compared with 39 per cent of those under thirty-five years. This makes some sense, since neo-orthodoxy as a major theological view did not come into its own until after the older age group had completed their formal theological training.

This table indicates both theological position and age are important in attempting to explain clergy's views on civil rights. In other words, we cannot fully explain liberal civil rights views among younger clergy as a simple artifact of their being theologically more liberal. Perhaps this can be seen more clearly in Table 47, which shows the interaction of age and theological position for the statement on Negro irresponsibility.

TABLE 47

BOTH THEOLOGICAL POSITION AND AGE AFFECT
RACIAL ATTITUDES OF CLERGY

	Funda-mentalist	Conserv-ative	Neo-orthodox	Liberal
"Negroes could solve many of their own problems if they would not be so irresponsible and carefree about life."		% Agreeing		
Under 35	43	20	11	8
35–44	42	22	12	10
45–54	47	32	16	18
Over 55	63	47	30	26

Among fundamentalists, 43 per cent who are under thirty-five years of age agree with this statement. The proportion agreeing increases with each age group: 42 per cent among those in the age group thirty-five to forty-four, 47 per cent between ages forty-five and fifty-four, and 63 per cent among those who are fifty-five years of age or over. This same age pattern holds for every theological position. But also note that a consistent pattern exists for theological position *within* each age group. For example, while 43 per cent of the fundamentalists under age thirty-five agree with the statement, the agreement in this age group drops to 20 per cent for those who call themselves conservatives, 11 per cent for the neo-orthodox, and 8 per cent for the liberals. Again, the pattern essentially repeats itself for every age group.

To state this finding somewhat differently, for every age group the theologically liberal tend to be more liberal in their views on civil rights than are neo-orthodox, who in turn are more liberal than conservatives, who are more liberal than fundamentalists. Reading across the columns also shows a patterned relationship by age within each theological group. Younger fundamentalists are more liberal than older fundamentalists on civil rights, younger conservatives are more liberal than older conservatives, etc. In short, both age and theological position make a difference in a clergyman's views about civil rights.

This same pattern generally holds for all eight of the civil rights items we have examined in this chapter (see appendix). However, it is not always as clear as the example presented here. The pattern tends to break down somewhat between liberals and neo-orthodox. This is not, however, surprising since the two groups were relatively close in their racial attitudes before age was introduced. Similarly, some inconsistent patterns can be observed for the age groups.

While we have seen that both age and theological position are important for predicting racial attitudes, the question that remains is whether one is more important than the other. A rough measure of the relative impact of age and theological position can be seen if we take the mean (average) difference for all eight attitude statements between the two extreme theological positions for each age group and compare these figures with the mean difference in attitude for the two extreme age groups for each theological group.

These figures are presented in Table 48. The average difference between fundamentalists and liberals for the eight civil rights items by age is approximately 20 per cent. The average difference between clergy under age thirty-five and clergy fifty-five years and over for the eight civil rights items by theological position is approximately

10 per cent. Thus, it can be seen that the theological position is roughly twice as important as age in explaining attitudes about civil rights.

TABLE 48

THEOLOGICAL POSITION IS RELATIVELY MORE IMPORTANT
THAN AGE IN PREDICTING CIVIL RIGHTS ATTITUDES

Mean difference between fundamentalists and liberals for eight civil rights items by age.

	$\bar{x}$ difference
Under 35	20.8%
35–44	20.5%
45–54	19.1%
Over 55	21.4%

Mean difference between clergy under age 35 and clergy over 55 for eight civil rights items by theological position.

	$\bar{x}$ difference
Fundamentalist	10.8%
Conservative	14.3%
Neo-orthodox	9.1%
Liberal	8.9%

SUMMARY. Protestant clergy in the national survey are overwhelmingly sympathetic toward the civil rights issue. This concern is reflected not only in attitudes about civil rights as a general principle, but also in terms of their sensitivity to the complexity of the problem and in the fact that they eschew simplistic scapegoating explanations. However, clergy are not unanimous in their views of all the various aspects of the civil rights struggle that we raised. Liberal and neo-orthodox clergy are more sympathetic toward civil rights than are clergy whose theological orientation is conservative or fundamentalist. Also, younger clergy hold more liberal civil rights views than do their older colleagues. When the relative impact of both age and theological position was considered, we found that both do make a difference, but that theological position is the more important predictor of the two.

Extent of Clergy Involvement in Civil Rights Activity

While more than half of the clergy in our study expressed sympathy for students and ministers who have gone south to work for civil rights, it would seem fairly certain that the proportion of clergy who have actually been involved in some form of social protest is considerably smaller than this. Impressions that one gathers from the mass media would suggest that the actual number of activist ministers is quite small. However, the actual number of ministers who have at one time or another joined in a protest march, carried a picket sign, or engaged in some other form of direct social action remains unknown.

Unfortunately, the national survey did not obtain data on actual involvement in social protest. At the time the study was initiated, the number of clergy who were actively involved in social protest seemed quite small, and thus it seemed that asking such questions would reveal that only a small minority had been involved in protest—too small a number to merit the space in a questionnaire that was already so long we were not certain that clergy would complete it. Moreover, as was indicated in the introduction, the involvement of clergy in civil rights was not the major objective of the study.

Looking back, I am inclined to believe that clergy involvement in social protest was greater in 1963 and 1964 than I realized when the study was initiated. However, the greatest thrust in clergy involvement in protest came after the study was initiated and thus any behavioral data gathered in early 1965 would not be a very good measure of the extent to which clergy have been and currently are engaged in protest. Nevertheless, such data would have been invaluable for examining the social and theological beliefs of activist clergy.

Realizing the importance of clergy involvement in social protest, I began in the summer of 1965 to gather data on incidents in which clergy had become involved in conflict over the civil rights issue. These case materials vary enormously in terms of the nature of the conflict situations as well as the amount of data obtained. Many of the case studies involve individual clergy, but I have generally been more interested in incidents which involved groups of clergy. In many cases I have only newspaper accounts. In other cases I have gone into a community and spent two or three days interviewing persons who were key actors in the conflict. In five conflict situations I have developed fairly extensive data, including depth interviews with up to one hundred persons, position and strategy papers, newspaper accounts, financial records of the organizations involved, and detailed histories on the communities and conditions leading up to the conflict. In one case I have more than three thousand pages of material on a conflict situation that has continued for more than four years. Not all of these data are amenable to systematic analysis, but they do provide an important resource for drawing some general impressions on the extent of clergy involvement in conflict over civil rights.

To begin with, these data strongly suggest that the extent of clergy involvement in social protest is much greater than is generally believed. Several factors tend to camouflage the extent of their involvement. First of all, much clergy involvement in social protest never reaches local newspapers and only a small proportion what is printed locally reaches the national news media. Many clergy participate in social protest anonymously, or at least anonymous in the sense that their congregations are not generally aware of their activity. In many situations where congregations are aware of their minister's involvement in protest, this involvement is not overtly the focus of conflict that emerges between the congregation and the minister. Rather, the conflict takes much more subtle forms and often people are probably not even overtly aware of the basic issue. For example, a minister who has become involved in some form of protest may suddenly find himself subjected to criticism for neglecting his visitation duties or absenteeism from the ladies' missionary society. In one sense, these criticisms may be legitimate, for the more he becomes involved in activity outside the church, the less time he has for local parish duties. But in another sense, the criticisms are a covert way of handling dissatisfaction with his involvement in social action. Few liberal Protestant congregations would express dissatisfaction with their minister if he were to become the most popular speaker on the civic club circuit, or if he were to become deeply involved in state or national denominational life, for these activities lend prestige to the local congregation. Yet these activities also would be taking significant time from his local pastoral duties. Thus, a minister may encounter conflict with his congregation ostensibly for reasons other than his involvement in social issues.

Clergy tend to be highly mobile, serving one congregation for a few years and then moving on to another. Many clergy move on to a new congregation before the conflict reaches overt expressions of hostility. A new congregation provides a clergyman the opportunity to start anew in his interpersonal relations with his congregation. He can learn from past experience and try out new strategies of involvement in social action which will hopefully avoid conflict. It also gives him an opportunity to reassess his ministerial activities and most certainly many clergy, having experienced conflict over their involvement in social action, decide to withdraw from an activist role.[3]

Other factors tend to camouflage the extent of clergy involvement in social protest, as well as the conflict that this involvement generates. The selective reporting of the mass media has resulted in the overexposure of a few activist clergy. For example, one Episcopalian clergyman with a patch over one eye was present at several protest marches during 1965, which was a year of intense involvement of clergy in protest. The patch over his eye made him highly visible and reinforced the impression that there are only a few activist clergy who travel from one conflict situation to another. True, there was a small group of clergy who did participate in a number of protest marches across the country. But the high visibility of a few, such as the minister with the eye patch, or, for that matter, the Rev. Martin Luther King, Jr., produces a subtle impression that is contrary to fact.

But just how large is the group of clergy who have been involved in social protest? This is very difficult to ascertain for at least two reasons. First, civil rights organizations are, like other groups involved in social movements, very poor record keepers,[4] and newspaper reporters who cover these events are not social scientists. They operate under time pressures and thus have to rely on impressions rather than systematic data. Secondly, defining involvement is a very sticky proposition. Is a clergyman who goes to Washington and anonymously marches in a large group, but treads lightly over the civil rights issue from the pulpit, more involved than the clergyman who never considered carrying a picket sign or joining a civil rights group, but hits the civil rights issue head on from the pulpit? The answer to this question is not at all obvious. Thus, the absence of records plus the very problem of defining involvement preclude any neat statistics on clergy involvement in the civil rights struggle. However, data from a few case studies should serve to demonstrate my contention that the involvement of clergy in social protest is more widespread than generally believed.

Since 1963 there have been three events in which a rather large number of clergymen have participated. The first was the 1963 Civil Rights March on Washington. The second event was the Selma March in the spring of 1965. Since no records exist, it is impossible to determine just how many clergy were involved in each of these marches. Newspaper accounts vary widely, ranging from two to more than ten thousand clergy participating in each of these marches. In the spring of 1967, approximately 2600 clergymen and seminary students participated in a Clergy Mobilization March on Washington to protest the Vietnam war. To be sure, these figures do not represent a large proportion of the nation's clergy, and the significance one attributes to the three mobilization efforts depends on one's criteria of evaluation.

Local conflict situations are perhaps more revealing of the uneasiness of clergy about the civil rights crisis in this nation and the potential for clergy to become involved in the struggle. Several illustrations will be briefly discussed here.

In 1964 Cleveland faced a crisis situation in the public schools. Negro students were being bussed from the overcrowded schools in Hough to Murray Hill, a nearby racially tense Italian neighborhood, but were being assigned to separate classrooms, with separate lunch and recess periods, and they were denied use of some of the school's recreational facilities. In the fall of 1963 the Cleveland Board of Education had pledged "the fullest possible incorporation of transportation pupils into the receiving school's organizations consistent with sound educational procedure. . . ." By January 1964 only about 10 per cent integration had been accomplished. The indignation of civil rights workers over the lack of progress in integration was heightened when the school board president, Ralph McAllister, made a public statement claiming that the Negro children who had been integrated could not keep up with the white children in their classes. Civil rights leaders were quick to respond that McAllister's statement either reflected a belief of his own that

Negroes were fundamentally inferior, or it was an admission of the failure of the school system to provide equal and adequate education in the Negro schools.

Shortly after this sharp exchange, the United Freedom Movement, a loosely coalesced organization of civil rights groups, assembled for a protest march on the Italian neighborhood. Simultaneously a crowd of whites assembled in Murray Hill. A direct confrontation between the two groups was averted, but the incident touched off one of the worst outbreaks of violence in the city's history.

From this point, the conflict in the city intensified for nearly four months. While all this was happening, the school board was rushing to construct new schools in the Hough area. The City Planning Commission advised against the school construction sites, indicating that there was inadequate land and there had not been sufficient time to conduct adequate population projection studies. Civil rights leaders claimed, with some justification, that the sites of the new schools constituted gerrymandering which would result in resegregation.

During these critical months the clergy of Cleveland formed a group which they called the Emergency Committee of Clergy for Civil Rights. There was no formal membership in the organization, but ECCCR records indicate that 221 Protestant clergy and 10 Jewish rabbis were affiliated with the group. This constituted more than 40 per cent of the metropolitan area's white Protestant clergy. Even though some of these men were only nominally affiliated, this was still a very significant amount of support. More importantly, the proportion of clergy involvement was much higher among the members of the more liberal denominations.

Table 49 shows the number of churches in the Cleveland metropolitan area for various denominations and the number of clergy from each denomination who were associated with the ECCCR. The percentage figure in the right-hand column consists of the number of clergy associated with ECCCR divided by the number of churches. This figure overrepresents the number of clergy in each denomination who are associated with ECCCR, since some churches have multiple-staff ministries. Churches with pulpit vacancies would partially correct this figure.

Allowing for adjustments because of the inadequacy of the data, Table 49 still reveals (1) that the proportion of Cleveland clergy who were involved in the ECCCR was relatively high, and (2) that

TABLE 49

CLERGY PARTICIPATION OF CLEVELAND EMERGENCY
COMMITTEE OF CLERGY FOR CIVIL RIGHTS, 1964

DENOMINATION	NUMBER OF CHURCHES	NUMBER OF CLERGY PARTICIPATING IN ECCCR	%*
United Church of Christ	58	50	86
Episcopal	30	22	73
United Presbyterian	42	28	67
Methodist	49	27	55
Disciples of Christ	20	10	50
Evangelical United Brethren	14	4	29
American Baptist	35	9	26
Lutheran (all bodies)	89	14	16

* Per cent computed by dividing number of participating clergy by the number
of churches (see text). The data were compiled by Rev. Andrew J. White, at the
time a graduate student in the department of political science, Case Western Reserve University.

denomination, and hence theological orientation, is strongly related
to the probability that a clergyman will be involved. Episcopalians,
Presbyterians, and the United Church of Christ, all theologically
liberal denominations, have very high levels of participation. Baptists, Lutherans, and Brethren, theologically conservative groups,
have relatively low levels of participation.

The racial crisis culminated in early April of 1964 when a young
Presbyterian clergyman was crushed to death beneath a bulldozer
at one of the school construction sites. Shortly after this tragic event,
the Emergency Committee called for the resignation of members of
the school board. At that point, the local newspapers, which had
not been particularly sympathetic with the ECCCR activities, especially their engagement in picketing and civil disobedience, demanded to know who the members of the ECCCR were. Up to that
point, the ECCCR was largely anonymous except for a small group
of leaders. About 60 per cent of those clergy who had been associated with the group, or about one quarter of the Protestant clergy
in Cleveland, consented to have their names released to the press.

For many this was a critical decision, and at least a dozen paid
for their involvement with the loss of their pulpits. Two clergymen
who occupied very prestigeful pulpits in the city decided to leave

the ministry. At least four others occupying less prestigious pulpits made the same decision.

It is difficult to assess just what the Cleveland clergy accomplished by their involvement in the 1964 school crisis. On the one hand, the school board members who were most resistant to change, including the board president, were defeated in the next election. A new school superintendent, who seems more sensitive to the complexity of the city's educational problems, was hired. Many symbols of progress can be seen, but in many respects the problems remain basically unchanged. By admission of the school superintendent, the public schools are on the brink of financial disaster. The ghetto schools remain a source of continual tension, and there is no concrete evidence to indicate that the quality of education in these schools has improved.

The prestige of Cleveland clergy as a group seems to have suffered from their involvement. Community and business leaders remain distrustful of clergy. And clergy themselves have failed to provide the unity they achieved in 1964 to face the continuing critical problems of the city. The riots of 1966 brought bold, sweeping promises from the Council of Churches which remain almost completely unfulfilled. Martin Luther King, Jr.'s campaign in the summer of 1967 received virtually no organized support from white Protestant clergy. But this is another story. The significance of this episode is that a very significant proportion of the city's clergy did get involved in an incident which they perceived as critical.

In the fall of 1966, Detroit clergy became involved in a struggle with City Hall over the displacement of poor Negroes by an urban renewal project. Detroit has had a vigorous urban renewal program which, in spite of impressive accomplishments, has resulted in the elimination of a great deal of low-cost housing. By the fall of 1966, the housing shortage in Detroit had become particularly acute for large poverty-level families. At the same time a significant number of large, sound dwelling units had been vacated for urban renewal, but many were not scheduled for demolition for many months (up to eighteen months in some cases).

In September, the West Central Organization (WCO), a militant community organization with strong backing from several denominational bodies in Detroit, began applying pressure on the Housing Commission to permit these units to be occupied until they were actually to be demolished. When city officials refused to negoti-

ate the issue, the WCO, led by clergy, broke into and occupied a
house in the urban renewal area. Ten days of tense drama and
strategy followed, in which more than twenty clergy were arrested.
But clergy support of the WCO and its objectives was even stronger
than is suggested by the arrest of a score of ministers. In the heat
of the confrontation, 132 clergy marched to Mayor Cavanagh's office
and presented him with signed statements indicating that they were
prepared to go to jail if the city did not respond to the housing
needs of the poor. Mayor Cavanagh outmaneuvered the clergy and
avoided being forced to arrest them. But again, our concern here is
not with the success of clergy in their pursuit of conflict strategies,
but rather in assessing the degree of concern and involvement of
clergy in the pursuit of social justice. The 132 represent something
less than 10 per cent of all the clergy in metropolitan Detroit, but
this figure is misleading. With the exception of about a dozen Roman
Catholics, these men come almost exclusively from the more liberal
Protestant denominations and represent about a third of the clergy
of those bodies.[5] In other words, a significant proportion of Detroit's clergy felt strongly enough about this particular incident to
risk arrest, condemnation from public officials and the press, and subsequent conflict with their congregations in order to stand up and
give witness to their convictions.

These are, of course, only case studies and they do not constitute
sufficient evidence to verify the extent of clergy involvement in social protest. They exemplify other cases that I am aware of, but
I do not know how many similar incidents have occurred across the
nation during the past few years. The case studies are at least
sufficient to cast suspicion on the contention that the social activists constitute only a very small proportion of the clergy. The case
studies also serve to suggest an underlying generalization: *Given a
critical incident, the general sentiment that clergy express for civil
rights and the achievement of social justice is capable of being
mobilized in social protest.*

Attitudes of Church Laity About Civil Rights

If Christian laity felt as strongly about civil rights as clergy do,
there would be little basis for conflict. The evidence, however, indicates that this is not the case.

In January 1967, we asked a national sample of the American public how they felt about the civil rights issue, and particularly about the role of clergy in the struggle. The data were gathered in personal interviews as part of the National Opinion Research Center's Amalgam Survey, and constitute a representative national sample of 1504 respondents.[6] Two hundred Negroes in the sample are eliminated from the analyses presented here.

Respondents were asked to respond to attitude statements using one of four responses. The response categories were as follows: "definitely agree," "probably agree," "probably disagree," and "definitely disagree." The percentages reported here combine the first two categories, "definitely agree" and "probably agree." Where parallel items for clergy and laity are compared, the "probably agree" category in the six-point continuum of clergy data is combined with the other "agree" responses to make the two samples as nearly comparable as possible.

The first statement in the national survey parallels an item in the national clergy survey: "I basically disapprove of the Negro civil rights movement in America" (Table 50).

TABLE 50

APPROVAL OF CIVIL RIGHTS MOVEMENT IS NOT
SYSTEMATICALLY RELATED TO CHURCH ATTENDANCE

"I basically disapprove of the Negro civil rights movement in America."	% Agreeing
NATION	44
FREQUENCY OF CHURCH ATTENDANCE	
Every week	43
Nearly every week	46
2–3 times a month	45
About once a month	52
Several times a year	42
About once or twice a year	45
Less than once a year	50
Never	39

While less than 10 per cent of the clergy in our national survey reported that they did not approve of the civil rights movement, 44 per cent of the white American public reported that they basically disapprove of the Negro civil rights movement. Moreover, frequency of church attendance bears little systematic relationship to how one feels about this issue. Of those who report attending church every week, 43 per cent, 1 per cent below the national average, say that they disapprove of the civil rights movement. This proportion rises to 52 per cent among those who attend church "about once a month." However, this pattern does not continue. The next category, "several times a year," drops to 42 per cent agreement, and then rises again to 50 per cent agreement among those who report attending church less than once a year. While the differences are not particularly large, those who report that they never attend church are the *least* likely to disapprove of the civil rights movement, with 39 per cent agreement. The swelling in disapproval among middle-range attenders might lead some to conclude that a little church is worse than none at all. Actually, the absence of a systematic pattern plus the relatively small differences that are observed preclude drawing any bold statements or sweeping indictments. All we can really say is that on the basis of this single statement, church attendance is not systematically related to attitudes toward the civil rights movement.

To the extent that one believes that church attendance should affect people's attitudes toward brotherhood and social justice, there is an implicit indictment in the data, for church attendance doesn't seem to make any difference. The finding is consistent with the cries of church critics who contend that there is as much racial hatred among church attenders as there is among people who do not attend church—in fact, the data suggest that there is slightly more. But more importantly, Table 50 is consistent with the research finding reported in Chapter III that there is no significant relationship between religious commitment and belief about social issues.

While the last few years have seen a growing number of public opinion surveys on the racial issue, none of these studies has given adequate attention to the impact of religion on attitudes toward racial issues. For example, the otherwise excellent surveys of Lou Harris in 1963 and 1966 omit any data on religion other than the standard designation of "Protestant—Catholic—Jew."[7]

The only national survey, to my knowledge, which has included any measure of religious involvement is the 1963 National Opinion Research Center study.[8] In that study, respondents were asked,

"How strongly do you feel about your religious beliefs?" The response categories for this question were "very strong," "strong," "moderate," and "not strong." Responses to this question were then correlated with a "pro-integration" scale, which was based on responses to eight questions dealing with attitudes toward integration. Table 51 presents a summary of these findings. The higher the mean (average) score, the more favorable the attitudes toward integration.

TABLE 51

MEAN (AVERAGE) SCORES ON PRO-INTEGRATION SCALE
VARY CONSIDERABLY BY REGION
BUT NOT BY STRENGTH OF RELIGIOUS BELIEF

	REGION	
STRENGTH OF RELIGIOUS BELIEF:	NORTH MEAN SCORE	SOUTH MEAN SCORE
Very strong	5.00	2.34
Strong	5.15	2.86
Moderate	4.87	2.53
Not strong	4.30	2.37

Source: Paul B. Sheatsley, "White Attitudes Toward the Negro," *Daedalus*, Winter 1966, Table 3, p. 226.

In both the North and the South, those who reported that they felt "strong" about their religious beliefs scored highest on an eight-item pro-integration scale. In the North, those who felt "very strong" about their religion had high pro-integration scores, but in the South, they scored the lowest on the pro-integration scale. However, the differences in response for the different levels of religious conviction is not very great. This was an eight-point scale, and the difference between the highest and the lowest mean score on the pro-integration scale was only 2.81 points. This range was considerably larger when different age, income, education, and occupational groups were compared. Thus, this survey supports the conclusion that religious involvement does not significantly affect attitudes toward the race issue.

If church involvement is unrelated to attitudes toward civil rights, and those who attend church are no more liberal in their views about racial issues than those who do not, then it is possible to examine national public opinion poll data on racial attitudes in order to gain some insight as to how Christian laity feel about this issue.

Over the past two decades public opinion polls have indicated that Americans have shown a steady increase in favorable sentiment toward civil rights issues. Paul Sheatsley of the National Opinion Research Center believes that these polls reveal an unambiguous and dramatic change in the basic attitudes of whites toward Negroes, in both the North and South.[9] I would argue, however, that the growing positive sentiment toward civil rights is at the level of *general* values and does not necessarily reflect a growing acceptance of the *specific* implications of civil rights.[10] Whites are increasingly assenting to general statements which assert that civil rights and integration are a good thing, but this "liberalization" of opinion is not evident on specific issues that imply closer personal contact with Negroes.

Integrated housing is a good example. Brink and Harris report that in 1966 52 per cent of Americans reported that they would be upset if Negroes moved into their neighborhoods.[11] But this figure increases sharply among those who face some real probability of Negroes becoming their neighbors. The 1966 *Newsweek*-Harris survey reported that 76 per cent of the whites who live in neighborhoods where Negroes would like to move would be upset if this happened.[12] This resistance is even higher in some of the racially tense neighborhoods in Chicago, where 89 per cent of those who are descended from eastern European stock indicated that a Negro moving into their neighborhood would be upsetting to them.[13]

The growing proportion of whites who feel that the pace of racial integration is moving too fast would seem to reflect the fact that many Americans feel that as the legal barriers to integration are being knocked down, the issue is getting closer to home. The majority of white Americans believe that the Negro's life chances have improved rather significantly in the past few years, but virtually all of the research that has been done indicates that conditions have improved for only a relatively small proportion of Negroes, while for the majority conditions have remained unchanged or grown worse. Professor John Spiegel, director of Brandeis University's

Lemberg Center for the Study of Violence, summed up the current attitude of whites as follows:

> . . . the attitude of whites seems to be based on ignorance of or indifference to the factual basis of Negro resentment and bitterness. . . . If white populations generally had a full appreciation of the just grievances and overwhelming problems of Negroes in the ghetto, they would give stronger support to their city governments to promote change and to correct the circumstances which give rise to strong feelings of resentment now characteristic of ghetto populations.[14]

The Report of the National Advisory Commission on Civil Disorders arrived at a similar conclusion:

> What white Americans have never fully understood—but what the Negro can never forget—is that white society is deeply implicated in the ghetto. White institutions created it, white institutions maintain it, and white society condones it.[15]

Against this background, it is not surprising that clergymen who have become directly involved in the civil rights struggle, as well as many who have simply tried to interpret the complexity of the crisis from the pulpit, have become embroiled in conflict with their congregations. We will return later in this chapter to a discussion of the issue of racial prejudice, but first we want to examine the attitudes of laity toward clergy involvement in civil rights activity.

Lay Attitudes Toward Clergy Involvement in Civil Rights Activity

The large majority of the American public is committed to the general proposition that religion is a basis for moral strength and concern in society. Table 52 presents the response of the American public to the statement: "The best mark of a person's religiousness is the degree of his concern for others." Eighty-six per cent agree with this statement. Those who report attending church every week are slightly more likely to agree with this statement than those who attend less frequently. And those who report never attending church are somewhat less likely to agree than those who attend. Protestants are more likely than Catholics, who in turn are more likely than Jews, to agree that concern for others is the best measure of a person's religiousness.

TABLE 52

MOST PEOPLE AGREE THAT CONCERN FOR OTHERS IS THE BEST EXPRESSION OF RELIGIOUSNESS

"The best mark of a person's religiousness is the degree of his concern for others."	% *Agreeing*
NATION	86
FREQUENCY OF CHURCH ATTENDANCE	
Every week	88
Nearly every week; 2–3 times a month	84
About once a month; several times a year	84
About once or twice a year; less than once a year	85
Never	79
RELIGIOUS GROUP	
Protestant	89
Catholic	82
Jew	74

Furthermore, as an abstract proposition, most Americans feel that clergymen have an important role to play as moral leaders. Table 53 presents the responses to the statement: "Clergymen have a responsibility to speak out as the moral conscience of this nation."

TABLE 53

MOST LAITY FEEL THAT CLERGY SHOULD BE MORAL SPOKESMEN

"Clergymen have a responsibility to speak out as the moral conscience of this nation."	% *Agreeing*
NATION	82
FREQUENCY OF CHURCH ATTENDANCE	
Every week	86
Nearly every week; 2–3 times a month	85
About once a month; several times a year	83
About once or twice a year; less than once a year	77
Never	71
RELIGIOUS GROUP	
Protestant	84
Catholic	81
Jew	80

Eighty-two per cent of the American public agrees with this statement. Again, frequent church attenders are more likely to agree than less frequent attenders, and persons who report never attending are the least likely to agree. Differences between the three major religious groups are quite small.

Even though response to these two questions varies somewhat by religious groups and frequency of church attendance, a more important observation is that such a large percentage see religion and the clergy as sources of moral strength and responsibility.

Some differences in response exist within Protestantism, but they are easily interpretable. For example, Episcopalians, one of the more theologically liberal denominations, score lowest in terms of agreement with these statements, while Presbyterians, another liberal group, score the highest. Similarly, Baptists and Lutherans, both theologically conservative, score high and low respectively. The failure to find a consistent pattern of denominational response, on these two questions as well as on others to be introduced momentarily, may partially be accounted for by regional differences. However, it seems equally plausible that the absence of consistent patterns across denominations is a reflection of our earlier finding, which indicates that religious belief is independent of social ideology. Unfortunately, the number of respondents in the study is too small to produce reliable findings when denomination and region are controlled simultaneously. For this reason, denominational differences will not be analyzed in this section.

In spite of a general affirmation of clergy responsibility to be spokesmen on moral issues, a significant proportion of Americans reject various ways in which clergy might exercise this moral leadership. Four questions about specific ways in which clergy might be involved as moral leaders were asked in the survey. The first statement reads, "Clergy should stick to religion and not concern themselves with social, economic, and political questions" (Table 54).

While the large majority of Americans feel that clergy should speak out as a moral conscience, they apparently have quite restricted ideas as to what this means. Approximately half (49 per cent) of the respondents in the study feel that clergy should not speak out on social, economic, and political matters. But again, frequent church attenders are less likely to agree with this position than those who attend less frequently or not at all. No differences

TABLE 54

LAITY ARE DIVIDED ON WHETHER CLERGY SHOULD SPEAK OUT
ON SOCIAL, ECONOMIC, AND POLITICAL ISSUES

"Clergy should stick to religion and not concern themselves with social, economic, and political questions."	% Agreeing
NATION	49
FREQUENCY OF CHURCH ATTENDANCE	
Every week	46
Nearly every week; 2–3 times a month	49
About once a month; several times a year	48
About once or twice a year; less than once a year	57
Never	57
RELIGIOUS GROUP	
Protestant	50
Catholic	50
Jew	26

are observed between Protestants and Catholics, but Jews are much less likely to agree that clergy should stick to religion.

The next item in the questionnaire reads, "Clergymen who participate in demonstrations and picketing do more harm than good for the cause they support" (Table 55).

While four out of five persons agreed that clergy should speak out on moral issues, only half implied by their response that social, economic, and political matters have moral dimensions. On this question we see even further evidence of a restricted definition of the meaning of the response to the first question and what is perceived as an appropriate way to "speak out" on moral issues. Nearly three quarters (72 per cent) feel that demonstrating and picketing by clergy does more harm than good. The response to this item may not necessarily represent a contradiction to the earlier statement, but it does at least suggest that a clergyman's thoughts on moral issues should be spoken softly so as not to disturb the conscience of the nation.

Church attendance again is somewhat related to the way people answered this question. Seventy per cent of those who attend church every week agreed, compared with 78 per cent who report never attending church. Seventy-seven per cent of the Protestants agreed

TABLE 55

MOST BELIEVE THAT DEMONSTRATING CLERGY HARM THE CAUSE THEY SUPPORT

"Clergymen who participate in demonstrations and picketing do more harm than good for the cause they support."	% Agreeing
NATION	72
FREQUENCY OF CHURCH ATTENDANCE	
Every week	70
Nearly every week; 2–3 times a month	73
About once a month; several times a year	72
About once or twice a year; less than once a year	76
Never	78
RELIGIOUS GROUP	
Protestant	77
Catholic	63
Jew	58

that demonstrations harm the causes of clergymen, compared with 63 per cent of the Catholics and 58 per cent of the Jews.

A similar response was given to the statement: "I would be upset if my (minister/priest/rabbi) were to participate in a picket line or demonstration" (Table 56).

Exactly the same proportion (72 per cent) agreed with this statement as agreed that demonstrating clergy harm the causes they support. But note that frequent church attenders are slightly more likely to report that they would be upset if this happened. Jews are much less likely to report that they would be upset over their clergyman participating in a demonstration than are Protestants or Catholics. Catholics are somewhat less likely than Protestants to reject clergy activism, but this finding is not easily interpretable. It may simply reflect the fact that fewer priests have been involved in protest and thus the issue is less salient for Catholics. In other words, Catholics may be less likely to disapprove simply because fewer Catholics have been confronted with the reality or possibility of their priest participating in some form of social action. Activism on the part of Catholic priests has been increasing. If this thesis is correct, a current survey on this question might reveal that the dif-

TABLE 56

MOST PERSONS WOULD BE UPSET IF THEIR CLERGYMAN PARTICIPATED IN A DEMONSTRATION

"I would be upset if my (minister/priest/rabbi) were to participate in a picket line or demonstration."	% Agreeing
NATION	72
FREQUENCY OF CHURCH ATTENDANCE	
Every week	74
Nearly every week; 2–3 times a month	74
About once a month; several times a year	70
About once or twice a year; less than once a year	73
Never	65
RELIGIOUS GROUP	
Protestant	77
Catholic	68
Jew	43

ference in response between Protestant and Catholic laity has largely disappeared.

A final statement in this series deals with the role of the late Dr. Martin Luther King, Jr., as an exemplary Christian. This question was, of course, asked before his tragic death in April 1968. The statement reads, "Martin Luther King, Jr., is an outstanding example of making Christianity relevant and meaningful for our day" (Table 57).

The author of this study was quite frankly shocked when he saw the response to this question. Only 29 per cent of the sample agreed with this statement. The reader's initial reaction may be that the results reflect a reaction against Dr. King's stand on the Vietnam war. However, this is an unsatisfactory explanation since Dr. King did not make a major public address against the war until April 1967, three months after the survey was conducted. The response to this question lends additional evidence to the growing number of cries that American society has deep threads of racism. While most people applaud the general idea that equality for Negroes is a good thing, they remain either indifferent to or ignorant of the historical conditions which have placed the Negro in a disadvantaged competitive position. Hence, they reject almost any effort that is directed toward

TABLE 57

THE LARGE MAJORITY REJECT THE POSITION THAT MARTIN LUTHER KING, JR., WAS MAKING CHRISTIANITY RELEVANT

"Martin Luther King, Jr., is an outstanding example of making Christianity relevant and meaningful for our day."	% Agreeing
NATION	29
FREQUENCY OF CHURCH ATTENDANCE	
Every week	28
Nearly every week; 2–3 times a month	29
About once a month; several times a year	35
About once or twice a year; less than once a year	26
Never	28
RELIGIOUS GROUP	
Protestant	27
Catholic	30
Jew	59

changing these underlying conditions. Neither clergy in general nor Martin Luther King, Jr., specifically have been appreciated or respected for attempting to accomplish change. One might argue that it is not the goals that are objected to, but the strategies or tactics employed. But as the racial crisis in America has deepened during 1967 and 1968, this argument becomes increasingly hollow. What this argument really seems to be saying is that people are entitled to believe whatever they like and to work for the causes they believe as long as their efforts do not disrupt the status quo or disturb the consciences of those who do not share their commitment.

Church involvement, as measured by frequency of attendance at religious services, has little bearing on how people felt about Martin Luther King, Jr. Frequent church attenders were *not* more likely to feel that Dr. King represented an example of making Christianity relevant. In fact, those who attend church every week were slightly less likely than the national average to view Dr. King's ministry favorably. Occasional church attenders were actually the most likely to approve of Martin Luther King, Jr. But the most significant aspect of the response to this question is that so few actually approved of or admired Dr. King.

Catholics were slightly more likely than Protestants to approve of Dr. King's style of ministry. The proportion of Jews who felt that Dr. King's efforts were a relevant and meaningful expression of Christianity was twice that of the Christians.

That Christian laity do not view the church as an institution for social change is also seen in a recent study by Yoshio Fukuyama of 8554 participants of 151 local congregations of the United Church of Christ.[16] In a check list of ministerial activities, only 20 per cent of the white respondents felt that their clergyman should spend a lot of time "working for social justice." Of twelve ministerial activities, "working for social justice" ranked tenth. It should be kept in mind that the United Church of Christ is theologically one of the more liberal Protestant groups. Some perspective on white laity's perception of appropriate ministerial activity can also be gained by comparing their responses with the Negro respondents in Fukuyama's study. Seventy-seven per cent of the United Church of Christ Negro laity, predominantly middle-class Negroes, felt that clergy should be "working for social justice," and this response ranked first among the twelve ministerial roles.

Returning to our own survey, there is a striking consistency in the rejection of clergy involvement in the struggle for social justice. Approximately 70 per cent reject the various ways in which clergy are or might become involved, leaving only about 30 per cent who favor clergy involvement. In light of this consistency, Table 58 shows an interesting pattern.

Here we see that a slightly larger proportion (37 per cent) report that they are basically sympathetic with Northern ministers and students who have gone south to work for civil rights. Again, Protestants are less likely to approve of this kind of activity than Catholics, and Jews in large part (almost three quarters) approve. Those who report attending church every week are the least likely to approve of this kind of activity.

Response to the question of whether clergy should go south to work for civil rights also varies by region of the country.

Forty-five per cent who live outside the South are sympathetic with this type of activity, compared with only 24 per cent who live in the South. This finding suggests that whites are not nearly so opposed to clergy protesting against the prejudices of others as they are to having the issue brought home. This conclusion is impres-

TABLE 58

LAITY ARE LESS SUPPORTIVE THAN CLERGY OF PEOPLE GOING SOUTH TO WORK FOR CIVIL RIGHTS

"I am basically sympathetic with Northern ministers and students who have gone to the South to work for civil rights."	% Agreeing
I. *LAITY*	
NATIONAL	37
FREQUENCY OF CHURCH ATTENDANCE	
Every week	35
Nearly every week; 2–3 times a month	43
About once a month; several times a year	40
About once or twice a year; less than once a year	34
Never	38
RELIGIOUS GROUP	
Protestant	33
Catholic	43
Jew	70
REGION	
South	24
Non-South	45
II. *PROTESTANT CLERGY*	
NATIONAL	64
REGION	
South	43
Non-South	72

sionistically supported by the shift in the mass media response to the civil rights movement as its major focus has shifted to the North. In the spring of 1965 Chicago newspapers wrote glowing editorials praising the courage and conviction of Chicago clergy who went to Selma. Three months later, many of the same clergy were marching on City Hall in Chicago to protest the reappointment of Benjamin Willis, the Superintendent of Schools who had been broadly accused of thwarting school integration. Suddenly, these same clergy were seen by the same newspapers as "starry-eyed," "irresponsible," and "childish."

Comparison of clergy and laity on this item provides a striking contrast. While nearly two thirds of the Protestant clergy report that they are sympathetic with clergy and students going south to work for civil rights, only about a third of the Protestant laity feel this way. But clergy response to this statement also varies dramatically by region. While 72 per cent of the clergy in the non-South indicate sympathy for this type of activity, only 43 per cent of clergy in the South approve. However, even in the South, clergy approval is nearly twice as great as laity approval.

This is the type of question that might be subject to opinion change over the two-year time spread between the clergy and laity surveys (clergy were surveyed two years before laity). I would suggest that had the two surveys been taken at the same point in time, the spread between clergy and laity would be even greater. At the time when significant numbers of clergy and students were going south, which was the time period of the clergy survey, public sentiment was probably much more critical.

The differences between clergy and laity can also be dramatically seen in their response to the statement: "Negroes would be better off if they would take advantage of the opportunities that have been made available to them rather than spending so much time protesting" (Table 59).

While only about one third of the Protestant clergy express some sympathy with this position, 86 per cent of Protestant laity feel this way. Among laity, frequency of church attendance has little effect on response, though occasional attenders are slightly less likely to agree. Protestant and Catholic differences in response to this statement are not large, although Catholics are somewhat less likely to agree with the statement. Compared with the two major Christian groups, Jews are considerably less likely to agree, although nearly two thirds of the Jewish respondents do agree.

This same question was asked in the study of Faith Lutheran Church in Minneapolis. Eighty-five per cent of the respondents agreed with the statement, about the same per cent as agreed in the national survey. Within the ranks of those who attend church with some regularity, there was little difference in response. However, only 65 per cent of those who reported never or almost never attending church agreed with this statement—20 per cent less than attenders. Religious belief was also related to response to this question. Those who scored high on the Biblical Literalism Index (see discussion in Chapter II) were more likely to agree that Negroes

TABLE 59

CLERGY AND LAITY DIFFER SHARPLY IN BELIEVING NEGROES SHOULD TAKE ADVANTAGE OF OPPORTUNITIES MADE AVAILABLE TO THEM

"Negroes would be better off if they would take advantage of the opportunities that have been made available to them rather than spending so much time protesting."	% Agreeing
I. *LAITY*	
NATIONAL	86
FREQUENCY OF CHURCH ATTENDANCE	
Every week	87
Nearly every week; 2–3 times a month	89
About once a month; several times a year	82
About once or twice a year; less than once a year	85
Never	88
RELIGIOUS GROUP	
Protestant	89
Catholic	84
Jew	65
II. *CLERGY*	
NATIONAL	35

would be better off if they would stop protesting and take advantage of existing opportunities than were those who scored low on the index. Eighty-eight per cent of those who scored high agreed, compared with 78 per cent who scored low.

The response to this question serves to recall again the remarks of Stark and Glock on the effects of belief in radical free will:

> . . . traditional Christian images of man prompt those who hold them to put the blame for disadvantage upon those individuals who are disadvantaged. . . . The simple fact seems to be that a great many church people, because they believe men are mainly in control of their individual destinies, think that Negroes are themselves mainly to blame for their present misery.[17]

AGE AND EDUCATION AS DETERMINANTS OF ATTITUDES TOWARD CLERGY AND CIVIL RIGHTS. We saw earlier in this chapter that younger clergy tend to be more liberal in their views about civil rights. Popular psychology has long portrayed youth as more radical and intent on achieving social change. If this is generally true, then we would also expect to find that younger laity are more liberal in their views about civil rights as well as in their approval of clergy involvement in the civil rights struggle.

Table 60 summarizes all nine of the attitude statements asked of laity in the national survey, controlling by age categories. Three distinct response patterns emerge. The first items in the table (A and B) deal with concern for others as a mark of religiousness and the responsibility of clergy to speak out on moral issues. These are the most generally stated of the nine propositions. On these two general statements older persons show a somewhat greater tendency to agree than younger persons. For example, 90 per cent of those persons fifty-five years of age or over agree that "The best mark of a person's religiousness is the degree of his concern for others," compared with 80 per cent of those under age thirty-five.

A second pattern emerges for the general statements dealing with attitudes toward clergy involvement in civil rights (items C, D, E, and F). Here younger persons tend to be more liberal in their views. On three of the four statements the difference between the youngest and the oldest age groups is approximately 20 percentage points. For example, 60 per cent of those fifty-five or over agree that "Clergy should stick to religion and not concern themselves with social, economic, and political questions," compared with 39 per cent of those under thirty-five years of age. This is a considerable distance separating age groups and as we recall is comparable to the distance separating younger and older clergy.

Yet a third pattern appears for those statements which deal *specifically* with personal attitudes about civil rights issues (items G, H, and I). On these statements there is essentially no difference in the response of the various age groups. For example, 30 per cent of all three age groups under age fifty-five agree that "Martin Luther King, Jr., is an outstanding example of making Christianity relevant and meaningful for our day," and 29 per cent of those fifty-five and over agree with this statement.

The pattern observed here is intriguing. On the most general statements, which sound almost like platitudes, younger people are more critical and thus more likely to reject the statements. The second set of statements are essentially expressions of tolerance for clergy to

TABLE 60

THE RELATIONSHIP BETWEEN AGE AND ATTITUDES
TOWARD SOCIAL ISSUES AMONG LAITY
DEPENDS ON THE NATURE OF THE ISSUE

		% Agreeing			
		UNDER 35	34–44	45–54	OVER 55
A.	"The best mark of a person's religiousness is the degree of his concern for others."	80	83	90	90
B.	"Clergymen have a responsibility to speak out as the moral conscience of this nation."	78	83	85	85
C.	"Clergy should stick to religion and not concern themselves with social, economic, and political questions."	39	41	54	60
D.	"Clergymen who participate in demonstrations and picketing do more harm than good for the cause they support."	62	69	76	81
E.	"I would be upset if my (minister/ priest/rabbi) were to participate in a picket line or demonstration."	62	69	76	81
F.	"I am basically sympathetic with Northern ministers and students who have gone to the South to work for civil rights."	43	39	34	33
G.	"I basically disapprove of the Negro civil rights movement in America."	43	44	40	48
H.	"Martin Luther King, Jr., is an outstanding example of making Christianity relevant and meaningful for our day."	30	30	30	29
I.	"Negroes would be better off if they would take advantage of the opportunities that have been made available to them rather than spending so much time protesting."	86	84	86	87

express their own convictions in ways that may seem appropriate to them. On these statements, younger people are clearly more tolerant. The third set of statements move from tolerance of clergy behavior to expressions of the layman's own opinions on issues in the civil rights struggle. On these specific statements of personal sentiment about civil rights, age does not make much difference. Younger people are slightly more likely to approve of the civil rights movement and be sympathetic with clergy and students going south to work for civil rights, but their attitudes toward Martin Luther King, Jr., and Negro protests are no different from those of the oldest group.

Therefore, the data indicate that while youth are more tolerant of others' views and their right to follow their own consciences in seeking solutions to the civil rights problem, they are not themselves appreciably more liberal in their beliefs about civil rights than are older people.

Education is another factor in our culture which is widely believed to have a liberalizing influence on people's attitudes about race and tolerance for a pluralistic society. Table 61 presents the responses to the same nine attitude statements broken down by education. The pattern here is much more consistent. The two most general statements (items A and B), as with age, fail to reveal any systematic relationship to educational level. However, on all of the other statements higher educational level is associated with more liberal attitudes. On all but one of the statements, the distance separating the highest from the lowest educational groups is greater than the distance separating the youngest and the oldest age groups. Thus, education emerges as a more significant indicator of attitudes toward civil rights and the involvement of clergy in the civil rights struggle than does age. However, both age and education are better predictors of civil rights attitudes than involvement in church life, as measured by frequency of church attendance, since we have already seen there is little relationship between attitude and attendance.

The next logical consideration is whether the combined effect of age and education will provide an even better predictor of attitudes toward civil rights and clergy involvement. If this is so, we would expect the youngest age group with the highest level of education to be the most liberal in their views, while the oldest group with the lowest level of education would be the most conservative in their views. The data are not presented here in tabular form, but this analysis

TABLE 61

EDUCATED PERSONS EXPRESS MORE LIBERAL VIEWS ON SOCIAL ISSUES THAN THE LESS EDUCATED

	SOME HIGH SCHOOL	HIGH SCHOOL GRADS	SOME COLLEGE	COLLEGE GRADS
			% Agreeing	
A. *"The best mark of a person's religiousness is the degree of his concern for others."*	86	87	82	86
B. *"Clergymen have a responsibility to speak out as the moral conscience of this nation."*	83	81	84	83
C. *"Clergy should stick to religion and not concern themselves with social, economic, and political questions."*	63	47	38	23
D. *"Clergymen who participate in demonstrations and picketing do more harm than good for the cause they support."*	77	72	70	57
E. *"I would be upset if my (minister/ priest/rabbi) were to participate in a picket line or demonstration."*	77	72	69	59
F. *"I am basically sympathetic with Northern ministers and students who have gone to the South to work for civil rights."*	36	35	41	43
G. *"I basically disapprove of the Negro civil rights movement in America."*	53	43	33	28
H. *"Martin Luther King, Jr., is an outstanding example of making Christianity relevant and meaningful for our day."*	27	27	32	40
I. *"Negroes would be better off if they would take advantage of the opportunities that have been made available to them rather than spending so much time protesting."*	87	88	88	73

does not increase our ability to predict racial attitudes. Younger people in all educational categories tend to be somewhat more liberal in their views than older people, but the differences are generally small and several deviations from the predicted relationship occur. Thus, the combined effect of age and education improves our ability to predict attitudes toward civil rights and clergy involvement only very slightly. Education is, thus, the more powerful indicator.

While younger age and higher educational levels do result in more favorable attitudes toward civil rights and the involvement of clergy in the civil rights struggle, we should not lose sight of the fact that the general mood of the American public, regardless of church membership, frequency of church attendance, age, or educational level, is conservative. The large majority indicate that they believe that concern for others is a good indicator of one's religiousness. Similarly, a large majority assent to the abstract idea that clergy should speak out as the moral conscience of this country. Yet in their attitudes toward the civil rights movement and its leadership, and in their feelings about clergy involvement in civil rights, they seem in large part to contradict these general beliefs about the role of religion and the clergy in the achievement of a moral and just society. This is a perplexing and troublesome dilemma. How can Americans feel that religiousness is measured in terms of concern for others and yet seem to be so unconcerned and uninvolved in the continuing problems of the American Negro? How can they feel that clergy should be a moral conscience for society, yet so thoroughly reject American clergy's efforts to be prophetic?

THE NEW AMERICAN DILEMMA. A theoretical understanding of this apparent dilemma is at least suggested in the classic study of race relations by Gunnar Myrdal, *An American Dilemma.*[18] Myrdal's central thesis is that Americans live with two contradictory belief systems. On the one hand, they believe in the tenets of the "American Creed," which embraces the principles of democracy, equality, and Christian brotherhood, and on the other hand, they also hold views toward Negroes which are in sharp contradiction to these principles. Myrdal argues that in order to cope with these contradictory belief systems, Americans tend to introduce yet a third set of beliefs, which he calls *"mechanisms of rationalization,"* which have the effect of reducing the inconsistency. For example, a democratic principle is that all men have a right to participate in the democratic process, yet many feel that this is a right which should be denied to Negroes. An intervening "mechanism of rationalization" that will reduce this inconsistency is the belief that "Negroes are innately less intelligent than whites," or that "Negroes are less well educated than whites," and therefore should be denied this right to participate in the democratic process. These "mechanisms of rationalization" may or may not be empirically true, but they are believed to be true and thus have the effect of reducing the discrepancy or inconsistency for the individual who ascribes to the contradictory beliefs.

While Myrdal's book has been widely acclaimed as one of the most important contributions to the study of race relations in this country, there has been very little systematic testing of his central theoretical thesis by either proponents or critics of the theory. The major exception is a study by Professor Frank Westie.[19] In a probability sample of Indianapolis in 1957, Westie found evidence to support the Myrdal thesis. First of all, respondents were more likely to agree with "general valuation" statements about equality, democracy, and brotherhood than they were to parallel "specific valuation" statements which applied to Negroes. Secondly, respondents did tend to see that there was a contradiction between their general and specific responses. Thirdly, respondents did tend to introduce additional intervening propositions which would "explain" or "account for" this discrepancy.

Westie astutely notes that "We do not know (1) whether the conflict our respondents experienced in the interview exists for them outside the interview situation, or (2) whether it exists on an affective as well as a verbal or intellectual level."[20] This would seem to be a very important question to answer if we are to understand the American public's response to the racial crisis in this nation. Prior to the civil rights movement in America, the discrepancy in the contradictory values probably reached the cognitive level only infrequently for most Americans. But as the civil rights movement has drawn more and more attention to the realities of the Negro's condition in society, the awareness of this discrepancy in the cognitive process has begun to reach the surface with much greater frequency. Similarly, scientific studies have made it increasingly difficult for educated Americans to explain away the discrepancies with the "tried and true" rationalizations. For example, repeated studies have failed to confirm that

Negroes are "innately inferior."[21] The reduction of this conflict has been achieved by a greater willingness on the part of the American public to acknowledge that the general values of freedom and equality also apply to Negroes. Thus, the public opinion polls show a marked trend in the proportion of Americans who believe that Negroes should have an equal opportunity to get ahead, equal educational opportunities, the right to purchase a home that they can afford, etc. In one sense, this may represent real progress in breaking down the barriers of prejudice and discrimination. In another sense, however, this increasing "liberalness" is occurring at a *general* level, which serves to reduce the cognitive discrepancy between the principles held in the American Creed and the realities of the Negro condition in America, but the evidence does not support the contention that Americans are becoming significantly more liberal on *specific* valuations that imply the implementation of the general values. For example, the polls indicate that an increasing proportion of Americans believe that Negroes are entitled to equal educational opportunities, but it does not appear that Americans are significantly more willing to have Negroes attend schools with *their* children. The polls indicate that an increasing proportion of Americans acknowledge that Negroes should have the right to purchase a home according to their economic means, but this does not mean that Americans are increasingly more willing to have a Negro as *their* neighbor.

I believe that the evidence suggests that the "liberalness" of an attitudinal response on the race issue is a function of two things: (1) the probability that the view expressed implies direct interaction with Negroes, and (2) the intensity of the interaction implied. In other words, the greater the probability that intense interaction is implied, the less willing the American public is to agree with a specific attitude. If an attitude statement suggests a low probability of interaction and the interaction implied is at a low level of intensity, there is a greater likelihood that a person will agree with the statement. Westie suggests yet a third factor which must be taken into account in predicting response to attitude statements. Given two interactions of equal intensity, respondents will be more likely to assent to a statement which refers to a *fait accompli.*[22]

While data are again inadequate conclusively to verify this thesis, several sources of data do suggest its credibility. The first source of data is the Westie study. Table 62 presents the twenty value statements from the Westie study with the general valuation on the left and the specific valuation on the right. In every case, a greater proportion of respondents agree with the general than with the specific valuation. But a more careful examination of the items suggests further interpretations which are consistent with my contention that favorable civil rights attitudes are a function of the distance removed from the probability of interaction with Negroes, as well as the intensity of interaction implied.

The first three items in Table 62 deal with equal opportunities; equal opportunities to get ahead, equality before the law, and equal educational opportunities. Virtually everyone (98 per cent) agrees with these statements. When the specific implications of these statements are presented, the proportion agreeing drops off significantly, but a substantial majority still agree with the specific statement (60–79 per cent). Keeping in mind that this study was conducted in 1957, examination of the specific content of these items is suggestive of my thesis. Seventy-nine per cent, almost four fifths, report that they would not object to having Negro children attend school with their children. Considering the turmoil that has erupted over school integration, this response seems like enormously liberal sentiment. But two important factors should be kept in mind. First, the data were gathered before school integration became a tremendously salient feature of American race relations. Secondly, Negroes in Indianapolis, as in most other American cities, are residentially segregated so that the possibility of school integration seemed rather remote. Hence, since this statement did not imply actual involvement or interaction with Negroes, it was relatively easy to agree with. The same is true for the statement regarding Negroes sitting on a jury before which they might be on trial. The vast majority of Americans have never been on trial, don't anticipate ever being on trial, and hence it is hard for them realistically to envision the hypothetical situation. As a result, three quarters say they would not object. Having a Negro as a supervisor at work is a little more realistic for some persons, since they actually work with Negroes, and they are more hesitant to agree with this proposition than the first two statements (60 per cent). But, for the majority, the possibility of a Negro supervisor is rather remote, and hence agreement with the question is not too difficult.

The last two items in Table 62 demonstrate what happens to attitudes when the content implies interaction. The general statements

TABLE 62

PER CENT AGREEING WITH
GENERAL AND SPECIFIC VALUE STATEMENTS

	General Valuation Statement	% Agreeing	Specific Valuation Statement	% Agreeing
A.	Everyone in America should have an equal opportunity to get ahead.	98	I would be willing to have a Negro as my supervisor in my place of work.	60
B.	All people should be treated as equals in the eyes of the law.	98	If I went on trial I would not mind having Negroes on the jury.	76
C.	Children should have equal educational opportunities.	98	I would not mind having Negro children attend the same school my children go to.	79
D.	People should help each other in time of need.	99	If a Negro's home burned down, I would be willing to take his family into my home for the night.	64
E.	Everyone should have equal right to hold public office.	91	I believe that I would be willing to have a Negro representative in the Congress of the United States.	71
F.	Each person should be judged according to his own individual worth.	97	I would not mind if my children were taught by a Negro schoolteacher.	67
G.	I believe in the principle of brotherhood among men.	94	I would be willing to invite Negroes to a dinner party in my home.	29
H.	Public facilities should be equally available to everyone.	83	I would be willing to stay in a hotel that accommodates Negroes as well as whites.	61
I.	Under our democratic system people should be allowed to live where they please if they can afford it.	60	I would be willing to have a Negro family live next door to me.	35
J.	I believe that all public recreational facilities should be available to all people at all times.	63	I don't think I would mind if Negro children were to swim in the same pool as my children.	38

Source: Frank R. Westie, "The American Dilemma: An Empirical Test," *American Sociological Review,* Vol. 30, August 1965, pp. 531–32.

deal with housing and recreational facilities, two issues which at the time had some saliency for Indianapolis residents. On these items agreement with the general valuation statements is low, lower even than agreement with the specific valuation statements on most of the other issues (60 and 63 per cent). It is not necessary to mention Negroes specifically because these are issues where the *status quo* of the accommodative social structure has already been challenged. Many respondents understand that agreement with the statement implies intense interaction with Negroes. But when the context is made more specific (Negroes living next door and in the same swimming pool) the proportion agreeing drops off abruptly to a little more than one-third agreement.

Perhaps the most revealing illustration of this thesis is found in item G. Ninety-four per cent agree that they believe in the principle of brotherhood. For reasons which we need not analyze, Americans have long thought it appropriate to express brotherhood by establishing highly structured visitations between groups at specified times. National Brotherhood Week is the prime example of a highly structured and culturally acceptable time for violating the normal accommodative structure by breaking bread together with persons of other ethnic, racial, or religious groups. While this usually occurs on "neutral ground," i.e., a public place, home visitation is also usually acceptable. Thus, the specific value statement "I would be willing to invite Negroes to a dinner party in my home" is in keeping with the traditional American way of expressing brotherhood. But notice what happens. Only 29 per cent assent to the proposition, the lowest proportion agreeing with any of the twenty statements. What has happened? I would suggest that two factors account for this response. First, it implies a high degree of intimate interaction. Secondly, I would suggest that at this point in the interview the interviewee may question the credibility of the interviewer. The interviewer has explained that he is from the University of Indiana and that he is conducting research, but is he really? The interviewee may well be asking himself, "What happens if I say yes? Will I be asked to have Negroes into my home? Is this person really in my home under false pretenses?" In other words, this question implies a high degree of intimate interaction and it may well be *perceived* as a highly probable situation vis-à-vis the interviewer, who is unknown to the respondent.

This may be reading too much into the contextual situation, but

I don't believe that it is. We have already seen that those who view their neighborhood as a target for integration are more opposed to integrated housing than are those whose neighborhoods are "safe" from integration. Additional evidence which suggests the same pattern of response will be introduced momentarily. But before leaving the Westie data, it is informative to compare the response to the dinner invitation with the specific valuation of item D. This item states, "If a Negro's home burned down, I would be willing to take his family into my home for the night." Sixty-four per cent agree, which is more than twice as many people than agree that they would be willing to invite a Negro to dinner. While 99 per cent of the respondents agree that "People should help each other in time of need," we might legitimately ask why they should be so willing to help someone they wouldn't invite to dinner. The answer, I believe, rests in assessing the probability of the event occurring. In the first place, not very many people's homes burn down. Secondly, being residentially segregated from the Negroes, the probability that any individual white family would be asked to take a distressed Negro family in for the night is so remote as to be almost incalculable. Hence, while the level of interaction would be intimate, the probability of the event occurring is very, very low. Therefore, it is not very difficult for one to agree with the statement.

The Faith Lutheran Church study in Minneapolis reveals a highly similar pattern of response. The overwhelming majority agree that it is a Christian responsibility to be involved in the world and to care for others. For example, 84 per cent agree that "The Christian idea of love should move beyond one's family and friends to a compassion for the underprivileged and troubled in the world." Similarly, 79 per cent agree that "Concern for the welfare of others in society ought to be just as important to the Christian as his concern for stewardship and loyalty to the church."

But how is this concern for others manifest in their specific concern for the American Negro? Only a third of the members express sympathy with ministers and students who have gone to the South to work for civil rights. And only a third feel that the church has been inadequate in facing up to its responsibility in the civil rights struggle. Half of the members feel that Negroes could solve many of their own problems if they were not so irresponsible and carefree. And nearly two thirds feel that Negroes would be better off if they would take advantage of opportunities that have been made available rather than spending so much time protesting. Note the similarity between this response and the response to the same questions in the national survey. The response reflects what Professor Spiegel refers to as the "ignorance of or indifference to the factual basis of Negro resentment and bitterness."

The Faith Lutheran Church questionnaire also included items which were designed to tap our thesis that racial attitudes are in part a function of the distance removed from direct and intense involvement with Negroes. Tucked away in a suburb on the South Side of Minneapolis, a city with only 3 per cent Negro population, 69 per cent of the respondents agreed that "Negro families with adequate income to purchase a home in my neighborhood have a right to do so." And only 29 per cent said, "I would be upset if a Negro family moved into my block." But they were not so certain that their neighbors would respond so openly to Negroes. Sixty per cent, or twice as many respondents, reported that "Most of the people in my block would be upset if a Negro family moved into our block."

Since no Negroes live in this suburb, these are hypothetical questions and we can only speculate as to how accurately the responses reflect the feelings of the respondents or how accurately the respondents perceive the feelings of their neighbors. But a series of more specific questions suggests that they are not very comfortable with the idea of intimate contact with Negroes. Only 15 per cent say, "I would consider moving if a Negro family moved into my block," but the proportion increases to 46 per cent agreement with the statement "I would consider moving if 25 per cent of the homes in my block became occupied by Negroes." An additional 22 per cent report that they "probably agree" with this latter statement. Furthermore, only a third respond that they would be willing to sell to a Negro family who was able to afford their home.

Thus, even though the situations posed are hypothetical, and in this particular suburb highly unlikely to become a reality any time in the immediate future, the more intimate the contact implied in the attitude statements, the greater the proportion who reject the propositions. Note also how the more specific propositions open the door to introduce what Myrdal referred to as "mechanisms of rationalization." One Negro on the block would be all right, but if 25 per cent of the neighborhood was Negro, "property values might decline, and I have a right to protect my investment." "Negroes have a right to purchase any home they can afford, but I wouldn't sell my home to them because my neighbors would object and I have a responsibility to respect their wishes."

The same pattern is repeated in a study of a suburban Episcopalian congregation in 1962.[23] Table 63 presents the responses of the congregation to six statements dealing with the responsibility of the church and laymen in racial issues. The items are ordered from the most general to the most specific in terms of action implied. Response was on a five-point scale and the percentage reported here combines the "agree" and "strongly agree" categories.

As the items become more specific, the proportion who agree decreases sharply. Note specifically the contrasts in items A and E, and B and D. Eighty per cent agree that churches should encourage

TABLE 63

RESPONSE OF A SUBURBAN EPISCOPAL
CONGREGATION TO RACIAL ISSUES

		% Agreeing
A.	*Churches should encourage their members to support efforts to reduce racial discrimination in their communities.*	80
B.	*The Christian layman should examine his business to make sure it does not discriminate against Negroes.*	82
C.	*Churches should encourage their members to keep informed about the situation in their community concerning discrimination in housing, employment, public accommodations and schools.*	75
D.	*A diocese should cut off financial support from church institutions (hospitals, missions, etc.) that discriminate against Negroes.*	45
E.	*A Christian layman should work to make sure Negroes can buy property in the . . . area.*	29
F.	*Churches should encourage their members to give money to support the sit-in movement and the National Association for the Advancement of Colored People.*	13

their members to support efforts to reduce racial discrimination in their communities. In sharp contrast, only 29 per cent agree that Christian laymen should work to make certain that Negroes can buy property in their suburban community, a specific application of the general principle agreed to in the first statement. Similarly, 82 per cent agree that a Christian layman should examine his business to make sure that it does not discriminate against Negroes. But only 45 per cent would approve of a diocese cutting off funds from a church institution that is guilty of racial discrimination. Least approved is the proposition that churches should encourage members to give financial support to the sit-in movement and the NAACP. Only 13 per cent agree with this statement. In short, approval for civil rights is widespread when propositions are stated in broad, general terms, but as the propositions become more specific, and hence imply involvement on the part of an individual respondent, support diminishes sharply.

A final example is taken from a "real" situation rather than people's responses to questionnaires. On November 7, 1967, Carl Stokes was elected mayor of Cleveland by a narrow margin and thus became the first Negro mayor of a large city in the United States. His victory was interpreted by many as overwhelming evidence that Americans are now willing to elect public officials on the basis of their qualifications rather than their race. Actually, the Cleveland election demonstrated quite the opposite.

For many years public opinion polls have found that the vast majority of Americans agree with statements to the effect that "People should be judged according to their individual worth," or "Everyone should have an equal right to hold public office." While no such poll was taken in Cleveland just prior to the mayoral election, there is no reason to believe that Clevelanders would have responded any differently from the way the American public has responded for many years.

The candidacy of Carl Stokes provided an opportunity to translate a general valuation into a specific action. When Stokes faced Mayor Ralph Locher in the primary, the city was in deep trouble. The city's racial tensions over the past several years had erupted in the nation's worst riot of 1966 and there was much evidence to indicate that the tensions were growing worse. Urban renewal was a dismal failure and in January the Department of Housing and Urban Development cut off the city's urban renewal funds, the first such action by the federal government. The exodus of a quarter of a million whites, as well as many businesses, from the central city during the previous fifteen years had left the city on the brink of financial disaster, and in February the Moody Bond Survey reduced the city's credit rating. The federal government took another unprecedented step in May by cutting off several million dollars of construction funds because of the failure of the construction industry to comply with federal policies for assuring equal job opportunities for minority groups.

The list of failures is long, but in short, the city was in deep trouble.[24] The spring brought a long procession of reporters to the city to write about Cleveland as exemplifying the urban crisis in America. While all of the city's failures could not be placed on the shoulders of Mayor Locher, there was near consensus in the business, labor, political, and intellectual communities that he was a blundering and ineffectual administrator.

Even in the context of the failure of the incumbent administration, Stokes received only 15 per cent of the white votes in the Democratic primary. By all odds, Stokes should have been an easy victor in the general election. Only 10 per cent of the city's voters were registered Republican, and no Republican candidate had seriously challenged the Democratic stronghold on City Hall for a quarter of a century. With the endorsement of the Democratic party, the labor unions, and the two major daily newspapers, he should have been able to coast to an easy victory in the general election.

When the votes were tallied, Stokes won by a margin of only 1500 votes in the largest voter turnout in the city's history. When the chips were down, the large majority of white voters could not bring themselves to vote for a Negro. One poll just prior to the general election indicated that 90 per cent of the white Democrats who voted for Locher in the primary would cross party lines and vote for the Republican candidate. Post-election analysis revealed that the results of the poll had to be pretty accurate. For a large proportion, this was probably the first time they had ever voted for a Republican candidate. As Catholics, ethnic-group members, and union members, they had been lifelong supporters of the Democratic party. But when it came to translating a general valuation into a specific act of supporting a Negro candidate, the large majority of whites were unable to do so. Pre- and post-election surveys revealed that only a small minority admitted to overt prejudice. Many voters gave rather detailed and subtle reasons for crossing party lines, though most simply indicated that they thought the Republican candidate was the best qualified. Although most political analysts in the city felt that Stokes was the more qualified candidate, we need not go into a detailed analysis of the candidates' qualifications here. The point to be made is that evaluating the "qualifications" of the candidates became the intervening mechanism of rationalization whereby many voters were able to vote for the Republican candidate without perceiving any conflict between their general belief that Negroes should have equal opportunities and their specific behavior at the polls. What specific criteria were used in evaluating the candidates' qualifications and the fact that they had always voted for the Democratic candidate in previous elections without much concern for the candidates' qualifications are really irrelevant issues.

That a Negro candidate was elected mayor of a large city is a landmark in American history, but an analysis of how he won does not support the conclusion that white America is prepared to accept Negroes on their individual merits. To the contrary, the Cleveland election dramatically demonstrated the extent of resistance to fulfilling the specific implications of the American Creed. Stokes won with a large Negro turnout and the support of a minority of liberal whites.[25]

Myrdal's analysis of the American dilemma, written a quarter of a century ago, was enormously insightful and appears equally cogent today. Why, then, do we need to speak of a "New American Dilemma"? The new dilemma arises out of the fact that the civil rights movement has shattered many of the old tried and true mechanisms of rationalization. The many chapters of the civil rights movement have served dramatically to demonstrate that the Negro has not been a part of the American dream. The mass media reporting of brutality, discrimination, and disenfranchisement of Negroes has repeatedly stunned the collective American conscience. It is increasingly difficult for ignorance of Negro conditions to serve as a mechanism of rationalization. Moreover, the initial thrust of the civil rights movement was not against the prejudice and discrimination of the majority of white Americans, but rather of a minority in the South. Incensed by the Negro condition in the South, public sentiment began to say that freedom and equal opportunities ought to apply to Negroes also. Using Myrdal's theoretical framework, the specific valuation has become the general valuation: *"Negroes* should be treated as equal in the eyes of the law," *"Negro* children should have equal educational opportunities," etc. This shift in public sentiment is well documented in the public opinion polls of the last decade, and the significance of this dramatic shift should not be minimized.

The new American dilemma arises out of the fact that a nation is now faced with implementing the specific implications of a new general valuation. Having acknowledged (1) that the Negro has not been a full participant in the American dream, and (2) that he ought to be, there is no turning back. The Negro's gains and rising expectations will not permit us to turn back. But the realization of the specific implications of the new general valuations constitutes another major step that the American public does not yet appear prepared to take. On the one hand it means that a Negro may live next door or that in a hundred other ways the intensity of interaction with Negroes may be increased. On the other hand it involves acknowledging the problems and changing the structure of a society that has historically placed and continues today to place the Negro in a disadvantageous position which makes it difficult for him to accomplish the American dream.

Ignorance has been and remains one of the strongest mechanisms of rationalization and defense against change which white America is unprepared to implement. But the dilemma intensifies because it is increasingly difficult to remain ignorant in the presence of media that continually bombard the public with information. What is an acceptable rationalization one day is destroyed the next. The mechanisms of rationalization become more subtle, but they are still operating. The floodgates for change have been opened, but the historical roots of prejudice are so deep that it is impossible for Americans to accept the specific implications of that which they have accepted as a general principle.

Clergymen, perhaps in part because they are as a group better educated than the average public, but also because they are the carriers and interpreters of an ethical and moral tradition, have become one of the vanguards for change. The data we have presented here indicate that they understand the implications of the Christian heritage more clearly than the general public or their lay congregations. That involvement in the life of the church seems to make little difference in laymen's attitudes toward the race issue would seem to suggest that clergy have not been particularly successful in communicating their concern and understanding to laymen. My interviews with clergy leave little room to doubt that some clergy have taken to the streets in protest marches as a desperate effort to dramatize to their laity their perception of the seriousness of the racial crisis. Yet this is only one reason why clergy have become activists, and it is a rather narrow perspective for understanding why and how they have become deeply involved in the civil rights struggle. We will turn to a more thorough analysis of the struggle for involvement in the next chapter. What needs to be emphasized here is that the disparity between the clergyman's and the layman's understanding of the civil rights crisis constitutes a very significant source of conflict within the churches. Whether he participates in a protest march or explores the implications of the Christian teachings from the pulpit, he is attempting to strip away the layman's mechanisms of rationalization. The closer he comes to succeeding, the more his laymen can be expected to resist.

Summary

The results of this chapter appear unambiguous. Clergy are extremely sympathetic with the civil rights cause. While the number of clergy who have been involved in some form of direct social action is unclear, case study data strongly suggest that a critical incident is capable of mobilizing a significant amount of clergy involvement.

Laity, on the other hand, are much less committed to implementing integration in American society. To the contrary, they tend to feel that the pace of integration is moving too swiftly. As far as clergy involvement in the civil rights struggle is concerned, the large majority oppose it. But at the same time, they feel that it is the clergyman's role to be a spokesman on moral issues. We have attempted to explain this discrepancy by introducing and elaborating a theoretical framework that was developed in Gunnar Myrdal's classic study, *An American Dilemma,* a quarter of a century ago.

The implications of these findings should be fairly clear. Conflict between clergy and laity in recent years over the civil rights issue is deeply rooted in fundamentally different views about civil rights and the role that the church and clergy should be playing in this struggle. What is perhaps surprising is that the overt conflict has not been even more serious.

V

The Struggle for Involvement

Introduction

Thus far we have seen that the ideological commitment of Protestant clergy to bring about civil rights and social justice in a number of areas is rather strong. It is also apparent that a large majority of laity do not share this level of commitment. Laity, as a group, are much less concerned about civil rights than are clergymen. Furthermore, the large majority of laity do not approve of clergy involvement in civil rights activity.

Given these divergent perspectives, it is certainly understandable how conflict has emerged in the churches. But if we consider further that laity, as members of a voluntary association, hold tremendous power because they control the financial resources of the church, we might ask (a) how is it that clergy have managed to get involved in the civil rights struggle at all, and (b) why has the conflict not been more serious than has been the case thus far? Furthermore, what are the prospects of intensified conflict in the years ahead?

I believe that the answer to the first two questions is that conflict, to this point, has been avoided because a large proportion of the activist clergy have been located in positions within the denominational structures which are insulated from direct reprisals from laity. In short, the most active group of clergy has not been parish pastors. But two factors threaten to intensify the conflict. First of all, the base of concern for social action is broadening among parish clergy. Secondly, laymen are becoming more sophisticated in their understanding of the organizational structure of the church and as a consequence are better able to resist clergy involvement.

The purpose of this chapter is to develop this thesis by examining the processes by which clergy have become involved in social action. We shall see that becoming socially active is a complex process and that a clergyman's personal conviction about civil rights is not always the most critical dimension in determining whether or not he will become involved. For some, the road to involvement is barricaded by congregational and denominational resistance. For those who ignore these restraints, the price they pay for involvement is often very great. For others, the hazards of becoming activists are diminished greatly by the support they receive from their denominations, fellow clergy, and a small minority of committed laymen.

The Road to Involvement

I had my first opportunity to observe the dynamics of the road to involvement during the early summer of 1965. Chicago had faced a long, hard battle over conditions in the public schools. In March and November of 1964 the Chicago school system had received two independent reports on school conditions. The reports were the result of the combined efforts of nearly fifty blue-ribbon educators selected from across the nation, and the two reports represented probably the most comprehensive examination that any school system had ever received. The first committee, officially titled the Advisory Panel on Integration of the Public Schools, was headed by one of the nation's most distinguished sociologists, Philip M. Hauser, of the University of Chicago. The second group was led by the equally prominent educator, Robert J. Havighurst, also of the University of Chicago. The two panels agreed that the time had come for decisive action on a number of educational policies and the reports presented far-reaching recommendations for changes in the public school system.

By the spring of 1965 it had become apparent that little action had been taken and that the work of these blue-ribbon committees was in danger of becoming just two more reports to be placed on a shelf. In fact, many informed persons felt that the school board, which had commissioned the reports, was deliberately attempting to suppress serious discussion and action on them.

Much of the brunt of the criticism of the school system fell on the shoulders of School Superintendent Benjamin C. Willis. The superintendent's contract came up for renewal in the spring of 1965 and the Coordinating Council of Community Organizations (CCCO), headed by a Negro schoolteacher, Albert Raby, made an all-out effort to block the renewal of Willis' contract. At an "unofficial meeting" of the Board of Education in early May, a straw vote was taken and seven of the eleven board members voted to fire Willis. Ten days later when official action was taken, three of the members changed their votes and Willis was retained.

Civil rights leaders were enraged and many felt that pressure had been applied directly from the mayor's office to persuade board members to change their minds. This turn of events led the CCCO and the NAACP to call for a massive school boycott. In an unprecedented court action, Circuit Court Judge Cornelius J. Harrington issued an injunction prohibiting the civil rights groups from carrying out the school boycott.

The civil rights leaders bowed to the injunction by the court and turned their energies on Mayor Richard J. Daley and City Hall. Demonstrations, which were to last throughout most of the summer, began on June 10. On that day, an estimated four hundred persons assembled at Soldier Field and marched down the middle of Lake Shore Drive to City Hall, where they staged a sit-in on La Salle Street.

The failure of the police to intervene in this obstruction of traffic during the rush hour drew sharp public criticism from Chicago's Mayor Daley. The following day, Friday, June 11, marchers again assembled at Soldier Field to march on City Hall. The marchers complied with police requests to march in only two lanes. However, at an intersection in Grant Park, police surrounded the marchers and demanded that they walk in a single lane. This was contrary to the marchers' understanding of the agreed-upon ground rules, and in protest 252 marchers sat down and were arrested. The following day the marchers were again stopped, this time at the intersection of State and Madison in the Loop, where 192 sat down and were arrested.

This was one of the first times that a large civil rights protest involving massive arrests had been witnessed in a Northern city. It was also one of the first times that ministers, priests, and nuns were present in large numbers in a Northern demonstration. I do not have exact data, but probably about one quarter of the 444 persons arrested during the first two days of demonstrations were members of the clergy. The Chicago newspapers, however, were either unaware of the extent of clergy involvement in the demonstrations, since many of them did not wear collars, or deliberately played it down. The Chicago newspapers typically described the white demonstrators as "the unwashed beard-and-sandal set," "high school and college youths in search of a Cause without any sense of what they were trying to accomplish," "Communist party members," "self-seeking, irresponsible elements," and "a *few* starry-eyed clergymen" (emphasis added).

An additional direction for the study of clergy involvement became apparent when, a few days after the initial demonstrations, I discovered that a number of the clergy who had been arrested were participating in an intensive one-month study program at the Urban Training Center for Christian Mission (UTC) located in Chicago. The Urban Training Center is an ecumenical program designed better to equip clergymen to minister to the inner city by informing and involving them in the political, economic, social, and spiritual problems of the metropolis.

There were forty-eight Protestant clergymen, all white but one, coming from seventeen states and representing seven denominations, participating in the June program at UTC.[1] The UTC trainees were given a detailed orientation to the Chicago school situation on the Wednesday before the initial march, and were informed that the training center curriculum would be suspended on Thursday so that those who wanted to could participate in the march from Soldier Field to City Hall. While it was emphasized that each trainee should follow his own conscience, and that they did not have to participate in the march if they did not want to, participation was unambiguously approved by the staff. (All but one of the staff members, an elderly gentleman in poor health, appeared for the march.)

On Thursday, forty of the forty-eight trainees appeared at Soldier Field and marched on City Hall. Friday, the number of UTC marchers declined to thirty-five, and on Saturday this number dropped to only twenty. Thus, as the conflict between the marchers and the police became increasingly intense, many of the UTC trainees dropped out of the protest. However, by Saturday afternoon twenty-five of the forty-eight UTC trainees had been arrested—ten of them who had been arrested on Friday and posted bond returned on Saturday to be arrested a second time.

This situation provided an excellent opportunity to learn about the processes involved in clergymen's decisions to participate in a civil rights protest. The uniqueness of the situation, in which approximately half of the trainees chose to be arrested and the other half chose not to become so involved, provides a quasi-experimental situation in which the differences between the two groups, who had been exposed to the same opportunity, could be examined.

With the help of a colleague, Dr. Raymond C. Rymph of Purdue University, I moved quickly to the Urban Training Center, located in a near West Side slum, and explained our interests to the staff members. With their approval and assistance we proceeded to gather a wide variety of data on the trainees, including detailed background records which the trainees had provided for UTC prior to their admittance into the program, personal interviews ranging from two to six hours with twenty-seven of the trainees and the entire staff, and two questionnaires that were mailed to the trainees after they returned home. On the shorter questionnaire, which focused on the UTC experience and attitudes toward civil rights, we received a 92 per cent completion response. The longer questionnaire, which was identical to the national sample, was returned by 60 per cent of the trainees.

What did we learn from this rather intensive examination of the forty-eight trainees? What features distinguished those who chose arrest from those who did not? On the face of it, we might have expected to find that those choosing arrest were more strongly committed to the achievement of social justice for Negroes in America than were those who did not choose arrest. Or in the words of an old folk song about labor-management conflict in Harlan County, Kentucky, when the chips are down, "whose side are you on?" This explanation seems plausible and is consistent with our cultural tendency to psychologize all human behavior. However plausible, the data do not bear out this interpretation. *We were not able to determine any significant differences in attitudes toward civil rights of those who were arrested and those who were not arrested!* Similarly, we failed to find any significant differences on several personality dimensions.[2]

In short, it was apparent that there were forces outside the individual psyche of these clergymen which were affecting their behavior. Our attempt to understand the behavior of these forty-eight clergymen thus shifted from a psychological orientation to a structural or sociological orientation. Several structural variables were examined, and as we shall see in the analysis which follows, the results clearly indicate that the clergyman cannot isolate himself or his decision from the social milieu in which he moves.

First of all, the action of an individual minister is probably not independent of the position his denomination has taken on the civil rights issue. If his denomination has repeatedly and consistently taken a strong pro-civil rights stand, then his involvement would be congruent with denominational policy. Where the position of the denomination has been something less than active involvement, the involvement of a member is unlikely to be met with unanimous approval by denominational officials. Thus, we would expect to find that the stronger the position taken on civil rights by the denomination of which the trainee is a member, the greater the likelihood that he will involve himself in the demonstration to the point of being arrested.

Of the five denominations with more than a single representative at UTC, two of them, the United Church of Christ and the Episcopal Church, have repeatedly taken strong stands on civil rights. The other three denominations, all Lutheran bodies, have taken positions that have been somewhat more modest in scope and less vigorous in actual lines of activity.

While the number of cases is small, this simple dichotomy between strong and moderate denominational commitment to civil rights is clearly related to the involvement pattern of the minister trainees (Table 64).

TABLE 64

CLERGY FROM LIBERAL DENOMINATIONS WERE MORE
LIKELY TO BE ARRESTED

	TOTAL	ARRESTED		NOT ARRESTED	
		N	%	N	%
American Lutheran Church	26	11	42	15	58
Lutheran Church of America	3	1	33	2	67
Missouri Synod Lutheran	4	2	50	2	50
United Church of Christ	6	4	67	2	33
Episcopal	7	6	86	1	14
Others	2	1	50	1	50

N = Number of cases.

Of the seven Episcopalians only one was not arrested and he was physically unable to march. Four of the six members of the United Church of Christ were arrested. One of the two not arrested was in Detroit speaking on the civil rights issue. Within the Lutheran denominations, on the other hand, considerably smaller proportions were arrested. If we combine the three Lutheran groups, we see that only fourteen of thirty-three, or 42 per cent, were arrested, as compared with 75 per cent for the two more liberal denominations. Thus, trainee arrest is positively associated with a strong denominational stand on civil rights.

A number of case histories indicate that Southern congregations fiercely resist the involvement of their ministers in the civil rights struggle. The actual degree of resistance of Northern congregations to the active involvement of their ministers in the movement is not as well documented, but the data presented in the previous chapter suggest that resistance is also strong in the North. Thus, we would expect the attitudes of the clergyman's congregation toward involvement in civil rights activity to be at least as important as the policy of his denomination in determining his decision to become involved in civil rights activity. In short, UTC trainees would act in a way which they perceived as acceptable to their parishioners at home. But what of men who do not serve a parish? Since the official position of all denominations has been in favor of desegregation, clergymen in non-parish positions should be able to involve themselves in the civil rights movement without facing serious reprisals. But again, the stronger the denominational stance, the greater the probability of non-parish clergy involvement. Similarly, ministers serving congregations that are substantially integrated should be relatively free to involve themselves in civil rights activities. In fact, they may be expected to do so. On the other hand, ministers serving all-white suburban congregations might expect to face resistance from their laity if they become actively involved in the civil rights movement. Physically separated from the Negro community, suburbanites would probably view any form of involvement as a threat to the established patterns of physical separation. In between is the minister who serves a congregation in the inner city. Many factors influence the response of the inner-city church to the Negro. Factors such as physical location of the church vis-à-vis Negro populations, financial status of the parish, socioeconomic and ethnic backgrounds

of the church membership, etc. influence the freedom of the inner-
city minister to become involved in civil rights.

The behavior of the UTC trainees was examined from the perspective of the typology suggested above. Examination of the types
of positions the UTC trainees occupied dramatically illustrates the
impact of social structure (Table 65).

TABLE 65

"STRUCTURALLY FREE" CLERGY WERE MORE LIKELY
TO BE ARRESTED

	TOTAL	ARRESTED		NOT ARRESTED	
		N	%	N	%
Inner-city—integrated	4	4	100	0	0
Non-parish	9	7	78	2	22
Inner-city—token or no integration	19	7	37	12	63
Fringe or Suburban	10	1	10	9	90
Non-metropolitan*	6	6	100	0	0

* Non-metropolitan is defined as outside of a Standard Metropolitan Statistical Area.

There were only four ministers from integrated inner-city parishes;
all four were arrested. These four represent three denominations,
suggesting that this involvement is independent of denominational
affiliation.

Next, we see that seven of the nine, or 78 per cent of the ministers
in non-parish positions were arrested. While each of these persons
is responsible to denominational officials or boards, it would appear
that the absence of responsibility to a specific parish membership
"frees" one to act according to his conscience or some other reference system. In examining the two deviant cases, we found that one
came from the most conservative denomination represented at the
training center, and the other was not in the city during the marches.

In dramatic contrast, nine of the ten suburban ministers *did not*
get arrested in the demonstrations. The one deviant case expressed
considerable ambivalence about remaining in the suburban church
he was serving at that time. Four of the suburban church ministers
did not even march in the demonstrations. Thus, independent of

their own personal views, the positions of their respective denominations, the position of the UTC staff, and the views and actions of their fellow ministers in the training program, suburban clergymen would appear to have responded to this choice in terms of their congregations' expectations.

Seven of the nineteen (37 per cent) ministers in inner-city churches that were not integrated were arrested, thus occupying an intermediate position, as predicted, between inner-city integrated and suburban ministers. We asked these ministers how they felt the "influentials" of their congregations would react to the possibility of church integration. Of the twelve who were *not* arrested, two said that the influentials would be openly opposed to integration, five reported that the influentials would verbally go along with integration but would probably be pretty uncomfortable if Negroes actually came into the church, and three reported that the influentials would probably go along with "token integration" but would probably resist a serious attempt to develop a truly integrated congregation. In short, most of the inner-city ministers who were not arrested had reservations as to the willingness of their congregations to go along with racial integration.

On the other hand, of the seven inner-city ministers who were arrested, only one felt that the influentials in his congregation were opposed to church integration. Three of these men were serving congregations with token integration. Thus, inner-city ministers did not act independently of their congregations' views on integration, or at least their perceptions of their congregations' views.

In dramatic contrast to the inner-city clergy, the dominant response of suburban ministers was that they *did not know* how the influentials of their congregations felt about integration. In the inner city, the physical proximity of Negroes makes the issue of integration much more salient. Inner-city clergy think they know how their congregations feel about integration, and they tend to act in a manner which is consistent with what they perceive to be the feelings of their congregations. Suburban ministers, on the other hand, claim that they do not even know how their congregations feel about integration. Nevertheless, it would appear that there is a latent uneasiness, as they act almost unanimously in avoiding involvement in the conflict situation which *might* be upsetting to their congregation. Thus, it would appear that resistance by the congregation to ministerial involvement in the civil rights movement is by no means limited to the South. Wherever a minister is directly responsible to an all-white congregation, there is a real possibility that he will be shackled by their direct or subtle opposition.

An unanticipated finding was the fact that all six of the ministers from the non-metropolitan communities were arrested. Why this should happen presents an intriguing question. There are several possible explanations, and it is not possible to untangle the interactions of these several factors.

An immediately plausible explanation of the propensity of the small-town ministers to choose arrest is derived from the unusual situation of small-town ministers receiving urban training at the request of their denominations. This may have been taken by these men as an indication that they would soon be moved by their denominations to a metropolitan situation. In other words, they may have felt that they need not concern themselves too much about the attitudes of their current congregations because they could expect an early transfer to an urban position.[3]

A second possible explanation is to be found in the demographic structure of the non-metropolitan areas. Except for the South, rural areas and small towns have small proportions of, if any, Negroes. The question of civil rights, thus, remains largely an academic one. Therefore, to a non-urban congregation, their minister's participation in a civil rights demonstration is little more than an intellectual extension of their non-involved "tolerance" for civil rights.

A third possible explanation for the non-metropolitan ministers' behavior is based on a process of selective perception of the congregation's position. The familiar process of perceiving what one wants or expects to perceive may operate here. As there are probably no Negroes in the community, a civil rights sermon would probably draw little criticism from the congregation. This would lead the minister to conclude, perhaps erroneously, that the congregation supported his position.

The age of the non-metropolitan ministers offers still another possible explanation for their behavior. The average age of the non-metropolitan ministers was 30.2 years, compared with 38.0 for the total group, a difference of 7.8 years. As noted earlier, popular psychology and history have long linked youth to radical behavior. Thus, the ministers' behavior may reflect the independence of youth, and a more critical attitude toward the existing social structure which has nothing whatsoever to do with their parish. They are in a non-metropolitan parish because non-metropolitan parishes are not the prize positions, and the prize positions do not normally accrue to youth.

But independent of their personal convictions, why do they act unanimously and without hesitation? Do they not have some concern for what this may mean for their careers? I doubt that they act without concern for their careers. What this does suggest, however, is that their career aspirations lie someplace other than the suburban church. This suggestion is supported by the Bridston and Culver study of more than 17,000 seminary students, which indicates that *only* 33 per cent aspire to a parish ministry.[4] In other words, these six non-metropolitan clergymen may not have weighed how this experience would influence their chances of getting into a suburban position, because they did not aspire to this type of position. If these non-metropolitan ministers aspire to inner-city careers or non-parish careers, then far from being a detriment to their careers, the arrest may be worn as a badge of courage.

This leads us to a consideration of the relationship between age and involvement in civil rights activities (Table 66).

The average age of the UTC ministers who were arrested was 36.2 years, compared with 39.4 years for the non-arrested. This difference does not hold for all denominations, especially those with a very

TABLE 66

ARRESTED CLERGY WERE YOUNGER THAN THOSE WHO WERE NOT ARRESTED

	ARRESTED		NOT ARRESTED	
	N	Mean Age	N	Mean Age
American Lutheran Church	11	35.7	15	41.6
Lutheran Church of America	1	38.0	2	34.0
Missouri Synod Lutheran	2	29.0	2	40.0
United Church of Christ	4	41.5	2	41.5
Episcopal	6	36.7	1	33.0
Others	1	31.0	1	28.0
TOTAL	25	36.2	23	39.4

small number of participants. The difference is quite marked for the American Lutheran Church, the largest group, where the average age difference between arrests and non-arrests is six years. Thus, arrest appears to be independent of age in the more liberal denominations, while in the denominations taking a more moderate stand on civil rights, the young clergy are more likely to be arrested.

Although it was clear that the staff of the Urban Training Center favored involvement in the civil rights demonstrations, including arrest for civil disobedience, it is unlikely that this sentiment was universally shared by the ministers. Thus, one might predict that there would be a tendency for the undecided minister to turn to his peers for guidance. It is impossible to reconstruct the mental processes of the ministers at the moment of arrest, and it is nearly as difficult to determine after the event the earlier feelings of the participants. However, one consequence of such dependence upon peer support can be measured. If an undecided minister was seeking peer guidance, a likely candidate would be his roommate. That roommates should be close peers seems particularly plausible considering the fact that the training session had only been in process a few days and other peer alliances had probably not had adequate time to develop. Therefore, if ministers tend to behave as their roommates behave, the seeking of peer support is at least suggested.

Roommates were arbitrarily assigned alphabetically, subject to late cancellations and registrations for the program. The presence of a systematic bias in the assigning of roommates, thus, appears unlikely. Of the fifty ministers who had roommates, thirty-two acted with respect to arrest just as their roommates did, and only eighteen deviated from their roommate's behavior.[5] Arrestees were no more conforming than non-arrestees. These data suggest, thus, that peer identification was an important aspect of the decision-making process. Having a roommate who was getting arrested probably made it easier for those who were in doubt also to choose arrest—or possibly more difficult to avoid choosing arrest. By the same token, those who were not in sympathy with civil disobedience probably found it easier to avoid going with the crowd when their roommate shared their sentiments.

To summarize the discussion thus far, we have seen that while those UTC trainees who chose arrest were not systematically different from those who did not choose arrest in terms of attitudes toward the civil rights issues and personality characteristics, they did tend to be different in terms of *structural* variables. Arrestees tended to be younger, coming disproportionately from denominations that had taken a strong stand in favor of integration, occupied positions that were not directly responsible to all-white congregations, and tended to have roommates who also chose arrest.

While a single case study clearly does not provide conclusive proof of the social dynamics at work in clergymen's struggles to respond to what they perceive as critical social issues, it does provide a theoretical framework from which other evidence may be examined. Before we turn to other evidence it might be useful to speculate a bit more as to the meaning of what was observed at the Urban Training Center.

The major thrust of the argument thus far has been that certain kinds of structural conditions made some clergy *freer* to engage in social action than others. But this may be too narrow a perspective. It may be that what is involved is not greater or lesser amounts of freedom to act, but rather the fact that different obligations are attached to different social positions. The positions described can be aligned along a continuum varying from heavy obligation to the parish on the one hand, to heavy obligation to the denominational structure on the other. Thus, a minister who serves a prosperous suburban parish that is conservative on the civil rights issue faces an entirely different set of obligations or role expectations than the minister who works for a church bureaucracy that has taken a strong position in favor of an activist approach to achieving integration. In between is the minister who serves an inner-city parish that is partly dependent upon the denomination for financial support.

The generalization, thus, becomes fairly obvious—the more dependent the minister is upon denominational leaders, the more pressure he is under to reflect their beliefs in action. This should not be interpreted to mean that ministers who are dependent upon denominational leaders are always obligated to take a liberal stance. In some instances their denominational leaders may be more concerned with institutional maintenance than change and thus reject active clergy involvement in social issues. Furthermore, the types of positions that denominational leaders hold within the organization will significantly influence how much attention they must give to problems of institutional maintenance.

Similarly, the more dependent a clergyman is on his local congregation, the more important it is that his public pronouncements and actions reflect their views. If he ignores this basic structural dependence, he is likely to encounter conflict.

Still another interpretation of clergy involvement in social issues might emphasize factors which are antecedent to the clergymen's current position. Different types of ministers get recruited into different types of positions. Thus, we might expect to find that ministers whose views on civil rights are conservative are being differentially recruited into all-white suburban parishes, while ministers who most strongly support the civil rights movement are being recruited into integrated parishes and denominational bureaucracy. In other words, a minister's civil rights stance may precede rather than follow his position in the church structure.

One would be surprised if some selectivity of this sort is not operating in filling positions. However, at the same time, it is also plausible that attitude formation does not stop with entrance into a job and that positions themselves affect the rate and direction of attitude change. Just as a minister in a denominational position may come to feel that he has a responsibility to become more actively involved in the civil rights struggle, so also may the minister who has been appointed to a suburban parish undergo a process of resocialization so that his views become more like those of his congregation. Moreover, the clergyman may not be aware of the subtle changes which take place as he undergoes attitude and behavior change so that his views become more congruent with his position.[6]

The UTC observations do not support this interpretation, but it must be remembered that there were some rather unique selective factors in the recruitment of clergymen for the UTC program. Being selected for the program resulted both from the initiative of the potential trainee and from nomination by a church executive. Whatever the source of recruitments, one would expect trainees to be somewhat more liberal than "average" clergymen. Comparisons of the beliefs of the UTC trainees with the national survey data provide cautious support of this proposition.

Thus, the fact that UTC trainees from suburban and inner-city, non-integrated churches were not less liberal in their attitudes toward civil rights than the other trainees probably cannot be generalized to broader groups of clergy. What is suggested is that a clergyman's decision to get involved in a conflict situation is a complex interaction of the nature of the situation, his position in church structure, his own personal convictions, and the structural pressures to get involved or remain silent.

Still another way of viewing the UTC incident is from the perspective of social deviance. Using Robert Merton's typology from his classic paper on "Social Structure and Anomie," ministers who participate in civil rights demonstrations might be classified as "innovators."[7] They accept the cultural goal (integration) but see the institutional means (legal process and Negro self-improvement) as inadequate to achieve the goals. Many of the UTC trainees brought with them an awareness of the growing tension between what the church teaches and what the church does about brotherhood. Inasmuch as involvement may be viewed as an attempt to reduce this, it can be argued that these ministers brought with them a predisposition for involvement.

Social-deviance theory suggests a number of factors that can result in the emergence of deviance. Seen in this perspective, the Urban Training Center provided many of these factors to prompt "deviance" or involvement. First, the ministers were introduced to a deviant-role model, i.e., they were shown a pattern of behavior which included social activism. To be sure, they had been aware of clergy involvement through the mass media, but now they were confronting the model in the flesh. Group involvement at the UTC provided an opportunity for progressive, step-by-step involvement. For those already favorably predisposed toward the "deviant" act of participation, each interaction with fellow trainees probably reinforced commitment to act. Furthermore, most of the trainees did not view arrest as an imminent possibility before they actually marched. Thus, we see evidence of progressive involvement through the process of group interaction. Also, from the perspective of progressive involvement, it is interesting to note that all twelve of the ministers who had *previously* participated in a civil rights demonstration and participated in Chicago were arrested in the June demonstration.[8] Among those who marched in Chicago but had not previously marched in a civil rights demonstration, only half were arrested.

Because they came to Chicago believing that the civil rights cause was just, their highly selective and intensive interaction in a subculture which shared their views and also supported direct action led them to believe that civil disobedience was an appropriate means of dramatizing social injustices. For some, the intense emotional involvement in the cause seemed to block out their ability to see the situation from other perspectives. But others who by independent objective criteria faced the possibility of sanctions by their congregation were not able to get involved to the point where they were able to ignore this reality.

In other words, for many of the trainees the UTC setting became a subculture with all of a subculture's characteristics; a group acting in terms of its own norms. While only slightly more than half of the trainees were arrested, most of them *perceived* that the proportion arrested was much larger, indicating that individuals felt the group was cohesive and unified. Several were noticeably disturbed to learn that public sentiment, as reflected through newspapers and television coverage, was opposed to their behavior.

Another structural variable not mentioned thus far is that of participation outside one's own community. When a minister participates in a civil rights demonstration in his own community, there is always the possibility that even though his congregation is willing to tolerate his behavior, members of the power structure of the community may bring pressure upon his laity to initiate reprisals. This is less likely when the minister is involved in civil rights activities in another community. Furthermore, it is easier for his congregation to view his behavior in a favorable light when he is not protesting against *their* prejudices or the injustices of *their* community.

Based upon observations of the Chicago demonstrations during the summer of 1965, our impressions are that the local parish ministry was not widely represented in the marches. Local ministers who marched tended to be one of three types: Negro ministers of Negro churches, white ministers of Negro churches, and non-parish ministers associated with seminaries and denominational offices.

This subjective impression of the Chicago situation is consistent with observations of civil rights activity in other areas. For example, in Little Rock during the 1957 desegregation crisis, Negro children were escorted through the hostile crowds to Central High School by seven clergymen, five of whom were from out of town. This pattern appears to be fairly typical of most civil rights demonstrations.

Implicit in the discussion thus far has been the argument that ministers' involvement in civil rights may also be viewed from an *organizational* perspective. The connection between factors related to church structure and civil rights involvement raises the question of whether there have been significant changes in the structural organization of the church which have made possible its involvement in the civil rights movement. If, in fact, it is true that those ministers who are involved in the movement occupy positions that free them from the conservative constraints of congregations, then the extent of involvement of the church is a function of the number and desirability of those particular types of positions. Forty years ago, for example, the extent of the church bureaucracy was much smaller than it is today, and the ecumenical organizations such as the National Council of Churches were fewer in number and also smaller in staff. Thus, it is altogether possible that forty years ago the church could not have been involved in the civil rights movement. Further evidence to support this position will be introduced later in this chapter.

The same questions about organizational structure in the church may also be raised for the society more generally. Increasing population size in congressional districts and increasing financial abundance in the nation, for example, have perhaps made congressmen less dependent upon the expectations of a select minority of their electorate. Similarly, it may be that the legal profession is less dependent upon a small minority of the population. To be sure, there is evidence that special-interest groups who are concerned with the civil rights movement and civil liberties have created their own legal staffs. But possibly even more significant is the fact that mass society does give a certain degree of anonymity to individuals as well as organizations. Thus, we may have an emerging social structure in which there is a decline in the amount of client-based constraints placed on professionals, which in turn makes it increasingly possible for them to advocate radical change.

The Urban Training Center incident dramatically portrays the way in which social structure either frees or imposes serious restrictions on a clergyman's ability to get involved in social action. But this is only a single case study. Is it possible to generalize these findings beyond the group at the Urban Training Center in Chicago?

Historical Perspective on Clergy Involvement

While there are a number of important books on the history of the involvement of the church and clergy in social issues, all the published studies tend to be weak on examining the social-structural context of involvement which has been outlined here. I am inclined to interpret this weakness in historical accounts as a reflection of the psychological orientation of our culture which I spoke of in Chapter II. Historians have recorded a great detail of speculation on the psychological and theological dimensions of clergy involvement in social change, but their reporting of the social-structural context of involvement has largely been the fortuitous consequence of recording great detail rather than the result of a concise sociological approach to history.

It is beyond the scope of this volume to develop such a comprehensive history of the involvement of clergy in social action. I can only report that my reading of many historical accounts of the Social Gospel movement suggests that the activist clergy have in large part operated outside of or been driven from the congregational structure of American Protestantism. That is to say, the activist clergy have either been in structurally free positions, or their activism has resulted in conflict which forced them eventually to move into positions that were structurally free. Where clergy have not been free from the reprisals of laity and denominational officials, they have either defended the status quo or remained relatively silent on social issues.

In the absence of a comprehensive investigation of this thesis, my argument must proceed with illustration. This is an unsatisfactory methodological approach which is at least as disturbing to this writer as it is to the sophisticated reader. The illustrations, thus, must be interpreted as suggestive rather than as a definitive documentation of the thesis.

TEXTILE STRIKE IN LAWRENCE, MASSACHUSETTS, 1919. One of the pivotal episodes of clergy involvement in social action was the textile strike in Lawrence, Massachusetts, in 1919. In February of that year, thirty thousand textile workers faced a wage cut. The United Textile Workers organizers encouraged the workers to accept the wage cut with a proportional reduction in work hours. The workers rejected this proposal and the union withdrew, leaving the workers with a poorly organized and inexperienced group of indigenous leaders.

The leadership vacuum was soon filled by three young Protestant ministers, A. J. Muste, Cedric Long, and Harold Rotzel. All three were pacifists and led the strikers in a passive-resistance movement. As the police and the textile industry increased the tempo of violence, it became increasingly apparent that the workers were committed to non-violence and determined to win. Six months later, in July, they did win. They received a cut in hours from fifty-four to forty-eight, a wage boost rather than a wage reduction, and the recognition of The Amalgamated Textile Workers Union.

The three clergymen who led this successful strike all fit the pattern of structural freedom. Muste had resigned from his Congregational pulpit two years earlier to protest World War I. Rotzel had resigned from a Methodist pulpit in 1917. Long left his pulpit to participate in the textile strike and did not return to the ministry. A fourth young clergyman, Bill Simpson, who participated in the Lawrence strike also left his pulpit. Simpson did not return to a pulpit but rather took up a ministry of peripatetic poverty, preaching to student groups, conferences, on street corners, or wherever there was a call or opportunity. A fifth clergyman on the scene in Lawrence was Charles R. Brown, at the time dean of the Yale Divinity School. He had been sent by the Massachusetts Congregation of Churches to prepare a report on the strike. In Brown we see the presence of the church but not the local congregation. Yale Divinity School and the Massachusetts Congregation of Churches were both removed from the immediate control of laity, though both received considerable disapproval from church laymen because of the sympathetic nature of Brown's report toward labor.

The local Protestant clergy in Lawrence maintained a strict policy of non-involvement, and a leading Catholic priest was openly hostile toward the strike. At one point the Massachusetts Federation of Churches made an effort to mediate the strike, but their offer was ignored by the textile owners. In short, the entire effort of clergy involvement came from outside of Lawrence and was spearheaded by clergymen who were not directly responsible to laymen. Local clergy either remained silent or defended the textile owners.[9]

COTTON MILL STRIKE IN GASTONIA, NORTH CAROLINA, 1929. In 1929 Gastonia, North Carolina, a small cotton mill city, faced a labor strike that was to make news around the world. In one of the truly classic studies of social history, Liston Pope describes the role of the churches in this strike in *Millhands and Preachers*.[10] Pope thoroughly documents the economic and ideological interdependencies between the churches and the cotton mills. For the laborers, religion was largely a form of escape from their desperate economic conditions. For the millowners and their white-collar employees, religion provided a sanction and legitimization for the pervading economic conditions.

Management and middle-class churchgoers believed that ". . . religion ought not to meddle in politics, except where moral issues, such as prohibition, are involved."[11] Clergy were well aware that the laity controlled the economic resources to keep them in line and few dared to challenge this authority. But for most clergy, the threat of economic sanctions was not necessary, for they had assimilated the ideology of the millowners. In the heat of the strike, labor organizers repeatedly declared that they considered the clergy among their worst enemies. Furthermore, millowners were well aware that clergymen were important allies in their struggle to prevent labor from organizing.

The influence of the church was both subtle and direct. The subtle influence is demonstrated in the following comment by a mill official: "Belonging to a church, and attending it, make a man a better worker. It makes him more complacent—no, that's not the word. It makes him more resigned—that's not the word either, but you get the general idea."[12] Pope did get the idea, for he found that churchgoing laborers were among the most inactive during the strike. The millowners understood too, and after the strike one mill required job applicants to produce a letter of recommendation from their pastor. Pope reports that mill executives and ministers alike felt that the system worked so well that it was continued for a decade.

This was only one of many ways in which clergy supported the millowners and their ideology. Pope reports:

> The overwhelming weight of evidence indicates that the conduct of ministers in Gaston County afforded a powerful sanction to the prestrike economic structure . . . in the cultural crisis of 1929 Gastonia ministers revealed that their economic ethnicways were products

of the economic system in which they lived, with no serious modification by any transcendent economic or religious standard. They were willing to allow the power of religious institutions to be used against those who challenged this economic system; and themselves assisted in such use.[13]

But what of *outside* support from clergy and denominational structures? Pope reports a few denominational and church council pronouncements of sympathy and resolutions for moderation. But Gastonia, North Carolina, was too far removed physically and socially to draw the active support of the small group of Social Gospel ministers who had been active in New England. Pope reports that within Gaston County, there were only two or three ministers and an equal number of lay preachers who supported the strike in any way. And their influence must have been rather minimal since Pope is not certain whether the number was two or three. Furthermore, Pope reports that these were men who already ". . . stood largely outside of the economic and religious privileges of the Gastonia community. . . ."[14] "Salaried ministers of 'respectable' churches, with assured status in the prevailing culture, universally opposed the strike. . . ."[15]

In a postscript to *Millhands and Preachers,* Pope makes an observation which appears to remain virtually unaltered today: ". . . religious institutions can be a source of cultural transformation only as they transcend the immediate culture in which they function . . . only if they achieve larger structural independence. . . ."[16]

CALIFORNIA MIGRANT MINISTRY. For more than three decades the California Migrant Ministry, founded by the National Council of Churches, has conducted a ministry to Mexican and Filipino migrant fruit and vegetable workers in the lush agricultural valleys of central California. During the early years of the ministry much of the effort was aimed at charitable services. For example, day care centers were established and food and clothing were gathered to help migrant workers through the off season. But in recent years the Migrant Ministry has directed its attention more and more toward self-help programs for the migrant workers.

In September 1965 two migrant farm worker unions, the Agricultural Workers Organizing Committee and the National Farm Workers' Association, went on strike against several large farms, owned primarily by the DiGiorgio Fruit Corporation. In the midst of the conflict was the Migrant Ministry, headed by a young Presbyterian minister, Rev. Wayne Hartmire.

The cry of *huelga* (strike) rang out across the nation in this historic effort to organize migrant workers. But much of the publicity and controversy that grew out of this strike was not the result of unions attempting to organize workers, but rather that clergymen were so deeply involved in the conflict. Magazines and newspapers snatched up the story of the "crusading clergy." Other clergy from across the state of California and the nation responded with support in a variety of forms. Several "observational teams" of clergy arrived in the tiny town of Delano to assess the situation and write reports and make recommendations for further church-related action. The observation teams were comprised of Protestant, Catholic, and Jewish clergy, and their response was almost unanimously sympathetic toward the strikers and the Migrant Ministry. Many who came to observe joined in the picket lines and several followed Rev. Hartmire and his staff to jail for "trespassing" or "disturbing the peace."

My efforts to assemble data on the sympathetic clergy visitors indicate that the large majority were not parish pastors. They came from the National Council of Churches, state and national denominational staffs, colleges, and seminaries. The Migrant Ministry itself is sponsored and supported by the Northern and Southern California Council of Churches, again a structure which is removed from direct laity disapproval. Funds for the support of the ministry come to the Council of Churches from a variety of sources so that it is difficult for any one group or church to apply strong sanctions against the council or the ministry.

Nevertheless, after the conflict during the fall of 1965, the California Council of Churches and several supporting groups were under fire to cut off their support for the Migrant Ministry. At the Episcopal Diocese of San Joaquin convention in February 1966, the members approved a resolution "opposing the *procedures* of the California Migrant Ministry in the Delano grape strike." Several local congregations in the Delano area withdrew financial support from the Migrant Ministry. In May of 1966 a motion was put before the Northern California Conference of the United Church of Christ, "that the Conference Board of Directors be instructed to take action to get the Migrant Ministry out of the business of organizing unions and picket lines." The motion was rejected only after a long battle in which non-parish clergy took the initiative in defending the role of the Migrant Ministry.

Perhaps the strongest church protest against the Migrant Ministry came from the Delano Ministerial Association. They referred to the Migrant Ministry staff as "outside agitators" and deplored their tactics. In a widely circulated public statement they declared:

> The Delano Ministerial Association has gone on record that it has not fostered nor does it encourage any ecclesiastical demonstration or interference in the farm labor situation; and it looks with disfavor upon any non-resident church or clergy making such expressions. The Association recognizes its chief competency in the spiritual area, and feels that such controversial matters should be handled through properly established channels, that justice and peace might prevail.[17]

In another statement, a spokesman for the Association argued:

> We're here as spiritual leaders, to bring the people to God. We are not to give advice on economic matters. We resent very highly the fact that other clergymen have come into the area and destroyed the image of the church. There's no moral issue involved. The clergy have no business to be involved.[18]

Whether all of the parish clergy in the Delano area shared this sentiment is not clear. What is clear, however, is that the potential sanctions by the farm owners in the area were too great for any of the local parish clergy to risk speaking out in defense of the Migrant Ministry and the migrant laborers. Thus, as was the case in the Lawrence, Massachusetts, and Gastonia, North Carolina, labor disputes, the local parish clergy either remained silent or defended the status quo. Only those who were free from direct sanctions were able to pursue a course of action that was in sharp opposition to the existing power structure.

Structural Restraints in the South and the Role of Outside Agitators

When the Supreme Court handed down its historic decision in 1954, every major Protestant denomination in the United States, including Southern-based churches, moved swiftly to pass resolutions commending the wisdom of the Court. The Southern Baptist Convention meeting in St. Louis in 1954, the same year as the Court decision, passed a resolution stating:

> . . . we recognize the fact that this Supreme Court decision is in harmony with the constitutional guarantee of equal freedom to all citizens, and with the Christian principles of equal justice and love for all men . . . we urge our people and all Christians to conduct themselves in this period of adjustment in the spirit of Christ . . . we pray that God may guide us in our attitudes to the end that we may help and not hinder the progress of justice and brotherly love.[19]

The same year, the General Assembly of the Presbyterian Church in the United States (predominantly Southern denomination) adopted a resolution that among other things called upon the local churches to ". . . admit persons to membership and fellowship in the local church on the spiritual basis of faith in the Lord Jesus Christ without reference to race."[20] In 1955 and 1956 respectively, the Episcopal and Methodist churches, the two other major bodies with substantial membership in the South, issued official statements commending the Supreme Court decision and pledging support in its implementation.

In the years which followed, additional statements were issued by virtually every denomination. These statements tended to contain stronger language and more detail as to the responsibilities of Christians on the race issue. But implementing these ideals in the local congregation proved to be more difficult than passing resolutions in national assemblies. Those ministers and laymen who cast their votes (usually anonymously) in national or regional conventions stood alone when they returned home to carry out the implications of their resolutions. In the years immediately following the Supreme Court decision, few congregations in the nation achieved even the goal of token integration.

The school desegregation crisis in Little Rock, Arkansas, in the fall of 1957 was critical not only in terms of indicating the federal government's determination to implement the Supreme Court decision, but also in clarifying the role of the church in this struggle. Fortunately, two social scientists, Ernest Q. Campbell and Thomas F. Pettigrew from the Harvard Laboratory of Social Relations, were present to record the church's struggle for involvement in this historic episode. Their observations, recorded in *Christians in Racial Crisis,* are very insightful and deserve a much wider audience than they have received.[21]

Campbell and Pettigrew found that only five of the twenty-nine ministers they interviewed were segregationists. Yet in spite of their personal convictions favoring desegregation and the official position of their denominations, the Little Rock clergy remained relatively inactive during the city's racial crisis. During the days of the crisis the churches were so ineffective that there was almost no mention of their role in the major news dispatches from Little Rock. The opportunity for moral leadership by the Little Rock clergy passed by, like the Sunday offering plate, with quiet dignity to someone else.

While on the surface paradoxical, Campbell and Pettigrew see this silence as emanating from cross pressures or conflicting role expectations. The minister is an actor in three reference systems: (1) his own personal convictions, *self-reference system* (SRS); (2) the position of his denomination and fellow clergy, *professional reference system* (PRS); and (3) the expectations of his congregation, *membership reference system* (MRS). While his self-reference system and his professional reference system favor desegregation, his membership reference system is largely committed to maintaining the status quo.

If the minister goes against the expectations of his congregation and takes a strong stand for desegregation, he faces the possibility of losing members from his congregation, financial resources, and even his job. An aggressive stand in favor of desegregation, thus, could lead to a cleavage in his congregation that would bankrupt the church financially as well as spiritually.

Because of this possibility, denominational officials may even impose sanctions on parish clergy to conform to the expectations of the laity. Denominational officials have a responsibility for the preservation of the institution, and in some cases this responsibility may be viewed as more important than their commitment to civil rights. It seems apparent that denominational leaders, like the parish clergy, are caught in a conflict between supporting a creed and encouraging action which may have serious deleterious consequences to the organization. In the case of the Little Rock ministers, extremely strong pressures were brought to bear on them to conform to the expectations of their congregations, and most of them did.

But remaining silent can be a very difficult task for the minister who feels strongly about the racial issue, and several of the Little Rock ministers refused to be totally silent. However, they generally employed diversionary tactics which avoided a head-on confrontation of their convictions with the convictions of their congregations. Campbell and Pettigrew describe seven techniques to avoid head-on confrontations which they observed in Little Rock.[22] The first and most widely used technique was an appeal for *law and order*. A group of fifteen clergymen who initially signed a public statement protesting the action of Governor Orval Faubus in calling out troops to prevent compliance with the Supreme Court order later retreated from this position and called for a meeting to pray for peace and order. A second approach is identified as the *messenger of the Lord* technique. Here the minister does not purport to be expressing his own personal views but rather claims that his is the voice through which God has chosen to communicate. A third approach is identified by Campbell and Pettigrew as the *exaggerated southerner technique:*

> The basic essentials for the use of the *exaggerated southerner technique* are a good southern drawl and an impeccable southern background. A basic defense of segregationists is that birth, residence, or education outside the region invalidates a man's judgment on racial issues (unless, of course, he happens to believe in segregation). The home-grown integrationist, however, is difficult to oppose.[23]

A fourth approach is called the *every-man-a-priest technique*. While no doubt lessening the moral punch of his message, it permits the minister to state his own views with the minimum of offensiveness to his listeners:

> He prefaces his lecture with a statement something like this: "I am going to state my own opinions. We believe in freedom of opinion in our church, and you, also possessing free access to knowledge of God's will, may hold a different opinion, which I assure you I respect."[24]

The *deeper issues technique* was also frequently employed. This approach is addressed to abstract issues such as the "brotherhood of man" or "Christian love," but avoids specific reference to the racial issue. The *segregationists are stupid technique* does not defend integration but rather points out the inconsistencies or lack of strength in the segregationist arguments. A final approach is identified as the *God is watching technique*. With this technique the minister does not identify his own position, nor does he even discuss the issue. The listener must translate for himself the implications of the minister's comments.

These techniques obviously vary in their effectiveness, both in terms of getting the message across and in terms of avoiding conflict with the congregation. It would seem fairly obvious that the more abstract a minister's comments, the less likely they would create conflict, but such techniques are also probably the least effective. But beyond whatever impact a minister's devious ways of preaching about the racial issue may have on his congregation, it is important to see this as an essential device for reducing his own internal conflict and guilt over not taking a more active role in the civil rights struggle. He may preach about the "brotherhood of man" and no one in his congregation hears this as having anything to do with race relations, even though the minister's conscience may be eased because he feels that he has spoken out on the issue.

In spite of the lack of aggressive leadership on the part of Little Rock clergy during the 1957 school desegregation crisis, those who did attempt to speak out paid a price for their convictions. Campbell and Pettigrew report that by early 1959 at least nine ministers had left their pulpits "as a reasonably direct result of the integration conflict."[25] I am personally aware of at least one more pulpit that was vacated shortly after Campbell and Pettigrew completed their book which was a direct result of the school desegregation conflict.

In January 1963, just a few months after James Meredith's stormy entry into the University of Mississippi, a group of twenty-eight young, native-born, Mississippi Methodist clergymen jointly signed and read from their pulpits a document which they entitled "Born of Conviction." The statement was a carefully worded affirmation that they stood united in their belief that the Christian tradition does not permit discrimination because of race, color, or creed. *By mid-1965 only nine of these clergymen remained in the state of Mississippi, and only two occupied the same pulpit as they had at the time they signed the statement!*

This dramatic incident is informative on several accounts regarding the process by which clergy get involved in social conflict. Shortly after the Meredith affair at Ole Miss, a small group, comprising a nucleus of the twenty-eight clergymen, began to meet periodically. They had been drawn together out of a sense of isolation and a feeling that racial hatred had intensified. Several of them told me that prior to the Meredith incident they had been able to speak about racial tolerance from the pulpit. But after Meredith's penetration of the "Cotton Curtain," even mentioning brotherhood from the pulpit brought angry rebukes from their congregations. One of them explained the formation of the group in this way:

> The racial hatred had become so intense that it was necessary to get together with someone in order to maintain some sense of sanity and reassurance of the credibility of our views on the racial matter. I would not say that any of us in the group were really radical in our views on the race issue. But even as moderates, we were so far out of step with the prevailing mood that we felt intensely isolated. At first we met simply to have someone else to talk with—where we could exchange views openly without the fear of reprisals. But as we talked there emerged a feeling that we ought to try and do something constructive. What emerged was the "Born of Conviction" statement.[26]

What happened with this group followed a pattern which I have observed many times in talking with clergy who have become involved in conflict situations. In fact, the pattern is so uniform that it suggests unique stages or phases in the process of involvement.

(1) A group of clergy define a problem as serious or potentially serious and join together to discuss it. At this first stage there is often no immediate notion that some organized action on the part of the group is desirable. Usually, the coming together of the group to exchange views is an end in itself. This is not to say that some members of the group do not foresee the possibility of some collective action, but the commitment to action is something that emerges as a unique product of the group.

(2) The group interaction serves to reinforce the members' sense of the legitimacy of their concern, and hence raises the level of the commitment of the individual members. The more a group has in common, the greater the impact of the interaction in reinforcing their initial attitudes. Where diversity in backgrounds exists, there is greater opportunity for individuals to discount the credibility of others' views as stemming from values or experience which is not shared. For example, a moderate Republican businessman would be

less likely to have his concern to do something about urban problems reinforced by a liberal college professor than by another businessman who is also a moderate Republican. The two businessmen share a great deal in common, while it is uncertain what values or theories of the college professor may motivate his concern. In the case of the twenty-eight Mississippi clergymen, their common heritage was extensive. Not only were they all young, native Mississippians and clergymen in the same denomination, but also many of them had been classmates as undergraduates and seminarians. Thus, the situation was one in which the common heritage was maximal.

(3) The next step on the way to involvement is the presentation of an opportunity to act. The opportunity must be defined by the potential actors as reasonable and consistent with previous behavior. If the proposed action is too radical when compared with previous behavior it will likely be rejected. It is doubtful that the Mississippi twenty-eight would have gone along with the suggestion that they all simultaneously resign their pulpits unless their congregations agreed to integrate their churches, because that would be a sudden radical jump. But signing a statement was a logical step. They were simply putting in writing the views they all shared.

Another observation is that in the initial stages of involvement actors seldom perceive that there may be negative repercussion from their action. None of the twenty-eight foresaw the consequences of their document. At the Urban Training Center, few of the marchers anticipated that their marching would result in arrest. Those who saw the possibility were veteran marchers and were prepared, if necessary, to go one step further.

(4) This leads to two additional observations. First, involvement proceeds by a series of progressive steps, each one constituting a little more serious involvement than the previous step. Secondly, in order for a person to become progressively involved, there must be some form of reward or reinforcement which the actor perceives as outweighing the negative consequences. This positive reinforcement may come from any number of sources; from the group itself, or from others who appreciate the behavior. The Chicago UTC group and the Mississippi twenty-eight again provide good examples of both the presence and absence of reinforcement. In Chicago, the UTC trainees were reinforced by one another, by Negroes who shared the jail cells with them, and by the UTC staff. There was

also immediate criticism. The press was unanimously opposed and in a few cases, the reprisals from home were immediate. But those who marched *and* were arrested the first day were much more likely to return on subsequent days, for it was in this context that the reinforcement of their acts was greatest.

In Mississippi, on the other hand, there were few reinforcements. The twenty-eight were physically separated by considerable distance so that it was not possible for them to maintain close contact. The immediate storm that was created by their statement was much greater than they anticipated so that there was grave reason for them to doubt whether they had done the right thing. The few who publicly supported them also received heavy repercussions. For example, the senior minister of a large church in Jackson who supported them was forced from the pulpit he had occupied for many years, and a sympathetic lay leader and editor of the Conference newspaper was also voted out of his position in the Conference. In short, in the moment of crisis, each of the clergy stood alone, with little reinforcement, and with lingering doubts as to whether he had done the right thing. I made a systematic effort to obtain information on each of the twenty-eight three years after the fateful January statement. To the best of my knowledge, none of them had signed any additional statements, marched, or ventured into any other form of civil rights activity that would give their congregations reason to criticize them. This is not to say that they all totally withdrew from the racial issue. I know that at least some of them did not. But their activities and words became more subtle. As I talked with several of them it became apparent that they were employing some of the techniques described by Campbell and Pettigrew above.

There are other implications which seem apparent from the Little Rock and Mississippi experiences. First of all, I think these cases dramatize how very difficult it is for a parish clergyman to get involved in the civil rights struggle. True, he can preach about brotherhood and point out the prejudices of others, but if he points the finger at his own parishioners in such a way that they understand, he must face the consequences of their anger and aroused guilt. This is not to say that parish clergy have not gotten involved; indeed, a great number have. In a good number of cases, a minority of laymen have supported clergy involvement. But this support has not come without a price, usually a loss of membership and financial contributions from others. While I have no way of knowing how many, I suspect that the number of congregations that have split wide open as the result of a clergyman's stand on civil rights is much larger than most people would suspect. But for every church that has split, there are probably a dozen in which the minister has moved on to another flock to avoid deeper conflict. Denominations are reluctant to release figures or publish them in a manner which is easily interpretable, but the number of clergymen who have left the ministry out of frustration and despair over their lack of freedom to pursue the type of social ministry they feel is appropriate is again probably much larger than most people realize.

The Little Rock and Mississippi experiences also provide a perspective for understanding the role that hundreds of Northern clergymen played in going south to work for the civil rights cause. The incidents of conflict between Northern and Southern clergy are numerous, but the implications of these case studies would seem to be that neither group fully understood the role of the other. Northern clergy tended to feel that Southern clergy were all as bigoted as their congregations or that at best they didn't have the courage to stand up for their convictions. The national survey data show that Southern clergy are somewhat less liberal in their civil rights attitudes, but on the whole are not dramatically different from non-South clergy. But the price of standing up for their convictions was much greater than most Northern clergy realized—almost certain loss of their jobs and a high probability that they would be forced to leave the region of the country that was home to them. This is a price which most Northern clergy who went south, who were in large proportion not parish pastors anyway, were probably not prepared to pay for their Southern excursion. At the same time, Southern clergy by and large failed to understand that the Northern clergy were playing a role they were unable to play. They tended to be critical of Northern clergy for upsetting a delicate balance but failed to see that the delicate balance had already been upset.

It is impossible to measure the impact of the role Northern clergy played, but it seems to me that their net impact was enormously important. Their clerical collars provided a legitimacy for the Southern movement, they almost certainly provided a presence which minimized violence, and their reports and testimony to the United States Congress and Justice Department provided a very important moral and political force in moving legislation through the Congress. Vice-President Humphrey has repeatedly acknowledged the crucial role of the clergy in the passage of civil rights legislation, and Senator Russell of Georgia has been quoted as saying that the Civil Rights Act of 1964 passed because "those damned preachers got the idea it was a moral issue."

Structural Freedom and the Non-Parish Clergyman

We have seen that the parish provides a difficult structure for a clergyman who is committed to an active role in the civil rights struggle. We have also indicated that a large proportion of the activists have not operated out of this traditional structure, but what is the evidence for this latter assertion? Part of the evidence is suggested by case studies such as the Urban Training Center in Chicago. Less systematic observations consistently reveal that non-parish clergy are more actively involved in social issues. During the past three years I have visited approximately twenty-five major metropolitan areas in the nation. I have consistently sought out someone who is well informed on the church, such as a director of the local council of churches, a campus clergyman, or a religion editor for a daily newspaper, and asked him who are the clergy who are most active in social issues. Without exception, the list is dominated by clergy who do not serve parishes or who have some form of specialized ministry in an integrated ghetto church.

One of the most important pieces of evidence in understanding the emergence of the new breed of activist clergy is a study by Hammond and Mitchell entitled "Segmentation of Radicalism—The Case of the Protestant Campus Ministers."[27] Hammond and Mitchell's study begins with a fundamental sociological proposition about organizational structures: All organizations face the dilemma of adapting to an ever changing environment while at the same time maintaining the basic purposes or goals of the organization. If an organization is too susceptible to change, its very reason for being may be lost or seriously compromised. On the other hand, the existence of an organization which is incapable of change may be threatened if it becomes irrelevant or obsolete because of the changing environment in which it exists. Sometimes the pressures for change are only very gradual. In other cases, the necessity for rapid change is very great. Cases of the latter are readily available. The perfection of the automatic washer forced the suppliers of washing machine wringers to diversify their activities very quickly or go out of business. And major breakthroughs in medical science have caused foundations dedicated to research and treatment of a particular disease to move rapidly to redefine their goals.

While many organizations face the necessity of rapid change as the result of changing conditions in their environments, organizations also face internal pressures to change. Some of these internal pressures come about because persons within the organization have recognized or anticipate changes in the external environment which will necessitate change within the organization. But internal pressures also come from those who would redefine the very *raison d'être* of the organization. The former are vitally important to any organization, while the latter, if permitted to run rampant, may seriously disrupt or even threaten the existence of an organization. Unfortunately, these two types are often not easily discernible and an organization which is to remain viable cannot afford to purge itself of all its members who desire change. At the same time, it cannot easily tolerate forces which are disruptive of its ongoing activities. In other words, these "radicals" must somehow be *used* as well as contained. Maximum organizational viability depends on an organization's ability to reap the leavening benefits of radicals without suffering too much from their disruptive influences.

Hammond and Mitchell argue that many organizations create social structures that, while not overtly recognized, function in just this way. As examples they cite "research-and-development" divisions in industrial corporations, "institutes" in universities, and "war colleges" in the military. They further argue that the "campus ministry" constitutes a major mechanism through which churches have siphoned off the "radicals" in their organizations.

The data they present provide convincing evidence that campus ministers are more "radical" (liberal) than clergymen who serve in a parish. Comparison of campus and parish clergy in my own study clearly corroborates the Hammond and Mitchell data. Table 67 compares campus and parish clergymen from my national survey on the civil rights items that were discussed in Chapter IV. On every item, campus clergymen are more liberal in their views toward civil rights than are the parish clergy. While the data are not presented here,

TABLE 67

CAMPUS CLERGY HAVE MORE LIBERAL VIEWS ON
CIVIL RIGHTS ISSUES THAN DO PARISH CLERGY

	CAMPUS CLERGY	PARISH CLERGY
	% Agreeing	
"The real obstacle to integration in this country is political leadership and not the people themselves."	8	14
"The racial crisis in America would probably be less serious if the Federal government had not intervened."	5	11
"Negroes would be better off if they would take advantage of the opportunities that have been made available to them rather than spending so much time protesting."	7	21
"Negroes could solve many of their own problems if they were not so irresponsible and carefree about life."	7	23
"I am in basic sympathy with Northern ministers and students who have gone to the South to work for civil rights."	72	50

comparison of campus and parish clergy on many other social and theological issues reveals the same pattern. The campus ministry, thus, does appear to provide a mechanism for filtering "radicals" out of the parish where they might be disruptive and at the same time retains them within the organization where they may fulfill a leavening function.

Hammond and Mitchell point to a number of ways in which this change-oriented role is realized in the campus ministry. First of all, the churches are able to recruit and hold persons who would other-wise find the ministry too confining. Secondly, the campus ministry is an environment in which innovative ideas can be developed and sustained. Not only is the campus a more permissive environment, but it also has structural features which tend to encourage greater interaction among clergy. Eighty-six per cent of the campus clergy reported that they had at least *weekly* contact with other campus ministers. Parish clergy have much less contact with their peers. Sixty-five per cent of the parish clergy reported that they met informally at least once a *month* with clergy from their own denomination and 57 per cent reported informal contact with clergy from other denominations. The proportion of parish clergy reporting formal contact with other clergy is even less. Thirdly, the creative influences of the campus ministry are returned to the churches via ministers who themselves return to the parish and through their clients (students) who become adult church members. Finally, campus clergy provide an innovative leadership role both within and outside the religious organization. Within the churches, campus clergy have been on the forefront of the ecumenical movement. Outside, as well as within the church, campus clergy have been leaders in the pursuit of social justice. In other words, the campus ministry provides an excellent example of a more general organizational phenomenon, namely the creation of a subsegment within a complex organization where radicalism can be tolerated and at the same time feed innovation back into the larger organization.

Hammond and Mitchell acknowledge that other structures such as monasteries, seminaries, and special orders have served the same function for the churches. However, I do not believe that they emphasize strongly enough the enormous implications of this observation.

One of the most important observations of my studies is that the churches have been systematically isolating radicals from the parish, and hence from potential conflict with laity, for many years. Today the radicals have saturated virtually every non-parish structure within the church. They are not only disproportionately located in the campus ministry, but also in denominational administration, college and seminary teaching, inner-city experimental ministries, some forms of chaplaincy and missionary work, as well as other specialized ministries. More importantly, the very structures into which the radicals have been filtered are those positions which maximize their power to bring about innovation and change. As teachers they have recruited and socialized young clergy into the ranks of the new breed. As administrators they have created new structures and provided new opportunities for innovation and involvement while protecting the innovators from the mainstream conservatism of the church.

It is difficult to tell to what extent this has been a deliberate strategy of change, and to what extent it has been a latent consequence of innovative clergy attempting to avoid conflict with laity. My own impression is that it has been much more of the latter than a deliberate change-oriented strategy. But this does not make the consequences and implications for the churches any less serious. Today, large segments of the Protestant denominations in America are dominated by innovative leaders who are no longer content to see the church continue to serve the status quo comforter role.

The most valuable data for examining the thesis that change-oriented clergy have tended to move disproportionately into non-parish structures is a survey of the beliefs of participants at the Triennial Assembly of the National Council of Churches in Miami in 1966. The survey was conducted by Dr. Glen Trimble, director of the Department of Research of the National Council of Churches.[28]

Participants at the Triennial Assembly consisted of three groups: voting delegates or alternates, accredited visitors, and consultants. As they registered, they were given the questionnaire and asked to complete and return it during the week of the Assembly. Since the questionnaire was anonymous there was no way of following up on non-respondents. A total of 521 usable questionnaires were returned, 223 from voting delegates or alternates and 298 from accredited visitors and consultants. This represented only a 37 per cent return from the voting delegates or alternates. The total number of visitors and consultants was not known, but the proportion returned from that group was believed to be slightly higher. This proportion of returns is less than social scientists like to have in order to feel confident that their findings are truly representative. Nevertheless, several factors would suggest that the findings are fairly representative of the participants at the Assembly. First of all, Trimble reports that the returns are representative in terms of denomination and region. In other words, they did not get a very high percentage of returns from some denominations and very low from others, and the same is true for regions of the country. A second reason which suggests the representativeness of the returns is that in my national clergy survey I did careful comparisons of clergy who returned questionnaires early and late with the total returns and found no significant systematic differences. One possible bias that is likely in the Miami survey is that participants who were most active in terms of program and committee assignments were probably less likely to have completed the questionnaire simply because of the pressures of time. It is problematic whether such persons are systematically different in their views than those who had less program responsibilities, but if there is a bias, I would speculate that the net effect would be to make the Assembly appear slightly *less* liberal than was the actual case. At most, any systematic bias in returns would make only a very slight difference in the over-all picture of the beliefs of the Assembly participants.

For purposes of this analysis, I have divided the Assembly participants into three groups, irrespective of whether they were official delegates. The first group, which I will refer to as *church executives,* consists of clergy who have full-time positions on the staffs of a denomination, a council of churches, or some similar non-parish administrative position. The second group consists of *pastors* to local churches, and the third group consists of *laity.*[29]

On the basis of my theory that liberal or innovative clergy have been systematically moving into non-parish structures, we would expect to find that the church executives hold more liberal views on both theological and social issues than do parish clergy. Similarly, on the basis of data presented in Chapters III and IV, parish clergy should be more liberal than laity on social issues. Before turning to the data, some additional matters should be introduced.

First, the National Council of Churches has long been viewed by many as a liberal body. While most of the major Protestant denominations in the country are members, conservative churchmen do regard the Council with suspicion and many denominations have had battles over their affiliation with this body. Three major conservative Protestant bodies, the Southern Baptist Convention, the American Lutheran Church, and the Lutheran Church, Missouri Synod, have not affiliated with the National Council of Churches. Other denominations, such as the American Baptist Convention, have individual congregations which reject affiliation with the NCC and prohibit their contributions to their denominations from being used to support NCC activities.

That the National Council of Churches should be a liberal body is consistent with our general theoretical framework. Control of the NCC is probably more in the hands of clergy than is control of any other church organization. To a very great extent, its day-to-day activities are carried out with clergy. Its contact with and dependence on the masses of rank-and-file laity is minimal. In short, the NCC has maximal structural freedom. This is, of course, not to say that it operates totally independent of the pressures of conservative laymen and clergy. But it is a large, complex organization that is far removed from the day-to-day pressures that a parish clergyman or a local church council may experience from influential laymen who disapprove of certain policies or activities.

Denominational executives and councils have considerable control over lay representation on NCC boards and committees. The process of electing lay representatives becomes only quasi-democratic with church executives largely controlling the slate of uncontested candidates. Furthermore, laymen who have the time and interest to participate in NCC activities may systematically be more sympathetic with its policies. Laity who oppose the general policies and activities of the NCC may find it easier to ignore rather than fight the mammoth organization.

If these general observations about laity participation in the NCC are correct, then we would expect to find that lay participants at the Triennial Assembly were more liberal than the rank and file of Protestant laity. Items which parallel questions asked in the Glock and Stark study as well as questions that have been asked by the Harris and Gallup Polls permit an examination of this thesis.

Belief in God is undoubtedly the most fundamental precept for one who belongs to a religious group and professes to believe in its principles and doctrines, but even on this most fundamental issue, doubt has come to weigh heavily on the minds of believers. Participants at the Triennial Assembly were asked to indicate which one of six statements most closely expressed what they believed about God (Table 68). Sixty per cent of the church executives responded, "I know God really exists and I have no doubts about it." Sixty-two per cent of the pastors and 78 per cent of the laity gave the same response. Failure to select this category by no means constitutes a rejection of God, but for most it represents a lingering element of doubt. A number of respondents had difficulty fitting their own beliefs into the structured categories. Ten per cent of the church executives, as compared with 5 per cent of the pastors and 4 per cent of the laymen, indicated that none of the statements represented what they believe about God. Laymen were actually more likely to select "unorthodox" statements. Four per cent checked "I

TABLE 68

LAITY HAVE STRONGER BELIEFS ABOUT GOD
THAN DO CLERGY

	NON-PARISH STAFF N = 256	PARISH N = 109	LAITY N = 115
"I know God really exists and I have no doubts about it."	60%	62%	78%
"While I have doubts, I feel that I do believe in God."	26%	28%	11%
"I find myself believing in God some of the time, but not at other times."	2%	1%	1%
"I don't believe in a personal God, but I do believe in a higher power of some kind."	1%	3%	4%
"I don't know whether there is a God and I don't believe there is any way to find out."	0	0	2%
"I don't believe in God."	0	0	0
"None of the above represents what I believe."	10%	5%	4%

don't believe in a personal God but, I do believe in a higher power of some kind," and 2 per cent said, "I don't know whether there is a God and I don't believe there is any way to find out."[30]

If there is doubt and difficulty in conceptualizing God, the figure of Jesus is even more difficult. Only 54 per cent of the church executives and 60 per cent of the pastors were able to affirm that "Jesus is the Divine Son of God and I have no doubts about it" (Table 69). Seventy-one per cent of the laity chose this response as coming closest to expressing what they believe about Jesus. Again, the wording of the statements constituted a problem, but much more so for clergy than laity. Fourteen per cent of the church executives and 15 per cent of the pastors, as compared with 3 per cent of the laity, found that none of the statements adequately reflected their own beliefs.

Those assembled in Miami were also asked to affirm or reject

TABLE 69

LAITY HAVE STRONGER BELIEFS ABOUT THE DIVINITY
OF JESUS THAN DO CLERGY

	NON-PARISH STAFF	PARISH	LAITY
"Jesus is the Divine Son of God and I have no doubts about it."	54%	60%	71%
"While I have some doubts, I feel basically that Jesus is Divine."	28%	21%	18%
"I feel that Jesus was a great man and very holy, but I don't feel Him to be the Son of God any more than all of us are children of God."	3%	5%	4%
"I think Jesus was only a man, although an extraordinary one."	1%	1%	1%
"Frankly, I'm not entirely sure there really was such a person as Jesus."	0	0	0
"None of the above represents what I believe."	14%	15%	3%

belief in several specific church doctrines. These questions, as well as the two discussed above, parallel questions asked by Glock and Stark in their study of church laity in California. Table 70 shows the percentages of each group at the Assembly plus the California study who indicated that each of the theological doctrines is "completely true." The predicted pattern emerges fairly clearly in this table. Church executives are the most likely to reject orthodox doctrines, and parish pastors are more likely to do so than laymen. A comparison of the California laity with the laity at the NCC Assembly fails to reveal a totally consistent pattern. The NCC Miami laity are less likely than the general California laity in Glock and Stark's study to affirm the virgin birth, original sin, and the miraculous stroll of Jesus across the waters of the Lake of Galilee. However, they are slightly more likely to believe in a life beyond death, and there is no essential difference in the proportions affirming the existence of the devil.

However, the failure to find broad differences between the religious beliefs of the NCC laity in Miami and those of the California laity is understandable since the available research shows no consistent relationship between religious involvement and liberality on social issues.

The differences in the religious beliefs of church executives, parish clergy, and laity are clearly established. Consistent with our findings on campus clergy, and in accord with our theoretical model, non-parish clergy are less likely to adhere to orthodox theological positions than are parish clergy. But even parish clergy are less orthodox than laity.

TABLE 70

| | NCC MIAMI ASSEMBLY | | | |
	NON-PARISH STAFF	PARISH CLERGY	LAITY	CALIFORNIA LAITY
	% who answered completely true			
How certain are you of the following religious beliefs:				
There is a life beyond death.	58	70	70	65
Jesus was born of a virgin.	22	27	46	57
The devil actually exists.	18	28	37	38
A child is born into the world already guilty of sin.	11	22	17	26
Jesus walked on water.	16	24	33	50

Will these same patterns of liberality hold on social issues? Unfortunately, the Miami survey included only two attitude statements on social issues, but these provide dramatic confirmation of my thesis. First of all, Dr. Trimble asked the participants in the Miami Assembly how they felt about the war in Vietnam (Table 71). Fifty-seven per cent of the church executives and 52 per cent of the pastors felt that the United States should begin to withdraw its troops, while 38 per cent of the laity felt this way. But the differences between clergy and laity are less dramatic when compared with national Gallup Poll findings. In November, just a few weeks before the Miami Assembly, only 18 per cent of the American public felt that the United States should withdraw its troops.

The differences between the three groups at the Miami Assembly become more dramatic when we look at the percentages who felt that the United States should increase the strength of its attacks on North Vietnam. Only 9 per cent of the church executives favored an increase in attacks on North Vietnam. The percentage of pastors who favored increased attacks was almost double that of the church executives (16 per cent), and the percentage of laity favoring this policy doubled again (32 per cent). But while almost four times as many NCC laity favored increased attacks on North Vietnam as church executives, they were still considerably less militant than the general public. Gallup found that 55 per cent of the general public favored such a policy of escalation.

TABLE 71

NCC MIAMI ASSEMBLY

Which of these statements comes closest to the way you, yourself, feel about the war in Vietnam?	NON-PARISH STAFF	PARISH CLERGY	LAITY	GALLUP POLL NOV. 1966
The United States should begin to withdraw its troops.	57%	52%	38%	18%
The United States should carry out its present level of fighting.	22%	24%	19%	18%
The United States should increase the strength of its attacks on North Vietnam.	9%	16%	32%	55%
Don't know (no response)	13%	8%	10%	9%

Dr. Trimble also asked the Miami Assembly how they felt about the rate of progress toward racial integration in the United States (Table 72). Fully three quarters (75 per cent) of the church executives felt that the pace had not been fast enough. Almost 20 per cent fewer (58 per cent) pastors felt that integration had been moving too slowly. Fifty-five per cent of the laity, or about the same as the pastors, at the Assembly felt this way. But this question dramatically demonstrates the liberal leanings of the NCC laity, for only 4 per cent of the white American public reported to Lou Harris in 1966 that they felt racial integration was not moving fast enough.

While the Miami Assembly survey asks opinions about only two social issues, the issues are perhaps the two most salient issues in America at the present moment. The results reveal that church executives, pastors, and laity who attended the NCC Triennial Assembly in Miami all depart dramatically from the general mood of the American public. Church executives reflect the deepest concern over the moral and political implications of the Vietnam war and race relations in this nation. Pastors are only somewhat less disturbed, and even the laity at the NCC Assembly vary significantly from the general climate of opinion in America.

In summary, both the campus-parish clergy comparisons and the National Council of Churches Triennial Assembly data support the

TABLE 72

NCC MIAMI ASSEMBLY

	NON-PARISH STAFF	PARISH CLERGY	LAITY	LOU HARRIS POLL* (WHITES, 1966)
How do you feel about the current rate of progress toward racial integration in the United States?				
Too fast	6%	6%	13%	70%
Not fast enough	75%	58%	55%	4%
About right	18%	32%	30%	14%
Don't know (no response)	2%	5%	3%	12%

* Harris question reads, "Do you feel Negroes have tried to move too fast, too slow, or at about the right pace?"

theoretical model suggested by the Hammond and Mitchell study, namely that innovative clergy have been systematically separated from the parish pastorate.

I do not have data on clergymen who are college and seminary teachers, but an examination of Dwight Culver's survey of nearly eighteen thousand Protestant seminary students strongly suggests that the innovators are also heavily represented in the ranks of college and seminary teachers, and that the seminaries are producing challenge-oriented clergy at a greater rate than at any time in the history of the churches.[31] In 1962 Culver asked seminary students what type of position they *expected* to occupy when they completed school. One third selected a non-parish type position. The proportion of non-parish positions varies from denomination to denomination, and while I do not have exact data, the proportion of full-time non-parish positions for clergy probably does not exceed 10 per cent in any Protestant denomination. Yet a third expected to be in a non-parish structure upon graduation from seminary. But more importantly, *nearly two thirds of these seminarians told Culver that they hoped eventually to be in a non-parish position!* The implications of Culver's findings have generally not been fully understood. The large majority of seminarians are highly skeptical of or alienated from the concept of the parish ministry. Most of these young men had not yet had any experience as pastors, yet they were aware that their visions of creating a church which is vitally involved in seeking solutions to the many complex social problems of our age is in sharp contradiction to the expectations of church laity, who are looking for personable young men who will do or say nothing to upset their comfortable pews. Moreover, there is evidence that this trend away from parish orientation is continuing. Faculty members at Yale Divinity School report to me that with each subsequent entering freshman class since the Culver survey, the proportion of students indicating interest in the parish ministry has declined. I suspect this is true for many other seminaries.

Summary

In previous chapters we have seen that clergy and laity are a good distance apart, not only on the civil rights issue, but in terms of the role that they see for the church in society. Clergy have come to see the church as an institution for challenging man to new hopes and new visions of a better world. Laity, on the other hand, are in large part committed to the view that the church should be a source of comfort for them in a troubled world. They are essentially consumers rather than producers of the church's love and concern for the world, and the large majority deeply resent clergymen's efforts to remake the church.

With this as background, we proceeded in this chapter to answer the questions: How is it that clergy have managed to get involved in the civil rights struggle at all, and why has the conflict between clergy and laity not been more serious so far? The answer to these questions is enormously complex and at the same time relatively simple. The simple answer is that a large proportion of the activist clergy are structurally removed from the parish and as such do not often feel the direct weight of laymen's reprisals. However, a significant proportion of the activist clergy who work within the parish structure have paid for their involvement with considerable conflict with their laity. The more complex answer must take into account how the activists managed to work their way into non-parish structures. It is not altogether clear whether this has been a deliberate strategy, or whether the action-oriented have simply gradually filtered into non-parish structures in order to avoid conflict. Either way, the evidence is fairly clear that the innovative, action-oriented clergy occupy a significant proportion of the non-parish positions in American Protestantism. As Protestant denominations have become more complex in their organizational structure, the number of non-parish positions has grown. Furthermore, the evidence suggests that the seminaries are producing an increasing proportion of clergy who are committed to a challenge-oriented ministry—far more than the non-parish structures can possibly absorb. Herein lies the most critical dilemma for the house that is already divided. In the final chapter we turn to a discussion of the implications of these findings and speculate about the alternatives and possibilities for the churches. Is the schism already too deep, or are there some possibilities for accommodation and reconciliation?

VI

Collision with Reality

Introduction

The central theme of this volume has been that the Protestant churches are in the midst of a web of crises. These crises are seen as emerging out of serious doubt about the most basic theological doctrines of Christianity and from a growing struggle over the meaning and purpose of the church. These two crises have in turn resulted in a third crisis, namely a crisis of authority. In this chapter I want to argue that these three crises have led to yet a fourth crisis: a *crisis of identity* for the Protestant clergyman. Having elaborated this final development, I will then attempt to look at these crises in perspective and speculate about their implications for institutionalized religion in contemporary society.

The Clergyman's Crisis of Identity

The crisis of identity emerges out of the clergyman's *internalization* of the other crises. The problem of identity, in essence, is the confrontation of the self with the question, "Who am I?" As the vast literature of social psychology and philosophy will attest, the processes by which the self internalizes a sense of identity is enormously complex. Yet we need not go into a full explication of the theoretical literature to understand the clergyman's crisis of identity.

Identity emerges as a product of social interaction whereby the individual internalizes the attitudes and values of others toward the world around him as well as toward himself. While identity is not solely the product of what one internalizes about himself from others, social interaction is an integral part of the process by which the individual gains a sense of who he is. *Socialization* is the process by which human communities transmit values and modes of conduct to the individual which are essential for the survival of society. From the perspective of the individual, socialization is the learning of what is valued by the human community, what is expected in the way of conduct, and a built-in (internalized) desire to conform to the community's values and patterns of conduct. To the extent that socialization succeeds in internalizing the values and patterns of behavior of a society, it succeeds in giving the individual a sense of identity, for he not only understands the nature of the social order, he is able to see where he "fits in."

But what happens when a human community's values are in a state of flux or transition? To be sure, if the changing values are central to every individual, the entire community experiences some strain. But the strain is most acute for those whose responsibility it is to define, sustain, and transmit the values in question. When the values in flux are as basic as the ultimate meaning of life itself, the amount of strain is understandably great.

The clergyman's crisis of identity emerges out of the fact that the value system he has the responsibility of defining, sustaining, and transmitting is in a most serious state of flux. The evidence presented in this volume leaves little room to doubt that this is so. The society is not sure what it believes and it is uncertain as to what the meaning and purpose of the church ought to be. Lacking a clear and coherent notion of the role of religious faith and religious institutions in a changing world, it also is confused about the role of the clergyman. The failure to ascribe clearly defined roles to the clergyman, in turn, leaves the clergyman with considerable ambiguity and lack of clarity as to his role in society.

Many of the factors which contribute to this identity crisis have been implicitly elaborated in our discussion of the crises of belief, meaning and purpose, and authority. These need to be underscored and others further elaborated.

Social roles and identity grow out of the process of interaction with other persons who are important in the development of a self or a sense of identity. George Herbert Mead, one of the early and great contributors to the field of social psychology, referred to such persons as *significant others*. In early childhood the significant others may be very limited, but as the individual approaches adulthood, the range and number of significant others increase sharply. The number and range of significant others will be influenced by social status, residence, occupational choice, etc. A miner in an isolated rural community, for example, will obviously encounter both a smaller number and narrower range of significant others who contribute to the development of his sense of self-identity than will a high-status urban resident who aspires to a career in public life. Those who choose the ministry as an occupation are exposed to a wide range of significant others, both in the process of training and in the fulfillment of their roles in this occupation. Their sense of identity, thus, comes not from a single source, but from many sources.

The clergyman's identity crisis does not grow out of the fact that he encounters so many significant others, but rather that (a) the significant others often lack a sense of what the clergyman's role is, and (b) to the extent that they do define the role, there is broad disagreement and conflict. In short, the clergyman encounters a world that tells him that his role, and hence identity, is ambiguous. This can perhaps best be understood by elaborating some of the conditions and factors which contribute to this ambiguity. We will begin with some of the factors that contribute to the layman's lack of understanding, which of course are fed back to the clergyman, and then move to some factors that are more easily attributed to the occupation itself.

To begin with, the layman finds it difficult to understand the role of the clergyman precisely because clergymen are such an extremely heterogeneous group with respect to what they believe, what they do, and their presentation of self in society. As we have seen in this volume, the beliefs of clergymen range all the way from the Bible-slapping fundamentalists who hold forth in revival tents to the *avant-garde* men of the collar who proclaim that "God is dead" and think of themselves as Christian atheists. While the numbers at either extreme are probably not very large, there is still a very large variation in beliefs existing within the middle range. There is, for example, the conservative position, which, while not accepting the Bible as literal truth, holds a great deal of it as divine revelation which fundamentally informs man of the meaning of truth. The language and style of this position may not be easily distinguishable from the neo-orthodox position, where interpretation of religious doctrine has undergone a considerable degree of transvaluation of meaning. Most laymen are aware that there is a difference, but being theologically unsophisticated, they are not very clear as to exactly what the differences are or what they imply.

Ministers engage in an extremely wide range of activities. In recent years they have been conspicuously present in the civil rights movement. Others have developed styles of ministry and approaches to life which make it difficult to distinguish their work from that of the clinical psychologist or psychiatrist. Others are slaves to a church calendar filled with ladies' aid societies, Sunday school picnics, midweek prayer meetings, and youth chalk talks. And still others seem to be indistinguishable from the executive secretary of the chamber of commerce. They are busy from sunup until late at night making speeches and serving on committees that "make their community a better place in which to live."

The ministers' presentation of self today also involves striking variation. Some have the clean-cut, smooth style of the Madison Avenue executive. At the other extreme is a pious presentation of self which could leave little doubt in anyone's mind that the parson has arrived on the scene.

In short, ministers are an extremely diverse group of people who defy the historical stereotype of the country parson, and cannot be pigeonholed into some simple typology. All of this is perplexing to the layman. Can the carriers of God's "eternal truth" come wrapped in so many different packages? Not fully understanding what this range of styles represents, the layman does not know how to respond to the clergyman and hence the clergyman does not get a very clear reflection from the layman as to what his role behavior ought to be.

Historically speaking, the clergyman has been viewed as a professional holy man. He was God's representative on earth charged with the responsibility of manifesting pious, godly virtues. He was not supposed to be like other men. To reveal his doubts and anxieties, to interact with other men as colleagues or intimate friends, or to manifest his "humanness" would represent a betrayal or evidence of weakness of his calling. His authority to speak in behalf of the Lord was intricately linked to his pious posture and was protected by maintaining a social distance from laymen.

Today, most clergymen no longer consciously maintain this "holy posture" and social distance from their congregations. Yet many, if not most, of them find that they are still unable to communicate with many laymen and relate to them openly. This is probably in large part due to the fact that laymen have internalized the stereotypical view of the clergyman and respond to him as if he were a holy man apart from others. When they interact with a clergyman they must "put on" their most polished pietistic style.

But possibly even more significant is the fact that the social distance is now being created by the layman. He is afraid to get too close to the minister because he fears that the minister will ask him for commitments of his time and money that he is unwilling to make. One avoids a minister as one avoids the leaders of any voluntary association who are constantly on the lookout for persons who can be coerced to serve on committees or make larger financial contributions to the organization.

The average church layman wishes to maintain an active but nominal commitment to the church in the same sense as he desires nominal membership in his lodge and professional organization. They are there for his convenience, benefit, and comfort, but it is necessary to preserve social distance to avoid being saddled with too many responsibilities for the system-maintenance tasks of the organization.

But perhaps an even more important reason the layman maintains social distance from the clergyman is his desire to escape what I have called the crisis of meaning. To him, the church *is* a source of comfort and meaning and he does not wish to engage in a dialogue on the meaning of meaning. He does not wish to be confronted with questions regarding the implications of his faith for his daily life and the troubled world he lives in.

Interaction, thus, seldom goes beyond the minimal formal role requirements. While the minister may desire to move beyond this level of interaction and find out who his layman is as a person, and reveal to the laymen that he is also a person, the layman is reluctant to do so because of the uncertainties of what this kind of relationship might lead to.

Another critical underlying factor in understanding the ambiguity of the clergyman's role is the very nature of the changing world. Science and technology have pushed men to become increasingly concerned with the secular. The varieties and opportunities for new human experience have never been greater. Where once the church had a monopoly, it is now in competition for man's mind and his time. Moreover, there is too much which man doesn't know, but which he views as within his grasp to learn, for him to be overly concerned about those things that appear beyond the domain of human knowledge. Science has challenged the clergyman's claim to relevance in all matters of life. Often when clergymen are viewed as relevant at all by much of contemporary society, their competence is thought to be restricted to moments of grief and great exultation, such as death and birth.

The changing world is also at the root of the clergyman's crisis of identity, because it has necessitated a re-examination of the doctrines of religious institutions. While theologians have been seriously involved in this re-examination for a long time, it is not easy to communicate to laymen. Clergymen are caught in a dilemma between proclaiming a doctrine of truth which presumably transcends the ages and being forced to adapt and reinterpret this doctrine in light of man's increasing understanding of the empirical world. For the clergyman as well as the layman, it is often difficult to differentiate between the reinterpretation of enduring truth and the more precarious and fatal procedure of peeling away layers of the onion until nothing is left. What fundamental truths are there which the church proclaims which will abide through the ages? The clergyman fears to let go of doctrine before having subjected it to the most careful scrutiny for fear that having done so will leave him in a logically indefensible position. At the same time he feels pressed to discard irrelevant baggage which may get in the way of others understanding the essential features of his faith. Compounding this dilemma is the lack of consensus as to what the bedrock fundamental truths are.

As the physician who has difficulty diagnosing a rare disease does not find it easy to speak frankly with his patient, so the clergyman who is caught up in the turmoil of re-examining the canons of his faith finds it difficult to communicate clearly and honestly with his client. If his utterings appear to be unclear it may be because, in fact, his own beliefs are in a state of animated suspension.

In their quest for continuity with the past and relevance for the present many clergymen have retained much of the traditional language of the faith while reinterpreting its meaning. They are anxious to communicate this new meaning to those who will listen. At the same time, they are fearful of upsetting the faith of many who find meaning only in inflexible, absolute world views. They know that questioning this faith may cause considerable psychological distress and may risk losing the layman's support, as well as creating strife and discord in the congregation.

The young minister's own imperfect socialization to the nuances of Tillich or the latest *avant-garde* theologian at the seminary, combined with the difficult task of communicating new meaning with old vessels, has often left laymen in bewilderment. To the theologically unsophisticated, it is frequently not clear just what the differences are between a Billy Graham, a Norman Vincent Peale, and a James Pike; between a conservative, a neo-orthodox, and a liberal.

In a world that presents increasing opportunities for the utilization of time, the laity often find other uses for time traditionally reserved for religious activities. If worship and participation in church functions are preserved at all, they are likely to be rigidly compartmentalized. The minister who demands more time from his laity and pleads that they join with him in examining the meaning of the faith in a changing world is likely to find himself left with only a handful of faithful followers.

We can further point to the increasing division of labor and specialization in contemporary society as a factor contributing to the ministers' crisis of identity. The roles that were once exclusively or nearly exclusively the tasks of clergymen have been taken over by a proliferation of other helping professions. Teaching, administering aid, counseling the troubled, and advising the young are examples of tasks for which clergymen once assumed major responsibility, but which are now the domain of others.

This does not mean, however, that the clergyman in his search for relevance and meaningful activity has abandoned these earlier roles. On the contrary, he has expanded them, and usually does so without the benefit of specialized knowledge developed by other professional groups. As counselor, for example, he may engage in helping persons with emotional disturbances, marital problems, occupational choice, alcoholism, financial distress, and aging. Each of these areas has developed a highly particularized knowledge and practitioners who devote full time to this kind of helping relationship. The typical parish minister may very well be called upon to help in all of these situations within a reasonably short period of time. Thus, he is simultaneously sharing old roles while broadening them into other areas. It is increasingly difficult for him as well as others to discern what is uniquely the role of a clergyman.

He probably has not taken on this multiplicity of activities solely out of his search for identity and relevance, for many of these roles have been thrust upon him. Contemporary men are probably less reluctant than were men of earlier generations to turn to others for solutions to their problems. Man's practical and pragmatic orientation toward life leads him to seek to resolve or eliminate tensions that result in unhappiness. Unaware of where to look for specialized help or unable to afford professional services, he frequently turns to the clergyman. A national survey taken a few years ago found that 42 per cent of the American population indicated they would turn first to their clergyman if they experienced emotional stress.[1] This exceeds by a considerable amount the proportion who would turn to any other source of help, including the family physician.

Another factor involved in the clergyman's crisis of identity is his isolation from colleagues. The country doctor can work in isolation from colleagues because he has an image of who he is and what he does and this identity is shared by the community. But where the image is cloudy, as in the case of clergymen, isolation may increase the crisis of identity, or, alternatively, contribute to the individual's avoidance of the problem.

For example, when there is no other professional around to question the justification of his activities, the minister may find it easier to take on a motif of busyness that is psychologically rewarding to him and acceptable to his congregation, but which neglects many of the long-range problems of the church. Filling his life with so much activity that he never has the time to be troubled with the question "why," is the path of least resistance. While this may be functional for the immediate needs of the individual, it is dysfunctional for the larger task of reinterpreting the essential meaning of the faith and the role of the minister in contemporary society.

The isolation of the minister may also discourage him from straying too far from the parish and the activities that have been thrust upon him. The clergyman who ventures too far out of the ghetto of his parish is not unlike the American Negro. He cannot always be certain that he is welcome, and it is sometimes difficult to distinguish between genuine acceptance and a polite but patronizing tolerance.

What I am suggesting here is that while there are structural factors that make it possible for individual clergy to avoid a crisis of identity, and many may very well take this route, this does not alter the fact that the profession itself is caught up in a gathering storm.

It would be an oversimplification to argue that the society is totally ambiguous in its understanding and expectations of the clergy. While a significant proportion of the public lacks a clear conception of the clergyman's role, there is also another significant proportion who have a very clearly defined set of role expectations. The problem emerges out of the fact that different subgroups have different expectations. As has been demonstrated throughout this book, one of the major schisms of expectations is between clergy and laity. I have also tried to demonstrate that the depth of the schism is increasing. A significant proportion of young men who are choosing the ministry today are doing so out of a commitment to the solution of critical social problems in society. The seminaries reinforce and help internalize this commitment, because a large proportion of the seminary professors share this set of values and role expectations for the clergy. The same is true of many church administrators who seek to create structures in which the new breed can work.

But the vast majority must carve out their ministry within the structure of the local parish. While the seminary socialization may provide some realistic orientation to the parish ministry, for many it comes as a cruel awakening to discover the realities of parish life and the disparity between their expectations of the ministry and those of their congregation. But even when the young seminarian knows what he is in for, it probably doesn't significantly cushion the trauma of his exposure to the parish. Somehow he had hoped that his style and sincerity would bring laymen to see the purpose and meaning of the church in his terms. Not only is he confronted with the rude awakening that it didn't turn out as he had hoped, he must also confront the reality that he is pretty powerless to do much about it.

For some, the disparity between their expectations and the expectations of their laity is so great that they leave the ministry. Others seek to relieve the conflict by locating a non-parish position, but within the institutional church. For the large majority, there is nowhere else to go, so they attempt to solve their identity crisis by bringing their own views more in line with the expectations of their congregation. Resocialization may take many forms, but it usually involves taking a more "mature" and "realistic" view as to how much or how fast the church can change. Filling one's life with work is another way in which the resocialization occurs. One simply doesn't have time to think about all the problems that once bothered him. But for others, the resocialization is never quite complete. There is the lingering awareness of dreams once held. The increasing number and high visibility of clergy in non-parish structures also serves to remind the parish pastor of visions and expectations he once held. Thus, he must live with another dimension of his crisis of identity: the disparity between his expectations and the expectations of his congregation.

In summary, the reasons why clergymen are not understood and, in fact, often misunderstood, are intricately related to and a part of their crisis of identity. In the past, the clergyman's role was relatively unambiguous. He was the spiritual leader of his congregation, charged with the responsibility of proclaiming religious truth, tending to the propagation and preservation of the institutional church, administering the holy sacraments, and tending to the individual spiritual needs of the congregation. These traditional responsibilities were exercised in the roles of preacher, teacher, priest, and pastor.

Modern man is less certain of what the role of religion is or ought to be in his own life, and concomitantly is uncertain as to who the clergyman is and what his business is about. He is not satisfied with the traditional role of the pastor, but he doesn't understand or approve of the role of the new breed.

The clergyman faces a crisis of belief, yet he is required to maintain some kind of coherent and consistent posture from the pulpit and in other aspects of his ministry. Laity make multiple and often conflicting demands of him, and he is required to spend a great deal of time engaged in activities for which he is ill prepared. He is not only isolated from parishioners by social distance, but he is also physically isolated from other clergy from whom he might gain support and some sense of identity. Finally, he is caught in a conflict between his own concept of a clergyman's role and the purpose of the church, and the expectations of his congregation.

All of these factors contribute to the demise of the clergyman's authority in terms of the traditional order of the social system. If he is to achieve more than token authority and loyalty, he must rely heavily upon his own charismatic qualities. But charisma breaks down quickly when his direction of leadership strays too far from the expectations of his congregation. Which way does he go? How does he develop a life style that gives him a sense of identity and fulfillment which is acceptable to those whom he serves and who control his life?

Some Thoughts for the New Breed

The nature of the evidence presented in this volume seems to me to be overwhelming. There can be little doubt but that Christians are widely divided as to what they believe are the central doctrines of the faith. What is absolutely essential doctrine to one is considered peripheral to another and irrelevant to yet a third. Enormous doctrinal differences exist among the various Protestant denominations, but doctrinal differences are also very great within denominations and even within individual congregations. Clergy and laity alike are having difficulty accepting many of the traditional doctrines of the faith, and apparently for the same reason—they no longer seem plausible in the modern world.

But the consequences of doubt or rejection of traditional doctrine have not been the same for clergy and laity. Doubt has served to shift the clergyman's emphasis away from the next world to a deeper concern about the meaning and implications of the Christian faith for this world. As clergy have become more concerned with expressing love and achieving social justice in this world, they have become increasingly uneasy about the institutional church which largely reflects a middle-class commitment to the status quo. While perhaps not consciously realizing what they were doing, those who have been most uncomfortable with the status quo posture of the church have found it easier to move into non-parish structures than to try and change the local parish. The growing size and wealth of denominations has facilitated the development of such structures. But the number of clergy who envision a new church has also grown so that it is not possible to absorb all of them in non-parish structures. Today, a substantial proportion of the pulpits in American

Protestantism are filled by clergymen who hope to see the church become more vitally involved in the world.

Doubt has not had the same effect on laity. They have maintained a loyalty to the church, but it is questionable whether they maintain a high level of commitment. Religion has become more privatized. Laity are more likely to say that what a man believes about religion is more important than what the church teaches. This privatization has stripped the church and the clergy of much authority. The layman can take it or leave it. Or, if he doesn't like what he is hearing from one pulpit he can easily transfer his membership to another congregation.

The increasingly bold stance of clergy on civil rights and other social issues has left a large proportion of the laity bewildered and resentful. Many feel that the church has no business speaking out on social and political issues. Others question the competency of the clergy to make pronouncements on such issues. For them, the church is a source of comfort in a troubled world. Their church may be largely confined to four walls, their friends, and a salaried comforter, but it is a church they want and need. For them, the church is not an agent of change, but rather a buffer against it. They do not understand what clergy are saying and doing, nor are they willing to lend consent on the assumption that clergy understand better than they the "will of God." The result is that clergy and laity are on a collision course. In a very real sense, the laity have one church and the clergy have another. If one takes seriously the implications of the fact that the organizational structures of the church have facilitated and encouraged the development of a new breed, then it seems hard to avoid the conclusion that the conflict that has been witnessed in recent years is only a prelude to what seems almost inevitably to be a much more serious conflict in the years ahead.

But the crisis over meaning and purpose is not confined solely to a conflict between clergy and laity. While some clergy feel that the church should be the *avant-garde* to bring about social change in a troubled world, others feel that the church should be involved in change only indirectly as individuals come to understand and apply Christian principles in their daily lives. Still others feel that the purpose of the church is to prepare people for another life and hence it has no justification for involvement in this world at all, except in an evangelical mission to save souls. In short, the conflict that divides clergy and laity also divides clergy among themselves. While laity are also obviously divided among themselves, I have not found this to be as serious a schism as the other two divisions. Yet, it seems logical to conclude that this will become a much more serious problem in the years ahead.

There seems to be little room to doubt that the sharp divisions over belief and the meaning and purpose of the church are resulting in a struggle over authority and power. Similarly, it would seem almost inevitable that this conflict will increase in the years ahead. As leaders of a voluntary association, whose power rests largely on the consent of the membership, clergy need to consider the implications of this power struggle much more seriously than I believe they have to this point.

Finally, it seems fairly clear that clergy are experiencing an identity crisis. Their roles are poorly defined and their source of authority is much less clear than it once was. While no systematic survey data have been presented here which attempt to measure the extent of identity crisis, its existence seems to flow logically from the other crises. It also seems apparent from my many personal interviews with clergy, though I would hasten to admit that my personal interviews constitute a biased sample since I have sought out clergy who have been involved in conflict. I have no doubt that the identity crisis is present. What is less clear is how broadly and with what degree of intensity it is felt by clergymen in America.

While the evidence seems overwhelming, it is at the same time fraught with considerable ambiguity. The ambiguity lies not so much in the seriousness of these crises, but rather in the prospects for the churches to seek viable resolutions of the conflict. The churches face a critical and all-embracing question: *Are the institutional structures of the church broad enough to accommodate persons who are widely divided on the doctrinal basis of the faith and on the very meaning and purpose of the church, or are the divisions already so deep and entrenched as to make accommodation impossible?*

The data presented in this study are insufficient to answer a question of this magnitude. However, I believe that the data are sufficient to indicate that the question is an altogether appropriate one to raise. It is perhaps the most important question that the churches have faced since the Reformation. Moreover, I see considerable evidence that it is being ignored, precisely because the implications are too staggering to be realistically confronted. Those clergy who are today speaking of an *institutionless* Christianity are perhaps the most guilty of abdicating responsibility, for the very fact that they speak in these terms would seem to suggest that they understand the implications of the conflict. But I do not believe they understand the implications of Christianity without an institutional base.

Assuming that my analysis of the conflicts within Protestantism has some validity, how is the conflict to be resolved? While I have some aversion to crystal-ball gazing, it does seem appropriate to outline the logical possibilities and to speculate on the implications of each.

From a theoretical point, at least, it would seem that the conflict could be resolved most easily if clergy were to retreat from their commitment to active involvement in social issues. But practically, this does not seem like a very realistic possibility. The evidence would seem to suggest that they are going to become more, not less, involved. However, we cannot exclude this alternative altogether. As clergy involvement intensifies the conflict within the church, they may come to see the implications more clearly and thus draw back in order to avert internal institutional disaster. This alternative would not necessarily mean that clergy would retreat to total silence or that they would publicly confess that their role is more appropriately that of comforter and helper in the local congregation. Rather it would represent a retreat to the more subtle tactics of persuasion that Campbell and Pettigrew discussed in *Christians in Racial Crisis* (see Chapter V). It would involve an acknowledgment by the clergy that the imperatives of institutional survival are at least as important as the social issues that they are involved in. And it would involve a longer-range view of changing the church and the world.

My own assessment is that while many clergy may take this stance, it is not likely to become the "official" posture of the new breed. In a real sense, this was the strategy of many of the Social Gospelers of another generation. The new breed's perception of the urgency of many of the social problems of this nation and the world doesn't leave a great deal of room for "gradualism." The evidence of their greater involvement seems apparent on several fronts. Clergymen are among the most active in attempting to establish some dialogue with black militants in the cities. During the past year, clergy have become more deeply involved in the protest against the Vietnam war. The pronouncements of church bodies seem to be becoming bolder, covering a wider range of issues and endorsing specific public policies. Witness, for example, the 1966 Geneva Conference on Church and Society and the 1967 National Council of Churches Conference in Detroit following the summer riots.

A second kind of resolution of the conflict could happen if comfort-oriented laity and clergy were to capture the major administrative and decision-making responsibilities of the denominations, expelling or reducing to insignificant roles all those who were unwilling to go along with their expectations for the churches. It is not easy to assess the possibility or probability of this occurring. Yet, it seems fairly clear that if the involvement of clergy in social issues increases, and the boldness of their positions intensifies, the forces of resistance within the churches will become more vocal and better organized to assert their will. The predicted *coup d'état* of the conservative forces in the Episcopal Church to take over the quadrennial meeting of 1966 in Seattle did not materialize, but this does not mean that it won't happen in the future. The pressure of the conservatives is more likely to be felt at the local, state, and regional levels. Without gaining complete control, they can block expenditures of funds to specialized ministries that are engaged in "radical" programs. Many metropolitan councils of churches and experimental inner-city ministries are already feeling the pressure.

But the pressure of conservative forces may be felt in another way which, in the long run, will have serious implications for the involved ministers. Many laymen, who do not understand or approve of the church's involvement in social issues, may simply withdraw. Their commitment to the church may not be strong enough to fight for the kind of church they want. The loss of their financial support may be great enough to force considerable programmatic cutbacks, thus eliminating a significant number of the "structurally free" positions in the church.

A third route to conflict resolution would be for the clergy to stand united and invite those laymen who are not prepared to go along with their concept of the church in society to withdraw. While this is an option that some clergy would like to play, it is not very realistic. In the first place it assumes there is consensus among clergy, which there is not. Secondly, if it is considered a calculated power play on the part of clergy to get laity to mend their ways or see the light, it is probably unrealistic. Thirdly, if it assumes that the churches can suffer great losses in membership and financial contributions and survive to become more actively involved in the world, it is naïve. The overhead of the churches in the form of salaries and property mortgages is enormous. Even a modest cutback in operating budgets would seriously affect the operations of the institution. The institutional church is built around and financially geared to the local parish. Any sudden reorientation to this organizational structure would have the most serious consequences for the entire institution.

A fourth possibility is that many clergy may decide that the only way for them to pursue a course of involvement in the world is to leave the church. Indeed, many have already done so. During the course of my study I made considerable effort, without much success, to obtain denominational records on the number of men leaving the ministry. Incredible as it may seem, some denominations do not maintain the kind of uniform records that would make such data easily calculable. Other denominations consider such records a closely guarded secret. I also found that data on seminary dropouts was extremely hard to obtain.

In the national survey I asked clergy whether they had ever considered leaving the ministry for some other vocation. Twelve per cent said that they had considered such a possibility *very seriously*. An additional 16 per cent said that they had considered the possibility of another vocation, but not seriously. While I don't have data on other occupations, this proportion may not be any higher than one would find in other occupations.

As might be expected, the proportion reporting that they are very seriously considering leaving the ministry varies by denomination and age. The denominational range is from 8 per cent among Episcopalians to 16 per cent among Methodists. Those under thirty-five years of age are more likely to say they are seriously considering leaving the ministry. In this age group, the proportion ranges from 10 per cent among American Lutherans to 22 per cent among Methodists. The amount of attention the denomination gives to liturgy and ritual is also associated with consideration of leaving the ministry, with high liturgical emphasis being associated with a low desire to leave the ministry. Only 9 per cent of the clergy in denominations with high liturgical emphasis (American Lutheran, Episcopal, and Missouri Synod Lutheran), compared with 15 per cent of the denominations with low liturgical emphasis (American Baptist, Methodist, and Presbyterian), reported that they were seriously considering leaving the ministry.

In sharp contrast to this finding in the national survey, I found in one of my case studies that 30 per cent of a sample of eighty-four clergy in a metropolitan area were seriously considering leaving the ministry. The case study occurred in a metropolitan area in which clergy had been deeply involved in the racial crisis for a long period of time, and many had experienced serious conflict with their congregations. When we examine whether the clergy themselves had been involved in the racial crisis, the figures become even more dramatic. Of those who had been involved in the racial conflict, 35 per cent reported that they were seriously considering leaving the ministry, as compared with 20 per cent of those who had not been directly involved. But even those who had not been directly involved in the racial struggle were more likely to report that they were considering leaving the ministry than so reported in the national clergy survey.

Two possible interpretations seem plausible. The first is that even though they were not directly involved in the conflict, the racial situation had seriously affected their morale. Some of them may have wished to be involved but felt they were not free to do so. A second factor which may possibly contribute to the large number expressing interest in leaving the ministry is the fact that the context of an interview is different from a self-response questionnaire. The question came near the end of a long interview (the average interview was an hour and a half) and in most cases considerable rapport had been established. By the time I reached the question there had been a considerable amount of reflection on the clergyman's problems, and thus probably a greater willingness to admit that he was giving serious consideration to leaving the ministry. The questionnaire, on the other hand, probably did not elicit the same kind of emotional involvement.

To seriously consider leaving and actually to leave the ministry are two different things. But the fact that so many would admit that they were considering the possibility is, I believe, a significant indicator of the conflict in the churches and of the clergy's identity crisis.

Actually to leave the ministry is a very serious and difficult decision. In the first place, the clergyman has taken a vow at ordination which he considers sacred. The nature of this commitment is considered more serious than, for example, the decision to become an accountant. But also of considerable importance is the hard reality that most clergymen are not very well prepared for other vocations.

Some clergy are beginning to talk seriously about a "worker-priest" role. It would seem to me that the worker-priest concept idealizes the potential for clergy effectiveness as change agents in other vocations. As mentioned above, most clergy are not well trained for other vocations. The types of occupations they are qualified for are in large part subject to the same, if not more serious, structural restraints than they encounter in the ministry. However, the worker-priest role may be important psychologically. It may serve as a transitional period between clergy status and lay status. As such, it may ease the tension and guilt that a man feels in leaving the ministry.

Again, it is difficult to assess what the prospects are for massive defections from the ministry. It would be helpful if we had data on the number of clergy who have left the ministry in the past decade. The various Protestant denominations ought to begin to assemble more systematic data on this phenomenon. The rate at which men leave the ministry is an important barometer of the extent of the conflict. Similarly, the churches ought to be collecting much more systematic data on the characteristics of those who are entering seminaries and those who drop out before completing seminary training. While seminaries are increasingly employing entrance examinations, the American Association of Theological Schools has yet to adopt standardized testing procedures, such as the Graduate Record Examination, used by most graduate schools in the country, which would reveal where seminary students rank with respect to national norms for college seniors.

While each of these four logical possibilities for resolving conflict would seem to have some probability of materializing, none of them seems to be very promising for the new breed who would seek to make the church not only relevant, but vitally committed and involved in the world. It would seem to me that *the only way that clergymen can hope to maintain and further develop their involvement in social issues is to begin to think seriously about a strategy for engaging laity in the struggle.* It is a fundamental sociological principle that the leadership of a voluntary association can only be so far out of line with the expectations of its constituency before that leadership is questioned. The data presented in this study leave little room to doubt that the leadership of the church is already dangerously separated from its constituency. Moreover, the leadership seems to be moving in directions that will inevitably widen the gap.

During the past four years the Protestant churches in America have initiated a number of experimental training programs for clergy, such as the Urban Training Center for Christian Mission mentioned in Chapter V. There is a general sense of euphoria about these training centers among church administrators. A National Advisory Conference on Generating Manpower for Mission, sponsored by the National Council of Churches in the fall of 1966, recommended that clergy training centers be established in every major metropolitan area in the country. With the exception of one outside consultant, nobody at that conference even mentioned the question of laity reaction to clergy involvement or of "generating manpower" among the ranks of laity.

I think this is a significant indicator of the depths of frustration that clergy feel toward the possibility of involving laymen. They seem to operate on the assumption that laity are an immovable force that must be worked around and not with. At the same time it is a significant indicator of the conflict that lies ahead. Having largely written off the layman, church administrators seem to think that it is possible to continue to program involvement, and that the laity will continue to pick up the bills. While this may work on a short-term basis, enduring programs necessitate broadening the base of support. The current programs designed to sensitize clergy to the many critical problems of the metropolis, without creating structures for them to work in, can only create greater frustration on the part of clergy and increase the gap of understanding between clergy and laity.

During the past three years I have talked with a considerable number of church executives and non-parish clergy about the prospect that laity might one day refuse to support the ministry of the new breed because they consider it too far out of line with their understanding of the role of the clergy and the church in society. Almost invariably the response has been a troubled admission that this is a very real possibility. Many cited specific instances of how they had already felt the pressure, both in terms of threats to jobs and cutbacks in financial resources. But when I asked what was being done to develop understanding and support among laymen for their ministry, I was usually told "not much," or given some rather vague responses which seemed to me to amount to about the same thing.

I do not mean to suggest that no efforts are being made to interpret the ministry of the new breed or to engage laity. The Ecumenical Institute in Chicago is a rather bold attempt to create sophisticated lay education. A number of other programs can be cited, but none of them approach the scope and intensity of the Chicago program. But assuming a high degree of effectiveness in these programs, which seems to me a highly dubious assumption, the number of laymen who have been reached is rather trivial.

In short, the amount of effort and success in creating sympathy, understanding, and involvement among laymen has not even begun to be commensurate with the magnitude of the task if the new breed are going to build the kind of base they need to sustain their involvement in the world. The task may be facilitated by training programs, but no amount of special programing, unless it is combined with a broad-based organizational strategy, is going to produce the needed results.

Clergy have developed a new understanding of the meaning and implications of the Christian faith. They have not succeeded in communicating this understanding to laity. The frustration and failure of most clergymen to succeed in this task has led many of them to withdraw from the task. The fact that the amount of church involvement has little impact on attitudes toward racial justice and a large number of other social issues would seem to me to be rather serious evidence of the clergy's failure to communicate the meaning of the faith as they understand it.

As one who feels there is a great urgency in seeking solutions to many of the problems that confront this nation and the world, I have come to have a great deal of sympathy for the involvement of the new breed. But at the same time, I have come to feel that involvement has become the easy way out for many of them. Facing the jeers and insults of an angry crowd of racial bigots or war hawks may be easier than facing a congregation that feels the Christian gospel is a source of comfort and protection from a troubled world rather than a radical charge to go into the world and make it more human. The former can provide a pietistic sense of self-righteousness. The rewards of the latter come slower and only as one begins to see the results in how men live.

While converting the Christians is perhaps a more difficult task than carrying a picket sign, the longer-range results would seem to be more promising for achieving significant social change. The magnitude of the task is nothing short of revolutionary. It is highly unlikely that any significant success could occur without considerable conflict. But all the evidence would seem to suggest that the years ahead are destined to be fraught with conflict regardless of what strategy clergy choose. The conflict may be so serious as to produce a total realignment of Protestant churches along the comfort-challenge dimension. Again, this may happen even if clergy do not make a concerted effort to bring laity into the struggle. But the more strongly clergy attempt to engage laity, the more solid will be the base of a new, challenge-oriented church. Without strong laity support the new breed could be forced almost completely outside of the institutional church. Before freely choosing this road, the new breed ought to consider the implications. Without attempting to assess the success they have had to date in effecting social change, and assuming they have had some success, it would be hard to separate this success from their institutional base. While they may not presume to speak "in the name of" or "for" the church, there can be little doubt that their voice takes on considerable legitimacy because they are the professional leadership of large religious institutions. A National Council of Churches lobby for civil rights in Washington may take a position that does not represent the views of a large majority of the rank-and-file laity. In fact, it seems quite clear that it does not. Nevertheless, the lobby gains its voice and exerts influence in the name of forty million Christians.

Small cadres of clergy without an institutional base would be as powerless as any other cadre of individuals seeking to effect change. They would have power and influence only to the extent they could organize and coalesce others who shared their views. In part, I am saying that to walk away from the institution of the church is to abandon one of the broadest bases of potential support for change that exists in American society. But at the same time, there are limitations on how much it can be used unless there is broad-based support and understanding. Moreover, its effectiveness will be directly proportional to the extent that the rank and file support its programs.

The readers who have followed me this far may feel that my next task is to outline a strategy for winning and involving the laity. While it would be easy to pull out some tried-and-true clichés about division of labor between those who define problems and those who solve them, I fear this is not a very satisfactory response for me or my readers. Unfortunately, I do not have a strategy for action which is a panacea for all that ails the church or society. Hence, I must conclude by saying that I hope my elaboration of the parameters of the crisis has added some clarity to the seriousness of the gathering storm, and that perhaps my efforts will serve to stimulate others to consider further the implications of these developments.

Before concluding, it is perhaps appropriate that I should make clear my own values and hopes with regard to the outcome of the conflict. Sociologists have traditionally eschewed taking such a stance, or for that matter, even admitting that their own values are entangled in their work. Sociology has achieved some respectability as a legitimate intellectual discipline, and with this legitimacy has come a greater willingness to admit that we too have values which we wrestle with. I need not repeat here all the pros and cons of whether a social scientist can be "value-free." My own feeling is that he probably can insofar as his research is without any social significance. But as soon as he sees that his research may have some implications for the world he lives in, it becomes very difficult for him to maintain a totally value-free position. This is not to say, however, that he cannot conduct reasonably objective research.

It is clear to me that my own values have obviously had a great deal to do with my choosing to research this problem. It is possible that my values have influenced the way I have interpreted the results of the findings. I do not believe, however, that my values have in any significant way biased my gathering, assembling, or presentation of the data.

From this last chapter it should be reasonably clear that my own values and sense of urgency for social change lie with the new breed. I hope they succeed in their effort to create a "new thing." I have stressed the need to pay more attention to laity, not because I want to see clergy off the streets, but because I feel they must face the issue of involving laity if they are going to avoid the consequences of the collision course they now seem to be pursuing.

I do, however, have some serious reservations about some of the directions in which some of the new-breed clergy seem to be heading. It seems to me that a passion for specific issues has led many to pronouncements and involvement without paying adequate attention to the ethical and theological basis of their action. Without at all implying that all the evidence must be in before one can engage in a morally responsible or politically effective act, I do believe that some clergy have been guilty of acting without having even the most elementary command of the issues.

The crisis of theological belief has enormous implications for the clergyman's involvement in social issues and his engagement in power struggles in the political arena. Because doubt and uncertainty are so widespread, the clergyman cannot state with authority, "Thus saith the Lord." The age of doubt demands an ethical and theological rationale that is defendable in terms of the Christian heritage. This involves something more than dipping into scriptures and pulling out a justification for any specific behavior. The world knows all too well that a scriptural text can be used to justify almost anything, including war, racism, and silence while a nation commits genocide.

If only for pragmatic reasons, the precarious authority of clergy necessitates their being right, at least most of the time, when they take a stand. To the extent that the course of events and the unfolding evidence tends to indicate that their stance on a particular issue was ill considered, their authority is undermined even further. I think it is important that these comments not be interpreted as a plea for silence where knowledge is lacking. If overzealous pronouncement is a form of cardinal sin, silence because one is ignorant is the other side of the coin.

It is not enough to be "morally right" or "on the side of the angels." If clergy are going to educate the laity, they must themselves be well informed. In some of my case studies I have gathered data on the clergy's reading habits. The results give me reason to question the competency of many clergy to speak out on social issues. But the issue is not so much whether they are well enough informed to have a "right" to speak out on an issue as it is the effectiveness of their message. Moral platitudes and clichés are not nearly as likely to be effective methods of communication and persuasion as are informed and logically developed expositions of an issue.

If clergy are going to assume roles as actors in the social and political arena, they have the responsibility to play the roles well.

Clergymen cannot afford to be amateurs with inadequate knowledge to speak on an issue. The better informed the clergyman is, the more difficult he makes it for the layman to level the "unqualified to speak" criticism. But the issue is more important than being invulnerable to criticism on this count. If clergy were better informed, they might have greater success in convincing laity of the validity of their position. Moreover, their sophistication might have the effect of encouraging laymen to become better informed on social issues.

Not only is there a need for greater interpretation of contemporary social issues, in my judgment there is also a most serious need for clergy to explore openly and honestly the crisis of belief. It has heretofore been assumed that theological issues are far too complex for laymen to grasp. I would submit that *unless* laymen are brought to understand the theological revolution they are going to continue to interpret it as a peeling away of the layers of the onion. If this happens, the institution will lose its last ounce of authority. Religion will become an increasingly private affair. As Peter Berger so ably put it, when religion becomes a private affair, ". . . one 'cannot really talk' about religion any more . . . religion no longer refers to the cosmos or history, but to individual *Existenz* or psychology."[2]

If understanding social issues is a prerequisite to interpreting them, it is equally important that clergy understand the major developments in theological thought before they can interpret them to laymen. The results of my national survey, however, reveal that clergy, as a group, are not well informed on contemporary theological thought, at least insofar as having read the leading theological figures of this century is an indicator of being informed. What I am suggesting, among other things, is that effective leadership demands competency. An effective leader must know why he believes as he does and must be able to communicate these reasons to others.

I would hesitate to conclude that clergy should work toward establishing *general principles* rather than articulating specific positions on every issue they get involved in, for at least two reasons. In the first place, what is a general principle to one is a specific position to another. Secondly, the evidence presented in this volume would suggest that people often do not understand the specific implications of a general principle, e.g., the meaning of brotherhood. If one is to be heard and understood, it may be necessary to spell out positions in rather specific detail.

At the same time, it seems to me that there is much to be said for the position that clergy should devote more attention to carefully working through some general ethical positions rather than responding to every problem that arises on an *ad hoc* basis. As I have attempted to wrestle with any number of social problems, I have discovered that the more I learn about a problem, the more I realize how complex and ambiguous the issues are. Realizing the complexity of the issues has seldom led me to withdraw to silence or to fail to stand up for my own position. But it has taught me to appreciate the fact that others whose positions are contrary to my own may have some degree of credibility. I don't think that I am here pleading for greater tolerance. What I am saying is that it seems to me that the very nature of the social order is one of great precariousness and ambiguity. Less dogmatic stands on some specific issues may result in a broader audience for the underlying general principles.

From where I stand, the task is not one of indoctrinating people to accept specific positions or programs. If this is the best man can do then he is a rather feeble species and *Brave New World* or *1984* cannot be far off. The task, rather, is to get more men to think more seriously about the nature of their world; their values, policies, and institutional arrangements. Even in the midst of their faltering authority, I know of no other group in our society that has a greater potential and, indeed, a graver responsibility for generating a greater concern for human destiny than the clergy. In the name of MAN, I hope they succeed.

Notes

PREFACE

1. For a penetrating analysis of the implications of this question see: Peter Berger, *The Sacred Canopy: Elements of a Sociological Theory of Religion* (Garden City, New York: Doubleday & Company, Inc., 1967).
2. The point argued here is developed more thoroughly in Thomas Luckmann, *The Invisible Religion* (New York: The Macmillan Company, 1967), Chapter 1.
3. J. M. Yinger, *Religion, Society, and the Individual* (New York: The Macmillan Company, 1957), pp. 3–5.
4. Oliver R. Whitley, *Religious Behavior: Where Sociology and Religion Meet* (Englewood Cliffs, New Jersey: Prentice-Hall, Inc., 1964), p. 42. This discussion presented here is significantly informed by Whitley's discussion. Chapters 1–3 of Whitley's book are recommended for a more detailed discussion than can be presented here.

CHAPTER ONE

1. Peter Berger, *The Sacred Canopy: Elements of a Sociological Theory of Religion* (Garden City, New York: Doubleday & Company, Inc., 1967).
2. Op. cit.
3. Charles Y. Glock, Benjamin B. Ringer, and Earl R. Babbie, *To Comfort and to Challenge: A Dilemma of the Contemporary Church* (Berkeley, California: University of California Press, 1967).
4. Harvey G. Cox, "The 'New Breed' in American Churches: Sources of Social Activism in American Religion," *Daedalus,* Winter 1967, pp. 135–50.
5. William Stringfellow, *My People Is the Enemy* (New York: Holt, Rinehart & Winston, 1964).
6. Ibid., p. 134.
7. Ibid., p. 140.
8. Ibid., p. 140.
9. Gibson Winter, *The Suburban Captivity of the Churches* (Garden City, New York: Doubleday & Company, Inc., 1961).
10. Ibid., p. 21.

11. Ibid., p. 27.
12. Ibid., pp. 75–76.
13. Ibid., p. 29.
14. Ibid., p. 77 (emphasis Winter's).
15. Ibid., p. 129.
16. Peter L. Berger, *The Noise of Solemn Assemblies* (Garden City, New York: Doubleday & Company, Inc., 1961).
17. Ibid., pp. 13–14.
18. Ibid., p. 67.
19. Ibid., p. 103.
20. Pierre Berton, *The Comfortable Pew* (New York: J. B. Lippincott Company, 1965).
21. Ibid., p. 16.
22. Ibid., p. 15.
23. Ibid., p. 80.
24. J. Howard Pew, "Should the Church 'Meddle' in Civil Affairs?" *Reader's Digest*, May 1966.
25. Ibid., pp. 1–2.
26. Ibid., p. 3.
27. Ibid., p. 4.
28. Ibid., p. 6.
29. *The Christian Century*, May 11, 1966, pp. 607–8.
30. For an illuminating discussion of the "Death of God" controversy, see Harvey G. Cox, "The Death of God and the Future of Theology," in William Robert Miller (ed), *The New Christianity* (New York: Delacorte Press, 1967), pp. 377–89.
31. John A. T. Robinson, *Honest to God* (Philadelphia: The Westminster Press, 1963).
32. David L. Edwards (ed), *The Honest to God Debate* (Philadelphia: The Westminster Press, 1963).
33. Eric Routley, in ibid., p. 82.
34. T. E. Utely, in ibid., pp. 95–97.
35. C. S. Lewis, in ibid., p. 91.
36. Bryan Green, in ibid., pp. 88–89.
37. Harvey G. Cox, *The Secular City* (New York: The Macmillan Company, 1965).
38. Paul Lehmann, "Chalcedon in Technopolis," in Daniel Callahan (ed), *The Secular City Debate* (New York: The Macmillan Company, 1966), p. 64.
39. Cox, *The Secular City*, p. 112.
40. Ibid., pp. 2–4.
41. Edwards, op. cit., p. 233.
42. Charles Y. Glock and Rodney Stark, *Religion and Society in Tension* (Chicago: Rand McNally & Company, 1965), Chapter V, "The New Denominationalism."
43. Glock and Stark, op. cit., pp. 117–18.

44. Ibid., Chapter I, "A Sociological Definition of Religion."

45. Gallup Poll, in *Information Service*, Vol. XLVI, No. 2, January 28, 1967.

46. W. I. Thomas (with Florian Znaniecki), *The Polish Peasant in Europe and America*, 5 Volumes (Chicago: University of Chicago Press, 1918–20).

47. Lou Harris Poll, in *Church and State*, Vol. 20, No. 3, March 1967, p. 4.

48. Historical perspective reveals the church to be increasingly a voluntary association. This is seen clearly in Berger, op. cit.

49. Max Weber, *The Theory of Social and Economic Organization* (New York: Oxford University Press, 1947).

50. Paul M. Harrison, *Authority and Power in the Free Church Tradition* (Princeton, New Jersey: Princeton University Press, 1959).

51. Lester Kinsolving, "Episcopal Extremism," *The Nation*, January 23, 1967, p. 108.

CHAPTER TWO

1. For a more detailed description of the nature and objectives of the campus and parish clergy survey, see: Jeffrey K. Hadden, "A Study of the Protestant Ministry in America," *Journal for the Scientific Study of Religion*, Vol. V, 1965.

2. A detailed methodological description of the survey will appear in a subsequent volume.

3. Detailed analyses of this aspect of the study will appear in a later publication.

4. Charles Y. Glock and Rodney Stark, *Religion and Society in Tension* (Chicago: Rand McNally & Company, 1965), Chapter 5, "The New Denominationalism."

5. Ibid.

6. Ibid.

7. A national sample by the same scholars reveals that the basic conclusions from the Bay Area study are generalizable to the nation. See: Rodney Stark and Charles Y. Glock, *American Piety: The Nature of Religious Commitment* (Berkeley: University of California Press, 1968).

8. "Faith Lutheran" is a pseudonym to preserve the anonymity of the congregation.

9. A detailed report of this study is currently being prepared by the author of this volume.

10. Stark and Glock, *American Piety: The Nature of Religious Commitment* (Berkeley: University of California Press, 1968).

11. Ibid., p. 213.

12. Ibid., p. 221.

CHAPTER THREE

1. Paul Lazarsfeld, Bernard Berelson, and Hazel Gaudet, *The People's Choice* (New York: Columbia University Press, 1948).

2. For example, see Wesley and Beverly Allensmith, "Religious Affiliation and Politico-Economic Attitude," *Public Opinion Quarterly*, Vol. 12, Fall 1948, pp. 377–89.

3. Elmo Roper, "The Myth of the Catholic Vote," *Saturday Review*, October 31, 1959.

4. Gerhard Lenski, *The Religious Factor* (Garden City, New York: Doubleday & Company, Inc., 1961); Bernard Berelson et al., *Voting: A Study of Opinion Formation in a Presidential Campaign* (Chicago: University of Chicago Press, 1954); Oscar Gantz, "Protestant and Catholic Voting Behavior in a Metropolitan Area," *Public Opinion Quarterly*, Vol. 23, Spring 1959; Scott Greer, "Catholic Voters and the Democratic Party," *Public Opinion Quarterly*, Vol. 25, Winter 1961; Angus Campbell et al., *The American Voter* (New York: John Wiley & Sons, Inc., 1960); Philip Converse, "Religion and Politics: The 1960 Election," University of Michigan, unpublished paper.

5. Benton Johnson, "Ascetic Protestantism and Political Preference," *Public Opinion Quarterly*, Vol. 26, Spring 1962; "Ascetic Protestantism and Political Preference in the Deep South," *American Journal of Sociology*, Vol. 69, January 1964; "Theology and Party Preference Among Protestant Clergymen," *American Sociological Review*, Vol. 31, April 1966.

6. Max Weber, *The Protestant Ethic and the Spirit of Capitalism* (New York: Charles Scribner's Sons, 1930).

7. The question asked was: "Admittedly, there are difficulties associated with describing oneself in terms of broad theological positions. However, within the following categories, which of the following best describes your own theological position at each point in your career?" Theological position was ascertained for four points in time: "on entering college," "on entering seminary," "on leaving seminary," and "now." The data reported here are for the current position. The theological categories offered were as follows: "fundamentalist," "conservative," "neo-orthodox," "liberal," "Universalist-Unitarian," and "other." The categories of "Universalist-Unitarian" and "other" were selected by only a small proportion of the clergy and therefore are not reported in this analysis. Only among Episcopalians did more than 1 or 2 per cent select the last two categories. Seventeen per cent of the Episcopalians identified themselves as "other" and the large majority of this group wrote in that they were "Anglican" or "Anglican Catholic." As a group, they tend to score between the conservatives and the neo-orthodox on responses to social issues, though they tend to be more closely aligned with neo-orthodox clergy than conservatives.

8. Rodney Stark and Charles Y. Glock, "Religion and Prejudice," University of California Symposium, Patterns of American Prejudice, March 24–26, 1968, Berkeley, California. (Proceedings of the symposium will be published by the University of California Press.)

9. Ibid.

10. Ibid.

11. Social class is based on the minister's ranking of the occupational background of the members of his church. The options on the questionnaire were as follows: (1) professional and managerial; (2) majority salaried white-collar workers, but also a considerable number of professional and

managerial people; (3) majority salaried white-collar workers, but there are also a considerable number of blue-collar workers; (4) majority blue-collar workers, but there are some white-collar, professional, and managerial people; (5) membership predominately blue-collar; and (6) membership about equally drawn from all occupational groups. The analyses presented here collapse categories 2 and 3 as white-collar and categories 4 and 5 as blue-collar. Personal interviews with eighty-five clergy, using the same categories, indicated that their perceptions of the social class of their congregations correlated very highly with independent criteria.

12. The percentages reported in these two paragraphs are for the "agree" and "disagree" responses on a six-point scale. If the "probably agree" or "probably disagree" responses are added to the responses reported, all three figures will increase approximately 15 per cent.

13. Howard Ellinson, "The Implications of Pentecostal Religion for Intellectualism, Politics, and Race Relations," *American Journal of Sociology*, Vol. 70, January 1965.

14. When the 1957 Current Population Survey data are compared with the Glock and Stark data (Tables 16 and 24) the Methodists do not conform to the rank order indicated. This reflects the fact that the socioeconomic level of Methodists varies by region of the country. In California, where the Glock and Stark data reported in Table 24 were gathered, Methodists tend to be of a higher social status than in some other areas of the country. In the more recent study by Stark and Glock (*American Piety: The Nature of Religious Commitment*, Berkeley: University of California Press, 1968) national survey data show that Methodists are less theologically liberal than Episcopalians and they fall between the two major Presbyterian denominations in terms of liberalness. Thus, this apparent discrepancy in rank ordering of denominations by social status and religious beliefs can be accounted for by the regional bias of the initial Glock and Stark study.

15. Herbert Schneider, *Religion in 20th Century America* (Cambridge, Massachusetts: Harvard University Press, 1952), Appendix, p. 228, as reported in N. J. Demerath, III, *Social Class in American Protestantism* (Chicago: Rand McNally & Company, 1965), p. 2, Table I-1.

16. Paul F. Lazarsfeld, Bernard B. Berelson, and Hazel Gaudet, *The People's Choice* (New York: Duell, Sloan & Pearce, 1944); Bernard B. Berelson, Paul F. Lazarsfeld, and William N. McPhee, *Voting* (Chicago: University of Chicago Press, 1954); Gerhart H. Saenger, "Social Status and Political Behavior," *American Journal of Sociology*, Vol. 51, September 1945; Oscar Glantz, "Protestant and Catholic Voting Behavior in a Metropolitan Area," *Public Opinion Quarterly*, Vol. 23, Spring 1959. The tendency for persons of lower status to vote for the ideologically more liberal party is also suggested in several cross-national studies: Robert R. Alford, *Party and Society* (Chicago: Rand McNally & Company, 1963); Rodney Stark, "Class, Radicalism, and Religious Involvement in Great Britain," *American Sociological Review*, Vol. 29, October 1964; and Charles Y. Glock and Rodney Stark, *Religion and Society in Tension* (Chicago: Rand McNally & Company, 1965), Chapter 11, "Religion and Radical Politics."

17. Charles Y. Glock, Benjamin B. Ringer, and Earl R. Babbie, *To Comfort and to Challenge* (Berkeley: University of California Press, 1967).

18. Ibid., p. 171.
19. Andrew M. Greeley and Peter H. Rossi, *The Education of Catholic Americans* (Chicago: Aldine Publishing Company, 1966).
20. Ibid., pp. 114–37.
21. Ibid., p. 137.
22. Charles Y. Glock, "On the Study of Religious Commitment," *Review of Recent Research Bearing on Religious and Character Formation*, published as a Research Supplement to *Religious Education*, July/August 1962, revised version reprinted in Charles Y. Glock and Rodney Stark, *Religion and Society in Tension* (Chicago: Rand McNally & Company, 1965), Chapter 2.
23. For a similar view, see: Robert N. Bellah, "Civil Religion in America," *Daedalus*, Winter 1967, pp. 1–22.
24. That laity spend little time seriously studying theological doctrine is clearly indicated in the Stark and Glock study, which shows that Christians have very little knowledge of theological doctrine (*American Piety*, Chapter V). Gallup Poll studies have produced the same finding.

CHAPTER FOUR

1. NORC Amalgam Survey, conducted February 1967, with a sample of 1504.
2. For a further discussion of some of the subtle dimensions of prejudice see: Jeffrey K. Hadden, Louis H. Masotti, and Victor Thiessen, "The Making of the Negro Mayors, 1967," *Trans-Action*, January/February 1968; and Jeffrey K. Hadden, "The Riot Report: A Glaring Omission," *Commonweal*, March 29, 1968.
3. A good example of clergymen redefining their roles to conform with the expectations of their congregations is seen in a study of rabbis by Braude. The classic seminary model for the rabbi is one of teacher and scholar, yet laity feel that the primary role of the rabbi is to be a spiritual leader. Braude finds that young rabbis tend to go through a process of resocialization during the first years of their ministry. They begin their ministries trying to exemplify the teacher-scholar role but they find that laity are not interested and, in fact, sometimes call them on the carpet for neglecting other roles which they perceive as more important. Faced with this dilemma, the young rabbi is forced to re-evaluate his own self-image. Is he a teacher, or is he something else? In re-evaluating himself, he also re-evaluates his congregation. He comes to feel that the members of his congregation have emotional problems which stand in the way of their accepting the serious, scholarly nature of Judaism. He thus comes to feel that it is "the task of the rabbi to alleviate these problems much as the analyst would attack any psychological problem—by establishing intense contact with the patient, in this case the individual congregant." By redefining the problem in this way, he not only reduces the conflict between himself and the congregation, which has emerged because of different role expectations, but he also reduces the internal self-image conflict. He is not really abandoning his primary role, but rather playing an intermediary role to prepare his congregation to accept him as a teacher. This process may take place over a

number of years while the rabbi is serving a number of congregations. (Lee Braude, "Professional Autonomy and the Role of the Layman," *Social Forces,* 39, May 1961.)

4. For the first time, to my knowledge, the Clergy Mobilization March on Washington to protest the Vietnam war in the spring of 1967 obtained a list of all participants. However, before I could get the list it had been merged with another mailing list and there was no way of differentiating the clergymen who had participated in the march.

5. Exact figures on the clergy who signed the statement indicating willingness to go to jail are not available since the only copy of the statement went to the mayor. A request to the mayor's office for a list of the signatures was not answered. Several of the leaders of the protest told us that the number of signatures was closer to 180 than 132. A list which was passed around at the demonstration for signatures had 137 names, but the leaders claim that many clergy were missed. The figure of 132 was uniformly reported in the press. We were unable to locate the source of this figure. The proportions reported in this text are based on the most conservative estimate.

6. For details on sampling procedures, write to the National Opinion Research Center, Chicago, Illinois.

7. William Brink and Louis Harris, *Black and White* (New York: Simon and Schuster, 1967).

8. Paul B. Sheatsley, "White Attitudes Toward the Negro," *Daedalus,* Winter 1966, pp. 217–38.

9. Ibid.

10. This point will be elaborated later in this chapter, under the subtitle "The New American Dilemma."

11. Brink and Harris, op. cit.

12. Ibid.

13. Ibid.

14. John Spiegel, "Six-City Study, A Survey of Racial Attitudes in Six Northern Cities: Preliminary Findings," June 26, 1967 (mimeographed).

15. Report of the National Advisory Commission on Civil Disorders (New York: Bantam Books, 1968), p. 2.

16. Yoshio Fukuyama, "Parishioners' Attitudes Toward Issues in the Civil Rights Movement," paper presented at the Annual Meetings of the American Sociological Association, August 1967, San Francisco.

17. Rodney Stark and Charles Y. Glock, "Religion and Prejudice," paper presented at the University of California Centennial Symposium, Patterns of American Prejudice, Berkeley, California, March 24–26, 1968.

18. Gunnar Myrdal, with the assistance of Richard Sterner and Arnold Rose, *An American Dilemma* (New York: Harper & Brothers, 1944).

19. Frank R. Westie, "An American Dilemma: An Empirical Test," *American Sociological Review,* Vol. 30, August 1965, pp. 527–38.

20. Ibid., p. 538.

21. For a more concise summary of the evidence on biological-intellectual status of Negroes, see Thomas F. Pettigrew, *A Profile of the American Negro* (Princeton: D. Van Nostrand Company, Inc., 1964), Chapter 5.

22. Westie, op. cit., p. 532.

23. The data presented here appeared in an interim report to the congregation. The name and location of the church are omitted to protect the anonymity of the congregation. I am indebted to Professor William Silverman of the department of sociology at New York University, who served as a consultant to the study, for bringing these data to my attention.

24. For a more detailed discussion of the situation in Cleveland in 1967, see the introduction to Jeffrey K. Hadden, Louis H. Masotti, and Calvin J. Larson (eds), *Metropolis in Crisis: Social and Political Perspectives* (Itasca, Illinois: F. E. Peacock Publishers, Inc., 1967).

25. Hadden, Masotti, and Thiessen, "The Making of the Negro Mayors, 1967," op. cit.

CHAPTER FIVE

1. There were a total of 54 persons enrolled for the June session of the Urban Training Center. Six have been excluded from analysis here because they were theological students. The remaining 48 were all ordained ministers serving in full-time church positions. The seven denominations and the number representing each denomination were are follows: American Lutheran Church, 26; Protestant Episcopal Church, 7; United Church of Christ, 6; Missouri Synod Lutheran, 4; Lutheran Church of America, 3; American Baptist, 1; and the Moravian Church, 1.

2. Personality instruments here included Edgar F. Borgatta, "A Very Short Test of Personality: The Behavioral Self-Rating (BSR) Form," *Psychological Reports*, 1964; "A Short Test of Personality: The S-Ident Form," *The Journal of Educational Research*, 58, July/August 1965, pp. 453–56.

3. Two of these men were appointed to inner-city parishes only a few months after completing the UTC training program.

4. Keith R. Bridston and Dwight W. Culver, *Pre-Seminary Education* (Minneapolis: Augsburg Publishing House, 1965).

5. This figure includes two seminary students who were attending the training program. See note 1 above.

6. See, for example, Lee Braude, "Professional Autonomy and the Role of the Layman," *Social Forces*, May 1961.

7. Robert K. Merton, *Social Theory and Social Structure* (Glencoe, Illinois: The Free Press, 1949), Chapter 4.

8. Two other trainees reported that they had previously participated in a demonstration, but they did not march in Chicago.

9. Details of the Lawrence strike were largely adapted from Donald B. Meyer, *The Protestant Search for Political Realism* (Berkeley: University of California Press, 1961), pp. 93–99.

10. Liston Pope, *Millhands and Preachers* (New Haven, Connecticut: Yale University Press, 1942).

11. Ibid., p. 74.

12. Ibid., pp. 30–31.

13. Ibid., pp. 328–30.

14. Ibid., p. 277.
15. Ibid., p. 274.
16. Ibid., p. 334.
17. *The Delano Record,* October 1965.
18. Ibid.
19. Resolution of the Southern Baptist Convention, June 2–5, 1954, St. Louis, Missouri.
20. Report of the Council on Christian Relations, adopted by the General Assembly of the Presbyterian Church in the United States [Southern], May 27–June 1, 1954.
21. Ernest Q. Campbell and Thomas F. Pettigrew, *Christians in Racial Crisis: A Study of Little Rock's Ministry* (Washington, D.C.: Public Affairs Press, 1959).
22. Ibid., pp. 99–105.
23. Ibid., p. 102.
24. Ibid., p. 102.
25. Ibid., p. 110.
26. Personal interview.
27. Phillip E. Hammond and Robert E. Mitchell, "Segmentation of Radicalism —The Case of the Protestant Campus Ministers," *American Journal of Sociology,* Vol. LXXI, No. 2, September 1965.
28. Some of the results discussed here were reported in an earlier article by Dr. Trimble ("A Study Report on the Miami Assembly: Some Characteristics and Opinions of 521 Church Leaders," *Information Service,* Vol. XVLI, No. 9, May 6, 1967). I am deeply indebted to Dr. Trimble for providing me the original data for reanalysis. The interpretations of the data presented here are, obviously, my own and do not necessarily reflect the interpretations of Dr. Trimble or the Department of Research of the National Council of Churches.
29. Grouping the participants in this way is obviously the most logical in terms of my theoretical interest. I did not treat voting delegates or alternates separately from accredited visitors and consultants for two reasons. First of all, such a breakdown sharply reduces the number of cases to be analyzed and thus restricts the amount of detail in the analysis as well as the confidence that can be attributed to specific findings. Secondly, Trimble's analysis shows that delegates and non-delegates do not differ greatly in their views. His results show that non-delegates are slightly less liberal, but this is largely attributable to the fact that there is a slightly greater proportion of parish pastors and laity represented in the non-delegate category.
30. The lay responses to this question are very similar to the Protestant lay response to the Glock and Stark study in California. See *Religion and Society in Tension* (Chicago: Rand McNally & Company, 1965), p. 91.
31. Keith Bridston and Dwight W. Culver, *Pre-Seminary Education* (Minneapolis: Augsburg Publishing House, 1965), p. 227.

CHAPTER SIX

1. Richard McCann, *The Churches and Mental Health,* Joint Commission on Mental Illness and Health Monograph Series, No. 8 (New York: Basic Books, 1962).
2. Peter Berger, *The Sacred Canopy: Elements of a Sociological Theory of Religion* (Garden City, New York: Doubleday & Company, Inc., 1967), p. 151.

APPENDIX

Supplementary Data on Clergy Attitudes

TABLE I

(Supplementary Data to Table 17)

AGE AND INTERPRETATION OF SCRIPTURES

	Episcopalian	Methodist	Presbyterian	American Baptist	American Lutheran	Missouri Synod Lutheran
			% Agreeing			
"I believe in a literal or nearly literal interpretation of the Bible."						
Under 35	5	11	14	27	24	72
35–44	11	16	16	41	43	73
45–54	15	23	23	55	60	79
Over 55	14	23	31	47	74	84
"Adam and Eve were individual historical persons."						
Under 35	0	9	11	20	28	85
35–44	2	17	11	43	47	88
45–54	6	24	22	59	72	92
Over 55	5	26	27	55	77	98
"Scriptures are the inspired and inerrant Word of God not only in matters of faith but also in historic, geographical, and other secular matters."						
Under 35	4	8	6	17	6	63
35–44	2	12	9	30	26	74
45–54	9	15	17	41	32	85
Over 55	8	17	21	42	50	90
"An understanding of the language of myth and symbol is as important for interpreting Biblical literature as are history and archaeology."						
Under 35	95	83	82	75	82	41
35–44	89	78	83	64	55	35
45–54	88	73	72	54	46	28
Over 55	81	68	58	57	46	28

TABLE II

(Supplementary Data to Table 18)

RELATIONSHIP OF AGE TO LITERALIST DOCTRINE

	Methodist	Episcopalian	Presbyterian	American Baptist	American Lutheran	Missouri Synod Lutheran
			% Agreeing			
"I believe that the virgin birth of Jesus was a biological miracle."						
Under 35	31	49	38	58	70	93
35–44	43	53	52	64	84	95
45–54	42	57	57	75	92	96
Over 55	48	65	61	68	92	98
"I accept Jesus' physical resurrection as an objective historical fact in the same sense that Lincoln's physical death was a historical fact."						
Under 35	45	73	61	60	83	97
35–44	53	68	70	68	91	93
45–54	50	69	67	70	89	89
Over 55	50	73	61	65	88	90
"I believe in a divine judgment after death where some shall be rewarded and others punished."						
Under 35	41	55	46	61	86	95
35–44	53	53	55	69	91	93
45–54	60	58	66	79	97	95
Over 55	59	57	66	73	95	94
"Hell does not refer to a special location after death, but to the experience of self-estrangement, guilt, and meaninglessness in this life."						
Under 35	65	58	61	45	26	6
35–44	53	58	55	33	20	6
45–54	54	62	49	25	14	6
Over 55	55	60	50	41	24	7

TABLE II (continued)

	Methodist	Episcopalian	Presbyterian	American Baptist	American Lutheran	Missouri Synod Lutheran
			% *Agreeing*			
"I believe in the demonic as a						
personal power in the world."						
Under 35	34	67	49	57	80	91
35–44	38	65	50	64	88	93
45–54	41	63	59	77	91	89
Over 55	40	58	57	70	91	90
"Man by himself is incapable of						
anything but sin."						
Under 35	39	47	49	37	71	85
35–44	34	45	47	33	69	85
45–54	35	44	46	45	78	86
Over 55	37	41	42	49	76	83

TABLE III

(Supplementary Data to Table 44)

CLERGY ATTITUDES TOWARD CIVIL RIGHTS
BY THEIR THEOLOGICAL BELIEF

	American Baptist	American Lutheran	Episcopalian	Methodist	Missouri Synod Lutheran	Presbyterian
				% Agreeing		
"I basically disapprove of the civil rights movement in America."						
Fundamentalist	27	9	*	26	9	6
Conservative	6	5	7	12	9	7
Neo-orthodox	2	3	4	6	5	2
Liberal	1	9	3	5	*	3
"For the most part, the churches have been woefully inadequate in facing up to the civil rights issue."						
Fundamentalist	63	66	*	66	67	35
Conservative	76	67	63	71	67	71
Neo-orthodox	86	78	72	79	91	80
Liberal	82	85	79	80	*	79
"Many whites pretend to be very Christian while in reality their racial attitudes demonstrate their lack of or misunderstanding of Christianity."						
Fundamentalist	82	83	*	68	75	71
Conservative	83	78	78	72	77	81
Neo-orthodox	86	83	79	81	86	84
Liberal	86	91	88	83	*	84
"The real obstacle to integration in this country is political leadership and not the people themselves."						
Fundamentalist	39	22	*	37	20	18
Conservative	20	11	13	20	11	14
Neo-orthodox	14	10	13	13	2	10
Liberal	14	3	13	16	*	11

TABLE III (continued)

	American Baptist	American Lutheran	Episcopalian	Methodist	Missouri Synod Lutheran	Presbyterian
			% Agreeing			
"The racial crisis in America would probably be less serious if the Federal government had not intervened."						
Fundamentalist	31	12	*	44	38	18
Conservative	13	9	15	22	15	12
Neo-orthodox	5	5	7	8	5	4
Liberal	5	0	6	6	*	5
"Negroes would be better off if they would take advantage of the opportunities that have been made available to them rather than spending so much time protesting."						
Fundamentalist	51	34	*	61	55	18
Conservative	28	22	23	36	29	21
Neo-orthodox	8	14	13	16	9	8
Liberal	4	15	13	13	*	7
"Negroes could solve many of their own problems if they would not be so irresponsible and carefree about life."						
Fundamentalist	53	44	*	64	55	29
Conservative	33	22	27	39	26	25
Neo-orthodox	11	13	14	20	16	8
Liberal	9	9	18	18	*	8
"I am in basic sympathy with Northern ministers and students who have gone to the South to work for civil rights."						
Fundamentalist	22	37	*	20	20	24
Conservative	41	42	43	28	32	50
Neo-orthodox	72	60	58	50	68	74
Liberal	79	65	64	59	*	77

* The number of cases is too small to compute statistically reliable percentages.

TABLE IV

(Supplementary Data to Table 45)

CLERGY ATTITUDES TOWARD CIVIL RIGHTS BY THEIR AGE

	American Baptist	American Lutheran	Episcopalian	Methodist	Missouri Synod Lutheran	Presbyterian
			% Agreeing			
"I basically disapprove of the civil rights movement in America."						
Under 35	2	4	3	7	8	1
35–44	7	4	2	8	7	4
45–54	8	4	9	8	9	7
Over 55	9	13	6	10	11	6
"For the most part, the churches have been woefully inadequate in facing up to the civil rights issue."						
Under 35	81	75	72	79	76	85
35–44	82	69	75	76	72	77
45–54	75	67	69	73	61	69
Over 55	67	67	58	73	58	67
"Many whites pretend to be very Christian while in reality their racial attitudes demonstrate their lack of or misunderstanding of Christianity."						
Under 35	88	83	87	82	81	88
35–44	85	79	81	78	80	80
45–54	83	78	83	77	74	82
Over 55	79	76	78	78	74	82
"The real obstacle to integration in this country is political leadership and not the people themselves."						
Under 35	9	9	10	12	6	11
35–44	15	8	11	13	9	10
45–54	22	15	17	19	13	12
Over 55	32	23	15	27	24	18

TABLE IV (continued)

	American Baptist	American Lutheran	Episcopalian	Methodist	Missouri Synod Lutheran	Presbyterian
			% Agreeing			
"The racial crisis in America would probably be less serious if the Federal government had not intervened."						
Under 35	6	5	10	7	11	3
35–44	10	5	5	13	11	6
45–54	15	5	13	14	15	9
Over 55	20	24	11	19	40	15
"Negroes would be better off if they would take advantage of the opportunities that have been made available to them rather than spending so much time protesting."						
Under 35	8	14	17	17	22	7
35–44	18	20	12	21	20	9
45–54	33	21	19	25	37	15
Over 55	39	42	30	32	60	27
"Negroes could solve many of their own problems if they would not be so irresponsible and carefree about life."						
Under 35	9	15	14	18	24	7
35–44	20	17	15	23	20	10
45–54	40	22	17	32	33	19
Over 55	49	48	41	40	53	31
"I am in basic sympathy with Northern ministers and students who have gone to the South to work for civil rights."						
Under 35	60	56	61	53	40	72
35–44	53	49	58	44	35	69
45–54	41	37	54	40	31	59
Over 55	47	30	43	40	20	51

Date Due

JAN 13 '78			
NOV 15 '79			
APR 13 '85			
... 11 '85			
OCT 13 '86			
F			